P9-EDW-776

SAFE
IN THE CITY

A Streetwise
Guide to Avoid
Being Robbed,
Raped, Ripped
Off, or Run Over

Marc "Animal" MacYoung
and Chris Pfouts

Paladin Press
Bouler, Colorado

Also by Chris Pfouts:

Lead Poisoning:
   25 True Tales from the Wrong End of a Gun
True Tales of American Violence

Also by Marc "Animal" MacYoung:

Cheap Shots, Ambushes, and Other Lessons:
   A Down and Dirty Book on Streetfighting and Survival
Fists, Wits, and a Wicked Right:
   Surviving on the Wild Side of the Street
Floor Fighting:
   Stompings, Maimings, and Other Things
Knives, Knife Fighting, and Related Hassles:
   How to Survive a *Real* Knife Fight
Pool Cues, Beer Bottles, & Baseball Bats:
   Animal's Guide to Improvised Weapons
   for Self-Defense and Survival
Street E & E:
   Evading Escaping, and Other Ways to Save Your Ass When Things Get Ugly
Violence, Blunders, and Fractured Jaws:
   Advanced Awareness Techniques and Street Etiquette
   to Avoid When a Fight Goes to the Floor

Safe in the City: A Streetwise Guide to Avoid Being Robbed,
Raped, Ripped Off, or Run Over
by Marc "Animal" MacYoung and Chris Pfouts

ISBN 0-87364-775-0
Printed in the United States of America

Published by Paladin Press, a division of
Paladin Enterprises, Inc., P.O. Box 1307,
Boulder, Colorado 80306, USA.
(303) 443-7250

Direct inquiries and/or orders to the above address.

Contents

Preface

Before you can avoid being a victim of crime—whether in New York, Los Angeles, or points in between—you need to know something about your attackers. A lot has been written about the criminal mind, much of it by people who have never had the joy of looking at a criminal from the wrong end of a gun.

The most fundamental thing to realize is that a criminal has an entirely different mind-set than you do. This difference goes all the way down to basic assumptions regarding reality, behavior, morality, and values. For example, to a gangbanger killing is not morally reprehensible; it is a mark of manhood, a rite of passage that brings praise and kudos rather than rebuke.

The best way to explain criminals is by using the food chain. It's comically portrayed by a graduated line of fish, with the smaller fish getting eaten by the bigger ones. The food chain is a little more complicated than this, but the idea of being both the hunted and the hunter is critical for understanding criminal behavior. Criminals are predators, but they are only middle-line predators. While they are hunting you, others are hunting them—not only the police, but other criminals as well. In fact, they are more likely to be a victims of crime than you are! It is a matter of life and death for them to prey only on those weaker or smaller than they are and to avoid bigger predators.

A street criminal lives by a very basic philosophy: there are two types of people in the world, predators and food. The former are to be feared for the pain they can inflict, and the latter are to be victimized and used. The victimization can take many forms—financial support, rape, physical assault—depending on the criminal. The only thing that makes a street person hesitate about using violence against someone is the fear of greater retribution. But it's not just physical pain the criminal fears; it's the fear that he may be knocked lower down the predatory ladder than he is now and become a victim himself. In a world of sharks, a wounded shark doesn't last long.

Make no mistake, if you want to survive, you not only have to play the criminals' game, you must be better at it than they are. The good news is once you know their game, it is predictable and avoidable. Look at it this way: a criminal wants to achieve something. His goal determines what steps he must take to achieve it. To succeed he has to do certain things; this makes him predictable. It's sort of like if you were going to someone's house. Initially, there are several possible ways to get there, but the closer to the house you get, the fewer options you have. Finally you are left with no choice but to turn down a particular street. Crime has a similar pattern.

The pattern that all criminals follow is based on a five-step process, which we refer to as the five stages of an attack. (By *attack*, we aren't referring simply to a physical assault; we mean any action by a criminal, from aggravated harassment to robbery to rape.) The five stages are intent, interview, positioning, attack, and reaction. Notice that the actual attack is step number four in the process. The first three steps (intent, interview, positioning) involve the criminal deciding if he's going to risk an assault or not. It is during these first three phases that the attack can be aborted without physical conflict.[1] It is important to realize that this decision process involves multiple steps. A single phase by itself is not a threat. But when the first three steps are present, *you are in the middle of being set up for a crime!*

1) INTENT

This is a mental process entirely internal to the attacker. This is where the attacker crosses a normal restriction and is willing to, or has decided to, commit a crime or act of violence. It is at this time that the person becomes a predator; he is now actively hunting a victim. His intent could result from a conscious decision or as a by-product of mounting aggression. This shift in intent is reflected in the attacker's eye movement, physical body language, words, and verbal timing (his speech cadence). All of these signs are subconsciously recognizable to any observer. A very primitive part of you *knows* this guy is hunting you—just as it knows when someone isn't hunting you. Don't think this is some sort of esoteric mumbo jumbo; we do have this knowledge inside us. If we didn't, we wouldn't have made it this far. The very fact that you're here today indicates that your ancestors managed to get up the tree before the lion got them.

The most common problem "civilized" people have in a threatening situation is accessing the appropriate primitive response to their unconscious warnings. People facing a predator sense that something is amiss but have no clear idea what is wrong. On a surface and/or rational level there is nothing apparently wrong, just a guy (or guys) approaching. Deep inside of these people's brains, though, the cerebral cortex (aka monkey brain) is jumping up and down screaming, "Danger! Danger!" But, alas, most rational people don't speak "jungle" so they ignore the voice. When those bells go off in your head, listen to them! Don't blow off these impressions or decide to override them because you have to get to a meeting or you want to leave. Being five minutes late is better than being raped, robbed, or ripped off.

2) INTERVIEW

Contrary to popular belief, most criminal attacks aren't the "jump out of the bushes" variety that many people think they are. In most crimes, the attacker actually talks with his victim beforehand, but conversation is seldom related to what the criminal is really up to. This is a period of time where the would-be attacker assesses an individual for "victim potential." It is during the interview that the attacker is looking for blind spots, lack of awareness, opportunity, and excessive fear (either panic or blustering anger); testing boundaries; and summing up the odds of success. As odd as it may sound, this is one interview that you want to *fail!*

There are also five types of interviews: regular, silent, escalating, hot, and prolonged. Understand that these are broad categories that overlap. Depending on a person's reaction, interviews can switch from one type to another. For example, what started out as a regular interview, if met by verbal aggression, will often shift to an escalating interview.

Regular Interview: The regular interview is the most common. The criminal is looking for a lack of awareness about his intent and positioning as well as a victim's unwillingness to use violence. Often the interviewer asks the prospective victim for goods or services (such as matches, the time, spare change, or jumper cables) to see if the latter is willing to give. He is testing your boundaries. Once the precedence of giving is established, then it becomes a matter of how far he can go. The criminal is also looking for excessive nervousness regarding his presence. Some people will sense his intent and freak out; this tells the criminal that he's got a safe victim. Once he receives any of these signals, the criminal decides to continue.

A key point with rapists is that they will physically touch the woman they're interviewing. Often the initial touch is not particularly threatening; rather, it is to see if he can violate her boundaries. Touching is a critical thing to watch for when confronted by an aggressive male (see Chapter 12 for more info).

Silent Interview: A silent interview is the one people fear most. The criminal places himself in a position where he can see people passing by. He judges people by watching their body language and awareness of their surroundings. Once he sees someone he feels he can successfully attack, he acts quickly.[2] This decision can be reached immediately or after a time of quietly following the victim and watching him. This is the hardest crime to prevent because, by the time most people become aware of it, the attack is in full swing. From the victim's perspective, the criminal literally "just pops out of nowhere." Realistically, though, most of these attacks could have been prevented by occasionally looking around to see if anyone of ill intent is in the area or following you. This book will teach you to look in the places where this type of criminals lurks.

Escalating Interview: Escalating interviews begin calmly and normally and then increase in intensity until they explode in either violence or a criminal attack. Often, the person is approached in a seemingly friendly and mundane way, but the situation rapidly becomes unmanageable. The criminal pushes the boundaries incrementally to see if he can get away with it. Finally, when convinced that he can succeed, he will attack.

An example of this is a street person asking for spare change, then demanding more money. A request for spare change becomes, "Gimme a dolla," then, "Gimme five dolla," and so on. The way to halt an escalating interview is to draw a line and be prepared to defend it without hesitation.

Escalating interviews are especially common with date rapes. The man begins to escalate his demands for sex, or he violates the woman's space without verbal demands for sex. The woman tries to use reason to stop the process, or she becomes verbally hostile in an attempt to halt it—behavior that in a normal situation would work. But this isn't a normal situation; instead of preventing an escalation, her response may in fact be spurring it on. Another factor that may prevent reason from working is intoxication. It is estimated that 86 percent of all date rapes occur under the influence of alcohol.

An escalating interview is also common with packs. What starts out as an attempt to alleviate boredom by jerking someone's chain turns very ugly. For example, a person attempts to walk through an area where a group is hanging out. The next thing that guy knows, he's been robbed and assaulted. Why? Because he decided to go skinny-dipping in a school of piranha.

Hot Interview: During a hot interview, the attacker is openly hostile from the onset. This approach is usually reserved for male victims, but certain rapists may also use it as a justification for attacking women. In a hot interview the attacker makes a derogatory or hostile comment and uses the response as either a justification to attack or as a gauge for his chances for success. This approach is common in gay bashings. The attackers start out by calling the individual an obscene name. If that person counters with verbal hostility, the basher uses this as his excuse to attack. His twisted logic convinces him that the person's response justifies the attack. What the victim often doesn't understand is the attacker(s) started the gambit with the intention of escalating it beyond a verbal level.

Another kind of hot interview is basic bullying. The antagonist wants to see if he can get away with pushing you around. If he can, then he knows he's in control. The would-be attacker walks up and opens the conversation with something like, "Gimme some money, motherfucker!" Or the reverberating echo from high school: "What are *you* looking at?" If the person reacts in a fearful or overly defensive manner, the interviewer knows he has the advantage.

When someone comes at you in this manner, there are two basic ways to handle it: leave or prepare to take it to the mat. The latter is tricky, and even professionals know to back down from this sort of situation now and then. Normally, someone who's pulling a hot interview is already convinced he can win; otherwise he wouldn't have started the ball rolling.

Prolonged Interview: This last type of interview is normally used by professional robbers, stalkers, and certain rapists. A prolonged interview can literally take months. In the case of the professional robber, he and his team will "case the joint." They will go into the business that they intend to rob to see the type of security in place, the layout of the establishment, the entrances and exits, and other relevant factors. This can be done with only one trip (as with many store robberies), or it can be done through a long process of planning and watching the establishment (any gangster movie you can think of).

Certain rapists will employ a prolonged interview or, in this case, actually an ongoing silent interview. A rapist will spot a woman and then proceed to watch her over time until he learns her patterns and schedule. This is done without attracting the attention of the woman being interviewed.

Of late, a new form of prolonged interview has come to the attention of the public: stalking. A stalker uses a combination of interviews: prolonged, escalating, and hot. The stalker studies the patterns of the person he is pursuing, and his actions are spaced out over a long time. However, unlike normal prolonged interviewers, he lets the victim know he's after him or her. This situation often combines the antagonism of a hot interview with the increasing threat of an escalating one.

Fortunately, many states have passed stalker laws and can now do something about stalkers. If you can supply the police with records (especially video and audio) of the person's harassment, you'll have a stronger case. But getting this evidence takes time. What makes a stalker so dangerous is that the decision of when to move is entirely up to him. If he decides to strike during the period that you're accumulating evidence and you kill or injure him, you usually can prove your claim that you acted in self-defense. Don't threaten a stalker with the police. Instead, consult the police and begin to quietly gather evidence. The first notion a stalker should have that the police are on to him is when they knock on his door with a warrant. The thing to realize is that stalkers are a law unto themselves. Threatening them is only likely to set them off.

Practically speaking, though, the best ways to handle stalkers are highly illegal and, unless handled by a professional, likely to promote an attack on the victim or land the would-be

Galahad in jail. This is why it isn't advisable for someone's untrained brother or husband to try to handle these situations.

3) POSITIONING

Positioning involves the actual physical tactics necessary for an attack to occur. If the crim isn't in the right position, he can't attack successfully. No positioning, no attack—bottom line. Until he tries to get into position, everything could be innocent (yeah, right). This happens occasionally. However, when intent and an interview are combined with positioning, a very dangerous scenario ensues.

The attacker places himself in a strategically superior position from which to initiate his attack. Amazingly, there aren't that many positions available—only four. They are very distinct and obvious once you know them: 1) surprise, 2) surrounding, 3) closing, and 4) cornering. The objective of positioning is to close the distance between the crim and the victim, surround the victim, choose a location that cuts off escape routes, and ready a weapon in concealment. These specific actions have no other purpose other than attack. Once you know what to look for, someone moving into these positions is as obvious as if he were carrying a flare.

4) ATTACK

Once all the go-ahead signals and the attack criteria have been met, the actual attack/mugging/rape occurs. As we said, an attack doesn't have to be physical; if the person capitulates to the threats and yields to whatever the attacker wants, there often will not be a physical attack. In the case of sticking a gun in someone's face, the coercion is present even though the trigger is often not pulled. The mere threat, however, qualifies it as an attack.

5) REACTION

This is solely related to the attacker, and it usually occurs after the act. It is the emotional and psychological reactions the criminal has resulting from his action. It is mentioned here because, if the reaction occurs during the commission of the crime, the situation escalates into a more serious one.

Something about the way the victim reacts (often excessive fear) often triggers a "power trip" within the criminal. This can turn a simple burglary into rape/homicide. The criminal, experiencing the rush of power, realizes he can do whatever he wants: an emotionally crippled weakling suddenly finds himself with what his limited mind sees as unlimited power. Human nature often dictates that, when this happens, the results are vicious and bloody.[3] Fortunately, this is less common than many people would think. The bad news is that the rush becomes fixed in the person's psyche and often results in that person intentionally going out to commit this type of crime again for the same sensation.

Often, it is the rapist's reaction that results in the woman being harmed. After the actual rape, the man's rage often manifests itself in a different manner, and he physically assaults the woman. (For an in-depth look at rape, see Chapter 12.)

This is just a quick rundown of what a criminal needs to operate and what you need to avoid him. For a more detailed explanation, check out the video *Safe in the Street* (also available from Paladin Press).

NOTES

1. It is important to realize that situations arise where the first three stages are not done in sequence; however, all factors are still present. Also, the process can occur at an accelerated rate—remember that he's got experience doing this.
2. Recently, a study was done wherein videotapes of various people were taken to a prison and convicts were asked whom they would choose as victims. There was a 95-percent consistency rate of whom the criminals chose. Criminals read body language as a regular part of their lives.
3. This same reaction can be seen on a cultural level in

Vietnam, some African nations, and other third world countries. Once victory was achieved, the formerly "oppressed" new regimes loosed genocidal rampages that made the "oppressors" look like the Good Humor man. Just being oppressed, downtrodden, or persecuted doesn't automatically instill moral virtue, righteousness, or compassion when people suddenly find themselves in power.

L.A.

New York

INTRODUCTION

New York

The T-shirt has a picture of a snub-nose revolver on it. There is a big black X in front of the barrel, and it reads: "New York: You are here," with an arrow pointing to the X.

Out of the threads of T-shirts shall come the truth. Not too long ago, Sen. Daniel P. Moynihan of New York, who grew up in Hell's Kitchen in Manhattan, spoke out about the current conditions in his native city and what went wrong. As a yardstick, he compared the New York of 1993 with the New York of 1943. "We were a city of the same size, about 150,000 more persons than now," he said.

"Over on the West Side," Moynihan said, "we made a business about Hell's Kitchen and a street warrior caste, but in truth the neighborhood was in a way idyllic. In 1943 there were exactly 44 homicides by gunshot in the city of New York. Last year, there were 1,499." This isn't politicking by Moynihan, but a sort of open aching for the lost New York of years gone by.

Moynihan quoted a letter he received from Edwin Torres, a New York State Supreme Court judge, who wrote about the cowed acceptance of violence and crime that he sees in his courtroom—the day-to-day victimization that makes citizens do things like apologize for being in the way of a bullet. Torres wrote, "This numbness, this near-narcoleptic state, can diminish the human condition to the level of combat infantrymen who, in protracted campaigns, can eat their battlefield rations seated on the bodies of the fallen, friend and foe alike. A society that loses its sense of outrage is doomed to extinction."

New York: You are here. Doomed to extinction. Mayor David Dinkins didn't much like Moynihan's speech because it went on to point out that 50 years ago the city got things done—bridges and airports built, kids educated. Today it can't even fix a pothole or clean a subway platform.

In the sections of this book that focus on surviving New York City, I talk a lot about government and social conditions. The government has become in many ways more dangerous to the citizen and visitor than the idiot with a pistol. Government in this town, you see, is of the dollar, by the dollar, for the dollar. The average person is an annoyance to city government, and he or she is treated as such. Taxes are higher here than anywhere else in the United States, except in Washington, D.C. At the same time, citizens are not safe on the streets or in their homes, children are as likely to catch a bullet as an education in the schools, and God help you if you're old and pensionless in New York because no one else will. New York City is a special case in many ways, but especially this: Streetwise in the Apple means knowing how to watch out for the street predators on one hand and the governmental predators on the other.

This isn't just carping about taxes or lousy government. Those are general situations. I deal in specifics that are very harmful to the individual and certain pitfalls that are specifically designed to trap tourists. Part of our goal with this book is to give you some practical, potentially lifesaving knowledge about street criminals—their habits, patterns, and methods. All of this is from a couple of guys who have spent enough time slithering around in the gritty subcultures of the world to qualify for teaching credentials in the University of Dirty Deeds, College of Sharp Edges and Large Calibers. Beyond those lessons, we offer detailed, specific information on the latest criminal wrinkles in both Los Angeles and New York. These two cities are the trendsetters for street crime. Today it's happening in the Orange or the Apple—tomorrow it's going on in your alley.

New York consists of five boroughs: Manhattan, the Bronx, Queens, Brooklyn, and Richmond—also known as Staten Island. I have lived in all of them except the Bronx, and I have friends up there. This book mainly deals with Manhattan. The outer boroughs have neighborhoods that vary from the horse ranches on Staten Island to the meanest housing projects in Brooklyn. Manhattan is the place you see in pictures of New York, the island with the skyline and the skyscrapers, home to the Empire State Building and the recently bombed World Trade Center. It is one of the world's prime examples of a Big City—and it has its own rhythm, its own dynamics, and its own special brand of crime.

Some people love Brooklyn. I got shot there in a street incident some years back, and since then, to be honest, I don't go to or through the place unless I absolutely have to. Getting shot wasn't the first problem I've had in what was once called the Borough of Churches. These days it's more like the Borough of Early Graves. If you're a tourist, just avoid the place altogether. If you can't live without the Brooklyn Academy of Music, the Aquarium, Coney Island, or the Botanical Gardens, by all means go during daylight hours. This may not stop you from getting shot, but you'll be able to see where the holes are. Brooklyn at night is no place for camera-carrying, goggle-eyed, gee-whiz tenderfeet. Queens has just about zero to attract tourists except the two airports. There's Shea Stadium, but only if you dig the Mets. You can see all of Staten Island you'll ever want to see from the famous Ferry. The Bronx Zoo is cool, but watch yourself going in and out. Same for Yankee Stadium. And that's it for the outer borough section of the book.

A lot of the classic advice about self-defense goes down the tube when you talk about New York City. Awareness is always going to be your best ally in a tightly packed urban situation, and we will show you how to really observe the people around you. Some fighting and defense techniques begin with the admonition to guard your perimeter, which is impossible in New York. During rush hour in the trains and in the streets, your perimeter is your skin, literally. Outside of that, you frequently have no personal space, any more than one tooth has personal space from another tooth. If you are someone's special target, it's extremely difficult to prevent a sneak attack under these circumstances. Tight, rushing, tired crowds produce a very stressful situation that overloads the senses—so much so that focusing on the people around you is almost impossible. You can't look everywhere at once—it's too dense and too busy. What you can spot are patterns and strange movements.

Your best first line of defense in New York—during rush hour or any other time—is not to attract undue attention to yourself as a target. Number one: try not to look like a tourist, especially if you are a tourist. Standing around with your mouth open, gazing uncomprehendingly at a subway map, will draw the wrong kind of people to you. It may also draw a friendly person trying to help, but there are fewer of them than there are bad guys. Way fewer. In the subways, if you are lost, ask almost anyone. For some reason, New Yorkers in the subway system give honest, direct answers—something you will probably not get from token-booth clerks, if they lower themselves to answer at all.

Your clothing and accessories tell muggers a lot about you. Absolutely do not walk around with a huge expensive hotshot camera bag. This is like holding up a MUG ME sign. It tells the world that you are wealthy enough to afford tons of pricey photo and video gear and an expensive container for it all. I think expensive hotshot camera bags are stupid anywhere in the world outside of your own home. It's the same story everywhere— they attract muggers and thieves. I don't even like the brightly colored camera straps that have brand names printed on them. Low profile, that's the way to travel. Most people in New York, men and women, carry bags of one kind or another—back

6

packs, shoulder bags, briefcases, fanny packs. Use something like that instead of your camera bag. I've found that a backpacker's fanny pack will easily hold a 35mm SLR with a modest lens, along with a couple of extra rolls of film or an extra lens. And a man with a fanny pack is as common as a discarded beer can. You don't drive cars in New York, see, so you have to carry all your crap with you all the time on foot. You have a high-buck video camera? Fine. Carry it in a beat-up shoulder bag.

It's common to see people with cameras on straps around their necks. It's a bad idea. A mugger can grab the strap and choke you with it, pull you off your feet with it, or just grab the camera and boogie. When you're not actively using the camera, slip one arm through the strap along with your neck and keep the camera tight to the side of your chest. This makes it harder to grab, and if someone does pull on the strap, your armpit takes the force, not your vulnerable neck.

Another thing—always remember that you are in a hostile environment in New York. Give yourself the edge. A few weeks ago, I saw two people wandering around a not-so-hot part of town with Leicas around their necks. And not the $250 point-and-shoot, either, but the regular 35mm jobs that start at $2,500 and go up from there. The Leica is not a flashy-looking piece of equipment, but it's worth so much you might entice someone who didn't have robbery in mind at all. A simple tip: put a piece of electrical tape over the name when you're in the street. You know it's a Leica. It knows it's a Leica. Joe Junkie doesn't need to know that the little optical item hanging around your soft out-of-town neck is worth enough to support his drug habit for the next month. The idea is to prevent Joe Junkie from having those kinds of thoughts.

This goes double for jewelry. Basically, leave it at home if possible, especially necklaces and those ever popular gold chains. Kids love to snatch chains, and if it's a good one, it'll tear hell out of your neck before it breaks. Watches are always a target, and a watch tells the attentive mugger a lot about you.

If you have a real Rolex, leave it at home and buy one of the counterfeits on the street for your visit to the Apple. They look so close it's hard to tell the difference, and they cost less than $40 if you buy them right (Canal Street or 14th Street). A little consumer information: There are a lot of con artists out there in the world hawking phony Rolexs. The easiest way to tell a cheap fake Rolex from a real one is that the McCoys have a sweep second hand, while the fakes, with their quartz movements, have a second hand that ticks around. That tip alone might save you the cost of a case of these books.

Walking around looking like a tourist doesn't seal your doom or anything like that. But it does draw a lot of attention from muggers and other whackos—and this is whacko central. We got 'em in all flavors.

Along with mental health troubles, which the city has aplenty, from the mayor's office on down to the subway tracks, New York has some very serious health problems that affect everyone—at least potentially. The city has the highest concentration of AIDS and HIV in the nation. Anyone you tangle with these days can kill you through the interchange of blood. This is a reality in New York City, as solid as a speeding Cadillac and just as dangerous. The city is also plagued with a fresh outbreak of tuberculosis at epidemic, if not endemic, proportions. Jacob Riis is probably rolling over in his grave— he devoted his life to eliminating the kinds of lightless, unventilated tenement buildings that made TB epidemic in the slums of New York in the 1800s. TB is communicable, although not easily, and it thrives on the lack of sun and air, as in prison cells and subway tunnels. If you end up on Riker's Island, our city prison, you could come home with TB as a souvenir.

Ever since it was the Dutch colony of Nieuw Amsterdam, the city has been a near-brilliant breeding ground for crimes of all kinds. Any kind of lock, with the exception of the high-priced exotics, is like a new kind of candy for the city's thieves. As an example, the city once bought 50 car boots as an experiment. They were all stolen. The first cast-iron building in the world, which once stood near the present site of the World Trade Center (other classic historic examples abound in SoHo), was stolen. A 16-year-old kid recently stole an entire subway train, and just a few years ago, Port Authority cops finally caught a serial thief who was responsible for the temporary disappearance of more than 50 buses.

Theft is not the entire crime picture, to be sure, but in the city, purposeful and/or opportunistic thieves are literally everywhere. After a while, the constant threat of imminent theft becomes as wearying as a ball and chain. In fact, it is a ball and chain. On top of that there is the random violence factor; the constant assault on the senses from the smell of urine and the staggering, sleeping, shitting (sometimes all at once) derelicts; being panhandled every 50 feet—it gets a little bit overwhelming. The wolves are constantly pawing at the gates (and peeing on them, trying to jimmy them open, painting names on them with spray paint . . .), you see, which makes it extra hard to be vigilant about your perimeter.

Many areas of the city are alternately threatening and benign on a block-by-block basis: this block is okay, the next one's treacherous. Sometimes, it's even broken down to different sides of the street—this one good, that one bad. And when in unfamiliar territory, these truths are often not self-evident until one is halfway down the block in question and right in the middle of Uh-Oh Land. Good and bad blocks change pretty often, too. There are specific ways to deal with suddenly finding yourself in World O'Shit that we will teach you: navigational aids, if you will, for the very dangerous waters of New York City.

When you find yourself within spitting distance of that "You are here" X, we hope to be able to show you how to successfully avoid going all the way to the mark. Whether in New York or L.A. or Abu Dhabi, the basics remain the same. From that root you're looking at local refinements; even then, you'll often find that the same things that were being used to try and rip off our great-grandparents are still being used successfully today and will probably be around another century down the line. Knives, forks, and spoons offer a time-tested, very effective system for eating. Criminals employ the same kinds of time-tested tools and methods, just as effectively.

New York City is doomed to extinction, and there's nothing we can do about it. In the meantime we can try and keep you safe.

L.A.

I once had a rather entertaining conversation with Jesus Christ on the Venice Boardwalk. To use street vernacular, I was "tripping with him." It was weird and entertaining and provided a few minutes of break from what I was doing. Now rapping with a MICA (mentally ill, chemically addicted) probably isn't your idea of fun, but it's all part of street life in Los Angeles—a life-style that, like it or not, has slowly enveloped the entire city.

I doubt that the bedraggled refugee from Camarillo State Mental Institute was actually the Savior; nor, in truth, do I think he believed it entirely himself. In short, we both knew he was insane, and once that was established, we could have fun with it. When it comes to self-awareness, the fact that a bum on the Venice Boardwalk knows that he was flipped out puts him miles ahead of the city of Los Angeles. The most terrifying thing about Los Angeles isn't the fact that it's insane, but rather that it thinks it's sane!

It wasn't until I began to travel the country that I realized that the evening news didn't consist of these regular topics: national and international events, sports, weather, and today's murders. There are places in this country where all activities stop in a house while everyone watches the report of a single murder on the news. It's so rare it's worth notice! I also didn't realize that in other cities the sound of gunfire attracted major notice. It came as a surprise to me that people couldn't tell how many blocks over or what caliber the gunshots were. Even my mother can do that. Just as surprising to me is that there are cities in America where gunshots are reported by an entire neighborhood, not just the houses next to where the shooting occurred.

In most parts of L.A. murder is just a matter of course. I laughed at the Arizona talk show host who solemnly told me that in 1993 there had been 16 gang murders in Phoenix by June. Sixteen! That's a weekend in the L.A. area. What was weird was that when I went out to check out the local talent, I discovered that pound for pound, the bad boys of Arizona's largest city were tougher than the L.A. homeboys. I'm talking down-to-the-bone tough, where your best shot might not be enough to put them away. They had to be that way to endure 115 degree weather. The thing was that for every criminal, there were five more honest folks who were just as tough. All over Colorado and Montana I've met honest folk who are not only made of harder stuff, but wouldn't hesitate to shoot you if you gave them cause. I've never met a west Texan who didn't have that stringy hardness you need to survive in an environment that would eat most L.A. criminals for lunch. It's not a matter of toughness that makes criminals dangerous, because there are many more people out there who are "tougher."

The thing is, the L.A. homies are more psychotic. They're "too many rats in a cage" crazy, ready to turn on each other with no provocation. You have to be pretty far off the edge before you blow someone away for just living somewhere or wearing a certain football team jacket, but that's all it takes in parts of L.A. In a land where victory usually belongs to the one who shoots first, they are always on a hair trigger. That is what makes them dangerous, not that they are "tough" in the traditional sense of the word.

While that may seem bad, what is equally distressing is the canvas on which they paint their deadly picture is only slightly less crazed than they are. It not only creates them, but it actively supports them. Normal life in L.A. is skirting the edge already—there is no way for it not to be when you have more than 4 million people. These pressures are constant for anyone who lives there, and they affect people. Even the most well-adjusted, mellow person in Los Angeles is closer to the edge than a normal person from another city.

If you're going to survive in L.A., you have to put up shields and tweak yourself up to be ready to handle situations at any time. I'm not talking about just crime either; you have to be ready to fend off the advances of the homeless people on every corner; deal with a traffic jam consisting of more cars than exist in some major cities in the West and Midwest; accept the fact that any direction you look, day or night, you're going to see someone; deal with the idea that to get anywhere in the city between 5 A.M. and 10 P.M. it will take at least an hour's travel time even if it's only 20 miles away (mind you, this is with normal traffic).

These are just the everyday frustrations and pressures that ordinary people endure in Los Angeles. When you go into the lower echelons of society, it gets worse. Everyone is willing to accept that the rich are different—well, guess what, so are the poor. There are many aspects of lower-class society to add that proverbial push to send people over the edge. I'm not talking only about the pressures of being poor, underprivileged, ethnic, suppressed, etc., which the guiltmongers like to throw in people's faces as justification for certain behavior. Those pressures do exist in the lower classes, but so do drug and alcohol abuse; mental illness; fetal alcohol syndrome and crack babies; crippling degrees of dysfunctionality; a higher percentage of physical and sexual abuse; broken homes; lower IQs; one in three children being born out of wedlock; broken families; child abandonment; a parallel economy based on drugs, stolen goods, and fraud; and, of course, the casual acceptance of violence. You put these factors into the equation, and you can just about kiss off any hope of normalcy.

Important safety tip here: crazy people don't come from sane environments. It's the guy who snaps and climbs up in a bell tower with a rifle whom you hear about, not the huge supporting cast of dysfunctional people who helped shape the lunatic with the semiautomatic. He's only noticeable because he's the most rabid. The bulk of the insanity lies hidden in the underlying structure that produced him. In many cases that merely means his family environment, its structure, and dysfunction.

In this case, that underlying picture is the L.A. life-style. L.A. residents accept as normal what is outrageous elsewhere. This may come as a shock to a great many people living in L.A., but in the rest of the western United States it is not normal to have a firefight going on down at the end of the street! Time between gunshots in most neighborhoods is measured by months, not hours. And even in other cities' "bad" neighborhoods, it's days between shootings, not minutes. What's normal in L.A. is considered twisted elsewhere, but everyone in L.A. accepts it because it's politically correct.

Just an example of how tweaked L.A. really is came during the riots that followed the first Rodney King trial. They were the "riots" to everyone except the L.A. media, who called them the "civil unrest." See, you shoot rioters, but civil unrest is an "expression of anger from a segment of the population" and is therefore acceptable. That's being open-minded to the point of falling in. People in L.A. have spent so much time listening to (and being confused by) rhetoric that they've lost sight of the limits and boundaries necessary for a society to function, especially one that totals 4 million people! Last time I checked, losing sight of limits is a common symptom among the insane. If that's the case, L.A. should be stuck in a rubber room.

Setting limits is a way of saying that some things are simply flat-out unacceptable; if you cross this line, this will happen. It may come as a surprise to people in Los Angeles, but there are a large number of cities and states that still have and enforce these boundaries. Miami and Detroit will shoot you just as fast for participating in civil unrest as for rioting. No trial, negotiation, or civil rights issues; "get off the streets right now or get blown away, your choice." Not in Los Angeles; we'll let it go for a day and a half and then give you until nightfall to continue looting and burning before we let loose the National Guard.

If you want to see a more common example of L.A.'s insanity, just look at the fiasco it calls the legal system. You do a drive-by shooting in Texas, and you're facing a death sentence. You do a drive-by shooting in Los Angeles, and you're looking at doing seven years max, with a high probability of being out in three. Texas is executing people all the time in spite of the appeals process. In California it is nearly impossible to get the death sentence; if you do get one, your lawyer can appeal it and get it stalled in legal mumbo jumbo for anywhere from 5 to 15 years, or until it's easier to reduce the sentence to life imprisonment—which again means being paroled after a few years.

Here's an example of the insanity that infects L.A. When Californians allowed themselves to be talked out of the idea of an eye for an eye, they allowed the criminals to run amuck. Now the criminals have nothing to fear from any punishment that the state can deal out. Prison used to be something to be afraid of; now it's a boy's camp. You're violating a prisoner's civil rights if you don't allow him cigarettes. Punishment is taking someone's TV away for a week. Putting low-level offenders in tent cities is decried as cruel and unusual punishment. This is the threat that's supposed to keep the criminal from misbehaving? Putting it simply, there is nothing bigger and meaner out there than the criminals, and they know it! They aren't afraid of the court system because they have no money or property to lose. If they get sent to jail, it just means they get to kick back with their homeboys and watch TV— *which is what they do anyway*! Sitting on their butts is the same whether they're outside or sitting in a prison cell, except that they eat more regularly in the joint.

Just as locks only keep out honest people, jail is only scary to an honest person. Back when everybody had a choice of working or starving, prison was a serious threat. While you were in the pen, your livelihood was slipping away; when you got out, you were an outcast from society. However to today's criminals, it's just a part of life. Most criminals are terminally unemployed or underemployed anyway, so they have nothing much to lose.

A lot of them aren't employed because the little amount of money they could make with a legitimate job wouldn't equal what the state pays them. Meanwhile, state services are a windfall to criminals. Selling food stamps is a thriving business. (Don't believe me? Just look what happened after the January 1994 earthquakes in L.A.—food-stamp fraud was a thriving enterprise by the second week.) Their state checks can be used to finance the purchase of the drugs necessary to get back into their real business. Now, the real pisser is that there are a whole bunch of guys in California prisons who are still collecting unemployment, welfare, and Social Security benefits! There are all sorts of social benefits available to the ex-inmate because, in many cases, he is considered "psychologically damaged" by prison and therefore unemployable. If this doesn't strike you as insane, I bet you thought Jimmy Carter was a good president, too.

It's in the area of self-defense that L.A.'s weirdness is in full bloom. You are more likely to go to jail for attempted self-defense in L.A. than any other place I've been. The system is disposed toward the idea that violence is wrong, regardless of your motives. In essence, this means that if you win, you've broken the law. The legally acceptable level of use of force has such a narrow margin that without years of specialized training, it is nearly impossible not to cross the line of "excessive force." Even if you don't get slammed with an excessive force rap for fighting back and hurting the guy who was trying to rip you off, you're still in for trouble. The criminals have caught on that they can sue you for hurting them. That's right; you can be sued for defending yourself or your property. If you have assets, there's some bottom-feeding lawyer who will be willing to take such a case for 50 percent of the settlement. And because of the way the system is set up, he's got a good chance of winning. You have a choice in L.A.: 1) being victimized or 2) getting arrested and being sued for defending yourself. It has gotten to the point that in order to be safe from expensive legal ramifications of being attacked by a criminal, you have to break the law afterward. God help you if you shoot a burglar or he should hurt himself while crawling through your window! That's California's legal system right now, and L.A. is the epitome of it.

Nobody, except the criminals, is happy with the California legal system. Part of the population felt that justice was not served with the Rodney King verdict. (Incidentally, that same segment of the populace had demanded that the chokehold be outlawed when a drunken football player died from being improperly subdued with one; a chokehold would have resolved the entire King altercation in seven seconds and without a beating.) The rest of the population felt that justice was not served when Reginald Denny's attackers were acquitted on what amounted to a technicality. (Since the district attorney couldn't prove premeditation or intent, it wasn't attempted murder despite the fact that they hit him on the head with bricks and hammers.) The criminal's intent is evidently more important than his actions. Isn't progressive thinking wonderful? Thanks to these wonderful examples of corkscrew thinking, everyone is now pissed at the system. One can hope that this will result in its being reevaluated and reorganized, but I wouldn't hold my breath. This means the criminals will just be getting worse.

L.A. is not a town to be in for the next decade or so. Anyone with any sense or money is bailing out. That means that whoever is left will have neither sense or money. For years, L.A.'s economy has been going downhill as major companies have left the state because of the high cost of operating there. California business laws and taxes have become so user unfriendly that many large companies have pulled out—first out of L.A., then out of the state. In short, the part of society whose productivity was able to support both the lower end of the job market and the nonproducers has up and left. What you have now is a big version of a steel town whose factory has closed—a 4-million-people-bigger version.

For more than 50 years L.A. has been the dumping ground for America's unemployed. I'm talking about grunt labor. Start with the Okies in the Great Depression, then count the seekers of job opportunities provided by World War II, skip the 1950s, throw in the hippies of the '60s, include the recession victims in the '70s and '80s—and add to this a constant flow of immigrants from points south of the border (and across the Pacific) seeking jobs. Now the jobs have dried up, but all the people remain.

If you live in the areas where these people live, I don't have to tell you about the problems that come from having them as neighbors. Drunken arguments in the middle of the night, car crashes with uninsured (and drunk) drivers, shots fired, dead cars on the street or front lawn . . . the list goes on and on. With the workers come nonworkers and problem cases who ride the coattails of society. Professional criminals, addicts, alcoholics, gangs, and thieves prowl in the working man's shadow everywhere else, but in L.A. they don't even bother to hide anymore. In some areas, they have taken over from the workers, and they are the only ones there—most of the time carping that they have all sorts of "institutional" or "societal" problems that have caused all their troubles. It is only a matter of time before they bring their troubles to your door—and trouble is coming. The failure of the authorities to suppress the rioters only showed them that they can get away with it. There will either be a next time, which will have to be suppressed with a superior firepower, or the situation will continue to spin out of control until you end up with the sci-fi cyberpunk-type situation where everyone is armed and armored while the city rots around them.

In addition to all this, you have those from other countries escaping oppressive governments. There is a not-so-funny joke that L.A. is the world's largest third-world country. It's not funny because it's not that far from the truth: L.A. has long been the magnet for refugees. Some of these are the rich folks who managed to bail out in time, but most are the grunts and unemployed. Although there has always been Hispanic casual labor gathered on corners, these days most of them are not Mexican, but Nicaraguan, Salvadoran, and Guatemalan—the new wave of grunts. The most overcrowded pit in L.A. represents better living conditions than what they left. (It may come as a surprise to most people, but if you watch tapes of the L.A. riots, while the blacks were busy being interviewed as to why they were looting their neighborhood, half of the looters were Hispanic. They weren't saying anything; they were just pillaging and avoiding the news crews. The L.A. Mexican community was quick to stand up and say, "It's not us! It's the newcomers from Guatemala and Nicaragua!" Having grown up in a barrio and being able to spot subtle facial differences between northern Mexicans and Central Americans, I had to agree with them. Most of the looters did look to be from farther south.)

Not all the migrants who come to L.A. are Hispanic. One of the fires that raged through L.A. in 1993 was started by a homeless Chinese refugee whose campfire got away from him up in the Altadena hills. What are they going to do to the guy, send him to jail? A roof over his head and three square meals a day; yeah, that'll teach him! The prospect of Hong Kong being taken over by mainland China in 1997 has caused a major influx of Hong Kong Chinese refugees. Down Orange County way, you have massive Vietnamese and Cambodian populations who came when Saigon fell in 1975 and afterward, when those same "peace-loving people of Vietnam" we'd been fighting invaded Cambodia. Of course, by then thousands of Cambodians had bailed out already rather than be slaughtered by the Khmer Rouge. The reason there are so many Thais in

L.A. (nobody would know whom I was talking about if I said Siamese) is that things were getting awfully ugly up in northern Thailand for a long while. These people left to stay alive and are now part of the L.A. scene.

Immigrants aren't necessarily losers; in fact, most of these people are actually hardworking if they get a chance. A friend of mine in Miami once described the Jamaicans getting off the boat in their lime-green polyester suits with suitcases in hand and having a job the next day. The same can be said for many of the immigrants: they come to work, not cadge from the system. Until the Koreans got nailed in the riots, they were the only outsider group willing to take a chance on doing business in South Central L.A. The number of Armenian businesses in Hollywood and Glendale (and of course the Japanese) proves that not all immigrants are rejects from the countries they left.

What makes L.A. a truly insane place isn't that it's dying economically; that's just the catalyst. A major factor is that California in general and Los Angeles in particular have been used as the nation's septic tank for more than 50 years. I'm talking not only about the unemployed, but the losers, misfits, criminals, and mentally crippled from all over the United States who were sent off to California. Most times it was unofficial, just a little pressure from the community or the local police, but on more than one occasion it was official. The most notable case was the serial rapist in Florida who was given a choice by the judge of either a long prison term or a bus ticket to California. He took the ticket. (Fortunately, he was met at the border by the California State Police who said, "Unh-unh, pal! You're going back to Florida.") Los Angeles is a wonderful place year-round for the homeless. They aren't likely to freeze to death in the winter as they are to the north, nor are they likely to bake to death in the summer as they are in the desert. And California's dole system is higher-paying than other states', so California here we come!

But now the cesspit is full. People are bailing out of Los

Angeles and heading for the hills. The problem is that it's the respectable folks who are getting out! If you live in another state, the next time you hear someone bitching about all the Californians who are ruining your state, realize that you're getting back better than you sent! (I would recommend, however, keeping them out of local politics.) On the other hand, if you hear displaced Californians complaining about the backwater nature of your home state, just remind them what a paradise their hometown is now because they were too liberal to put their foot down.

Los Angeles has one of the worst gang problems in the country. The gangs are the best example of the tip of the insanity iceberg that makes up L.A. They're everywhere; there is very little area in all of L.A. that isn't claimed as a territory by one gang or the other except select areas of the Westside, the Valley, South Bay, or behind the Orange Curtain (Orange County).

I personally have been the target of drive-by and freeway shootings and more than once have had the bad luck of being where two gangs decide to hash it out. These happened to me simply because I was in L.A. There is no way in hell that I would ever consider taking a job as a convenience store clerk or a gas station attendant—it's like painting a target on your chest. Those hard-to-understand little guys standing behind the 7-11 counter are braver than you or I, bucko.

The best way to avoid being a victim of a crime in L.A. is mobility. Criminals are mobile; they come and go as they please. If you're a fixed target, they can choose when and where to strike. If they can get you into a place where you can't move, they've got you. Your car is still your best bet if it's moving, but if it's parked, forget it. Mobility means the ability to move, not struggling to get into your car and losing time until you can get it moving. Despite the number of people there, L.A. is still open enough that you can usually prevent people from pressing against you as they do back east. If a criminal can get close to you, the only way to be safe is to be faster, meaner, and more vicious than he is.

Speaking of mobility, you'll notice I spend a lot of time talking about cars in this book. Cars are a way of life in L.A. People who have never been to L.A. don't realize the size of the whole mess. One day, out of curiosity, I sat down and figured out that there was a place in L.A. where you could drive for at least 75 miles in any direction and still be in urban sprawl. That's more than an hour without traffic to slow you down, and you're still in the city. The L.A. sprawl has encroached on five separate counties! Los Angeles itself has three area codes and regularly does business with four more that abut L.A. County.

The whole mess that is L.A. consists of the large city of Los Angeles and suburbs. The magnitude of the sprawl has incorporated cities in other counties as suburbs of Los Angeles. Orange County is now merely a suburb of Los Angeles. Like a smeared piece of artwork, it's confusing to tell where one begins and the others leave off. Los Angeles consists of several main areas that are generally divided into Downtown, Hollywood, West L.A., East L.A., Central L.A. (although it is often classified as part of something else), and, of course, South Central. There are districts inside each of these areas that were once independent cities or areas that have been incorporated into the monolith. For example, the West L.A. area is subdivided into Palms, Mar Vista, Venice, Fox Hills, Brentwood, and Westwood. Even Downtown is divided into the Business District, Chinatown, the Warehouse District, Little Tokyo, the Garment District, and Skid Row (Spring Street). New Yorkers may talk about 42nd Street or the Wall Street district with pride, but in L.A. if it doesn't cover at least 50 blocks, it doesn't even warrant a name.

Except for East L.A. and South Central (which are the pits wherever you are), you can't really label a whole area as good or bad. It's when you get down to the districts that you can begin to say good, bad, or indifferent. Understand that there are around 100 of these areas in the L.A. area, so I'm not going to bother explaining them all. There are certain districts whose only purpose seems to be separating the larger areas—so much so that unless you live there, you have no idea that they exist. For example Echo Park seems to exist for the sole purpose of dividing the Hollywood section from what's called Downtown. I dare even L.A. natives to find Mount Washington!

Surrounding L.A. proper are localized areas consisting of several smaller cities but classified as a whole. San Fernando Valley (called The Valley) is made up of Van Nuys, Encino, Reseda, Sepulveda, Woodland Hills, Chatsworth, Sunland, Pacomia, Burbank, Glendale, etc. Each of these cities is also subject to specific categorization (e.g., Encino is rich and Van Nuys is rapidly becoming a pit, while Sunland ain't a place you want to go if you're not a truck driver type). Glendale is divided into north (nice) and south (pit). The South Bay, consisting of Redondo Beach, Hermosa Beach, Torrance, and (though they deny it) Palos Verdes, is mostly nice except where it leans toward Hawthorne, Inglewood, and Lawndale.

Some cities have such a reputation that they define an entire area. Pasadena is the term used to describe nearly anything on the west side of the San Gabriel Valley. Anything farther east has markings on the maps saying, "Here be monsters" or, "Unexplored" to most L.A. residents. Incidentally, this also includes anything north of Zuma Beach (north of Malibu). The hatred San Franciscans feels for Los Anglenos is one-sided; most people in L.A. don't even know Frisco exists, nor do they care! Long Beach is along the same lines as Pasadena; it's so big it's used as a reference point for nearby cities. Whoever heard of Seal Beach, and who cares about San Pedro? Malibu holds Pacific Palisades and a few other areas as minor satellites.

Others stand out without being grouped. Beverly Hills and Santa Monica are the most notable (sorry West Hollywood), but only because they're unique while still being surrounded by L.A. Of course, with some smaller cities, like Culver City, nobody realizes they're passing through in the first place. L.A. picks up again on the other side anyway, so why bother? Many people feel this way about Orange County. Face it, Orangers, you've been assimilated! However, to outsiders (and indeed many locals), this huge mess is all grouped together under the heading of L.A.

Los Angeles is a city on the highway to hell. In some ways it's worse than New York, and in others it will never be that bad. I don't recommend L.A. for anyone who isn't half mad dog or thick-skinned enough to make a rhinoceros blush. On the other hand, if that does describe you and you're young and bold, give it a shot. I have lived most of my life cruising through L.A.'s street life, and I've had a blast doing it. There may be men too gentle to run among wolves, but I sure wasn't one of them. With this in mind, I share with you the information I have gathered over the years about crime and criminals in L.A. and how to stay ahead of them.

CHAPTER ONE

The Basics

Robbery by definition is the taking of something by the use (or threat) of force. It constitutes 35 percent of all violent crime and is the most unpredictable of all crimes. Its seasonal curve is different from other types of violent crime. Instead of August being its peak month (as with other offenses), robbery exhibits a gradual swell in October and November, peaks in December, and then slowly decreases from January to February (whether this is because all the ho-ho-ho brings out the sharks or some psychological factor is anyone's guess).

More significant than its unpredictability is the ease with which it can suddenly turn into a murder, assault with a deadly weapon, kidnapping, or rape. In any robbery there are two factors that determine if one of these extremes develops: the robber and you. Yes, indeedy do, folks, like quantum physics, you are part of the equation. In fact, you are 50 percent of the equation. The first factor is something you really can't control; however, the second factor is all up to you. Your reaction, as much as the robber's, can prevent a robbery from evolving into something else.

But unless you are both willing to and able of committing bone-breaking violence at the drop of a hat, the odds are with the robber if he decides to attack. He's got the advantages of knowing what he's up to, positioning, preplanning, and possessing a violent mind-set. If he has a weapon, all he has to do is strike or pull the trigger. It is your job to ensure that he never gets to the point of doing that. Under these conditions, any violence must be fierce enough to stop him but not prolonged. Any prolonged encounter against an armed opponent increases your chances of being seriously hurt. Instead, you have to engage him just long enough to create a means of escape.

There is no guaranteed-safe solution in dealing with a robber. Once it has gotten to the point where the robber has decided to make his move, it is generally safer to comply with his demand that you turn over your valuables. If you find yourself in excessive fear (which is the normal reaction the first time you're robbed), you have turned over all control to the robber. The good news about this is a majority of all robbers only want to get their loot and be done with you. Don't hesitate (and, for god's sake, don't argue); just give him what he wants as long as it stays a simple robbery. It's when he tells you to go somewhere with him that it is going to get ugly. In cases like these, the likelihood of it turning into an attack/rape increases.

WHO GETS ROBBED?

Although the actual number of robberies is high, the likelihood of any one person being selected is rather low. Factoring in bank jobs, liquor stores, markets, and gas stations, the fact is that about 250 out of every 100,000 people will be robbed. That's statistics; reality is—unless you work in a bank or convenience store or live in or adjacent to a pit of a neighborhood—your chances of being robbed are much lower than that.

On the other hand, just as watering holes are the hangouts for predators, there are places where your chances of being robbed go up. Criminals commonly hang out and stalk their victims in or near parking lots, automatic teller machines (ATMs), event centers or popular gathering places; on pathways to or from your car; and near waiting points for the public transportation system. Hitting your ATM in the middle of the night increases your chances of being robbed.

If you work in a high-risk job (such as bank teller, convenience/liquor store clerk, or gas station attendant), your chances of being robbed go way up. Businesses that have high customer traffic and deal primarily in cash are choice targets. A major department store is less likely to be robbed than a video store because most of the former's transactions are either credit card or check. In the same sense, a person is less *profitable* to rob than a store. However, stores are *harder* to knock over—which makes people *safer* to rob. See the pattern yet?

WHO ARE THE ROBBERS?

Robberies, unlike most violent crimes, are generally committed by two or more individuals. If a criminal has a weapon, he might brave it alone, but more often than not he's with a partner. An astounding number of personal robberies are committed without weapons. That sounds reassuring until you realize that this means these crimes are committed by packs, and one viewing of the Reginald Denny footage will convince you what a pack can do. When it's five against one, who needs weapons? But the good news is that, while one person can move unnoticed with a certain amount of ease, five people are hard to hide.

Robbery, like most violent crimes, is mostly a young man's crime. Your average robber is young, not too bright (or he'd be in a more lucrative form of crime), willing to commit violence, and often sliding into the deeper levels of addiction. Robbers still conform to the prototype hunters, preferring to prey on women, senior citizens, and young adults (early twenties). All three groups are less likely to fight back—the elderly because of infirmity, women because of cultural conditioning, and the young because of lack of experience. This doesn't mean that just because you are not in one of these target groups that you're safe. Nor should you think that the age of your assailant makes him any less dangerous. An older, more-experienced criminal may be more cold-blooded, but a scared kid is more likely to pull the trigger during an encounter. The good news is that a kid is more likely to veer off during the interview in the face of assertive behavior.

The movie *Grand Canyon*, which was set in L.A., showed a particularly ugly professional robbery. The man came out of nowhere, weapon ready, and demanded something that was visible and easily pawned. A Rolex is worth more money than likely would have been in the victim's wallet. When the criminal saw what he considered resistance, he fired his gun with no hesitation at the knee, a professional target. A professional robbery is nearly impossible to prevent, and, sadly, this type of robbery is becoming more common. In some cities, the criminals are simply walking up and shooting the victim without even speaking to him. The criminal takes the wallet/purse/watch off the wounded victim and leaves. Fortunately, most robberies are not this concise or professional and can be avoided with a little common sense.

TIPS TO AVOID BEING ROBBED

1) *Hide your money.* Never flash large wads of money. Criminal hang out in liquor stores, fast-food joints, convenience stores, gas stations, and public service buildings and watch to see who's got the most cash. Always keep your money low and your body between it and anyone who's looking.

2) *Be especially careful at ATMs.* This is the favorite hunting grounds of robbers, so before you approach a machine, look to see who's around. If there is someone who looks odd, go to another machine. If someone looks quasi-threatening but you're not sure, let him go first. Watch what he does after he's finished his transaction. Is he waiting around for

you to turn your attention to the machine? If yes, then don't. Get lost instead. Always check for anyone in one of your blind spots before you start your ATM transaction. Your attention is going to be focused on punching the numbers for a few seconds, so make sure nobody is around to close the distance during this time. Once you've finished punching in the numbers, turn away from the machine and see if anyone is approaching. This is one of the most common times for criminals to strike. For a smash and grab, all he has to do is knock you down and scoot with the money. If he's willing to hang around, he can nail you from behind and punch in "another transaction" to score major money.

3) *Parking lots are death traps.* The second most common scenario for a robber to strike is when you're heading toward your car. A parked car isn't safe. Most people, even if they see a likely mugger, will head for the car. Go out and time yourself and see how long it takes to get in, start your car, and get out of a parking spot. You'd lose. A good rule of thumb is not to let anyone near you in an empty parking lot, period.

Cross the street and do doublebacks to see if anyone is following you. If your suspect cruises on by after you've done a course change, it means that he wasn't up to anything. If he changes course to match you, go into a restaurant, bar, liquor store, or any other open business that is nearby. Your pursuer probably will disappear if you involve other people.

4) *Senior citizens are special targets of robbers.* A junkie who steers clear of a young, healthy person will strike faster than a snake at an old person. Junkies know that an older person can't defend himself against a lightning-fast attack. Knocking an elderly woman over and snatching her pocketbook

is probably the safest crime available to a junkie.

In urban areas where banks pulled out years ago because of low profits and high robbery rates, leaving only the check joints, nailing old people with their Social Security checks has reached epic proportions. These money-cashing joints will cash checks without ID for upward of a 20-percent take. The junkie hits the older person at the mail box, snatches the check, runs to the local check joint, and has it cashed before the check can be reported stolen. Or they wait until they see the old-timer leaving these establishments and strike then. Another common place to strike is when the person is heading to the store.

In addition to junkies, kids are also a major threat to older adults. Kids have grown more vicious over the years, and a 15-year-old with a gun is just as dangerous, if not more so, than an adult with a gun. Remember how important your wishes were when you were 15, and what you would have been willing to do for them? A kid with no scruples and a gun still has those overwhelming desires.

The best answer to crime against the elderly is to get out of the neighborhood. For those who either won't or can't move out, the sad truth is there isn't much that can be done to protect them. Enlisting the aid of an able-bodied man, a police officer, or even a Guardian Angel (if your city has a branch) to accompany groups of seniors will help. Make a schedule for heading to the store or picking up or cashing checks so everyone can go at once.

WHAT TO DO *BEFORE* YOU'RE ROBBED

1)   *Keep one piece of identification at home, not in your*

wallet. One of the worst problems of being robbed is the inconvenience of having to replace everything. It was scary to have a gun stuck up your nose, but you'll want to murder the idiot at the Department of Motor Vehicles who tells you he won't issue a license without a Social Security card (never mind the fact that your SS card was ripped off with your driver's license, and it'll take six weeks to get a new one). If you live in an area where you are likely to get robbed, you might also consider "losing" your original driver's license and requesting another from the DMV. After you receive the new license, you "find" the lost one and keep it at home as a spare.

2) *Make a list of all the credit card numbers and phone numbers you need to report stolen and stick it somewhere you won't forget.* The second you hit the door or can call home, start burning up those phone lines to stop those cards from being used. Have your spouse call if you're down at the police station, but stop them immediately. Hot credit cards are often sold to credit card specialists within an hour. Since most people spend hours freaking out or dealing with the cops before reporting cards stolen, the crim has hours to rack up charges.

3) *Keep your money and wallet separate.* Since the guy often just wants your money (unless he's got an immediate buyer for hot credit cards), it's not a bad idea to set it up so you're either left with your money or your wallet after a robbery. This is accomplished by carrying your money in a pants pocket instead of in your wallet or purse. A money clip keeps the money folded and prevents unsightly bulges, as well as leaving you with taxi fare home in case laughing boy gets your car keys. If the guy says, "Give me your wallet," you hand it over. If he

says, "Give me your money!" you say, "Okay, it's in my front pocket," and give it to him. In either case you're left with more than you would be if you kept everything together. You can get by on either credit cards or cash; losing them both, along with your ID, is going to cause you major problems.

4) *Have spare keys in case your key ring gets stolen.* Keep your car key on a separate ring in your pocket, or have a spare key magnetically held in place somewhere in your car's engine compartment. A spare house key hidden somewhere in your backyard also allows you to get into your own home.

5) *Replace the locks on your house and maybe the ignition to your car if your keys get stolen—before you're robbed again!* You can either call the locksmith from the police department and have him meet you at home or call your spouse and have him/her pick up new locks on the way home. However you do it, get those locks replaced immediately. If you have a garage, change the lock and start parking your car in it until you can get a new ignition lock. If you don't have a garage, park down the street (or on another street) until you can replace the lock. The guy's got your address and keys; anything that fits those keys is vulnerable.

New York

New York City is a big place: 12 million people in the metro area. Naturally enough, there's room for every flavor of robbery.

The tone of Manhattan has bred a few extra special strains, though, that are worth mentioning. All our general advice on avoiding robbery/assault situations applies on the streets of Gotham, and after you're in town for a while, your eyes will quickly learn to filter out the hordes of more or less honest citizens hurrying through the streets (and subways), as Joseph Conrad would have it, "trying to filch a little money from each other." Behind those hurrying mobs is a slower, more reptilian pattern of predators looking to make a score.

Not all muggers are addicts—in fact, the worst of them are not drug dependent at all. They're simply sociopaths who don't see any particular wrong in stabbing you and your wife to get some money to buy sneakers and go to Roseland with. They call it "getting paid" around the Apple. It is not uncommon for a knot of kids to head toward Manhattan on a Saturday night with nothing but knives in their pockets, fully expecting to mug up enough money for the night's festivities on the way—which is a good reason to avoid the trains after about 10:00 P.M., especially on weekends.

These kinds of robberies are almost explosive. Three, four, five teenagers, some blades. The intent is there, with bells on.

The interview can be done by all of them or one of them, and it can be quick as a snap. Positioning, especially in a subway car or on a platform, is the least of the problems. When you squeeze lemon juice onto a clam on the half shell it literally curls up. The same thing happens in a subway car when a gang of loud, rowdy youths comes pouring in one end. You can almost hear the prayers down the length of the car—"Not me, just keep going, not me!" If there's a crowd, it parts. Positioning, when you've got nothing to stop you, is easy.

If they do zero in on you, remember that these kids want money. That's their motivation. They want sneakers and dough for drinks at Roseland. And if they have the drop on you, just give it up.

The ATM and bank situation in the Apple is fairly tense at all times. Interestingly, some small gangs, always very well dressed, have begun robbing bank customers inside banks—and the banks, like any good New York robber baron institution, have claimed that they have no responsibility to protect customers on their premises. If you get beat for your wad inside the place, they claim not to be liable. The legal standing on this, as far as we can tell, has not yet been determined. It's this kind of attitude that has kept me true to a New Jersey bank all these years.

These robberies are not pistol stick-'em-up jobs; they're finesse affairs. Often, they seem to have a teller as an accomplice. When someone makes a sizable withdrawal, the teller signals the others. Sometimes the teller can't get their attention right away, which will make him or her stall before handing the money over. Other times they pass the cash through and then make a big, obvious gesture, which, if the customer notices at all, will probably look like waving at a friend. If a teller stalls or waves when you take out big cash, call him or her on it or insist on seeing the manager and explain what just happened. Whatever little fuss you kick up will probably be enough to draw all sorts of attention to you, and that's the last thing these thieves want. But if the fuss does not shake them off and you do get jumped on the sidewalk, the cops will have a real good place to start their investigation—with the teller.

Inside-the-bank robberies are almost like pickpocket jobs, except this is no fishing expedition. From the teller's signal the thieves know you've got money, and they saw where you put it. Now they need a distraction. Common ones are to squirt or spill some food on you or to drop some bills on the floor and then act like you dropped them. From there, wiping off your jacket or helping you pick up "your" money, they are in position for either a grab and sprint or to just do a cool pickpocket job on you. Don't forget, you tend to lower your defenses somewhat inside a bank. After all, there are all these cameras, and they have a guard and everything. Your money is here, and it's safe; now you're here and you should be safe too.

Not in New York, you're not. A variation of this spotter-type robbery happens at ATMs. This is one wrinkle the banks never talk about, but it's pretty common. Here, the spotter will be someone else in the ATM vestibule with you, most likely a very nonthreatening woman, well dressed—a legit customer doing some quick paperwork, you think. Certainly not a mugger. You take out cash, and she watches where you put it. With a gesture she communicates that to the strong-arm boys out on the sidewalk. You walk out, and they come up and grab you and go straight for the poke.

There are also straightforward armed robberies at ATMs, and way late at night is a good time to invite one into your life. Just say no until morning. Many city ATM rooms double as dormitories for the homeless in winter. The year round, many homeless claim an ATM as their home and function as doormen or doorwomen for tips. This is kind of an oozy situation, and I always steer away and look for another location. It's too easy for this situation to be something other than it appears to be—and in a strict interview sense, by showing that you're willing to turn your back on some skel and tickle the most intimate parts of your financial infrastructure, you've already demonstrated that you ain't too damn streetwise. Also, the next time you use an ATM, listen to it when it counts money—you can bet the homeless dude in the corner is. It takes a lot longer to count $300 than it does to count $40, which is something else the homeless know well. Also, around Christmas, the thoughtful robber barons at the banks usually raise the ATM cash limits pretty high, like $800 per day. That's for any card, whether you're participating in Christmas or Kwanzaa or not.

Two times, when it wasn't practical to go somewhere else, I chased loiterers out before using the machine. They don't have cards and can't get back in until someone lets them in, and they probably won't come back inside until you leave anyway if you've been forceful enough. I am always surprised by the numbers of package-laden shoppers and petite, oblivious women who will walk into an ATM room at night, alone, when three or four homeless guys are already in there. This is right up there with polishing your credit cards and counting stacks of hundreds in a bucket o'blood tavern as a way to get mugged. The machine rickety-ticks out hundreds of dollars, and these guys haven't got their crack money for the day, or their wine money, or food, or whatever is motivating them at the moment. By going in like that, you put yourself in a situation that is very tempting—maybe too tempting. You inject the intent into what is already a perfect combination of positioning and a satisfactory interview. Next thing, you're in trouble.

New York is probably the world capital of purse and chain snatchings; it's at least the U.S. capital of this sneaky, dangerous crime. Purse snatchers are real low on the criminal totem pole, down there with junkies. Curiously, this is a situation where New Yorkers love to help out if they can—there's something about the cowardly, jackal nature of the crime that sets everyone off—that and the fact that the perp is running down the street like a scared dog, which often triggers mob-vengeance and pack-sadistic kinds of feelings in people who would otherwise stand and watch. All kinds of people are willing to try and catch snatchers—it's absolutely amazing.

Prevention measures are pretty much common knowledge these days: ditch the chains, carry purses and handbags close to the body and with the clasp toward yourself to thwart pickpockets, of which there are also many in the city. Cameras with a long enough strap should be worn bandolier-style instead of just around the neck to prevent injury if it should get pulled on. Women can also keep their wallets and other real valuables in a small fanny pack worn at the front and demote the purse to a large makeup case. Many international travelers favor small document pouches that ride under your clothes bandolier-style and keep passports, money, credit cards, tickets, and other important items safe and concealed. These are very cheap, usually under $10, and available anywhere that sells travel items, from camping/outdoorsy stores to department store luggage sections. These pouches are a good idea when you're far from home—you could go through anything from a motorcycle accident to a riot and not lose your really important papers. And if you travel in scruffy neighborhoods, they're not such a bad idea here in America.

One of the more common and ominous wrinkles to this old game these days involves cutting the strap. This is said to absolutely be a one-moment-it's-here-the-next-moment-vanished situation. Suddenly, with almost no sensation at all, the strap is cut and the bag halfway down the block. Whether the perp is using scissors or a razor, this is one sprinter best left unchased. He has a weapon, a sharp one. Knowing that, you know that distance is your best self-protection ally. Let it go and count yourself lucky that you weren't cut in the bargain.

Letting it go is usually the advice given to victims of snatchings. But keeping in mind that assault on the criminal puts you into a dangerous spot legally—leaving you open for lawsuits—this is one time when you might be part of dealing some righteous street justice. Naturally, you should be well aware that the snatcher may be armed—although probably not with a gun—and realize that if trapped, even an unarmed snatcher will turn on you with that famous cornered-rat ferocity. Nonetheless, even a brief chase will more than likely get other New Yorkers involved and might just help you settle the score.

Let's take a fast detour into the subject of concealed pistols for a minute. A running person with a gun will have his hand on the piece to keep it from bouncing away. Watch a cop running sometime. A guy with a snub-nose revolver or small auto in a secure armpit rig does not need to hold the pistol while sprinting, but cops with a gunbelt do. Little pistols fit into pockets where they're not a problem, but larger guns, at least on criminals, usually end up tucked into the waistband of the pants front or rear, just like in the movies. As one old Mafia gunsel told me, "That's where it's most convenient, and you can draw without getting it all hung up in your cummerbund." That's if you happen to be gunslinging in your tuxedo.

Cops who are looking for armed citizens watch people running—in the rain, for a taxi, against a traffic light. If they run with their hand on their bellies, it's a safe-money bet that there's a pistol there. Keep this in mind when dealing with purse or chain snatchers. Also, as a general minute-to-minute rule, anyone who keeps adjusting something under his clothes—like at the waist—is probably armed with a gun. Cops know, especially because they're like that themselves, that people with pistols can't keep their hands off them. If this means some psychological bullshit to you, try and get past it. The pragmatic aspect is this: people fidget with their pistols. You can know this kind of a secret if you just keep your eyes open. People with hidden pistols are generally bad to be around in big cities because the pistols sometimes discharge. And if your purse snatcher is running along holding his belly, it's time to stop the chase.

But in the more usual case of an unarmed punk, chasing is, in my opinion, okay to do, and I base that on what I've actually seen in the streets: which is, sometimes the punk gets away despite the chase, and sometimes people join in and stomp the useless scum into a grease spot then buy each other a beer to celebrate, while the police can't find any witnesses.

There are horror stories of women chasing a purse snatcher into a park and getting raped for their trouble, and I'm sure that once or twice a snatcher has run back to shut up a screaming woman, but this is not the usual thing.

There's one young woman who would have her purse today if she'd only screamed. It was on 14th Street at night, which can be a pretty barren area. As they ran toward me it looked like she and her boyfriend were jogging toward a bus—there was no special speed involved, and no look of panic or anger. And it was a shame, because I had plenty of time to position myself to take this guy out; I had something serious on me to hit him with and the inclination to bop somebody. He was also half my size. But the girl didn't scream until they were past me, and I'm no sprinter. Even then, her scream was this impotent thing that ended high, like a question. He was a damn slow runner, but she ran out of steam before he did, and he rounded the corner and was gone.

I've also seen a friendly stranger jab a broom handle between a snatcher's feet, bringing him down hard on his face, with some street justice immediately following. Another time I saw a snatcher trapped at the corner of Spring and Lafayette Streets, running up and down the subway steps, back and forth across the intersection, chased by a small mob, until the police showed and he fell on his face a couple of times. And once, in Hoboken, New Jersey, I saw a purse snatcher who got trapped like a bug in a frying pan right outside the police station. Cops ran out from the station; cops arrived on motorcycles, in cars, on foot, in Cushmans. The kid disappeared behind a wall of blue for a few minutes, and when the cops broke it up and tried to get him to the jail, the guy couldn't walk and was bleeding from all the visible natural orifices and a few unnatural ones. Behind all the yuppie nonsense, Hoboken is a tough town with a 1920s night-stick style of law enforcement, and snatching purses tends to bring out that kind of response. It's not a stand-up kind of crime, and snatchers do not get respect from any quarter.

Here's a useful thing to keep in mind if you're chasing any-one: the best and easiest way to bring a runner down is to shove or hit him from behind, sending him ahead beyond his own point of balance. A runner is leaning heavily forward to stay balanced—an additional shove, not even all that hard, will drop him flat on his face. It's much easier to do this than involving yourself in a flying tackle or a body block, plus it doesn't wreck your clothes or involve you in a potential mix-ing-of-the-blood fight on the ground.

One last general rule about New York City and robbery: other than inside your own house, it's almost impossible to find any place to be alone in this town. There are so many peo-ple that you almost never find yourself alone on a street, in an elevator, even in restrooms. For that reason, anytime you are alone, be extra aware of your surroundings and anyone that comes to join you. Restrooms in office buildings have been the happy hunting ground for many muggers and rapists, especial-ly late at night or during lunch hours when most people are elsewhere. People have been robbed while perched on the thundermug. It's kind of hard to defend against this, as you're in a pretty vulnerable situation, and anyone with a key can come through the outer door. Keys to restrooms do wander from hand to hand at an alarming rate.

We shouldn't need to point this out, but if you happen to encounter a bathroom where a sporting lady is entertaining a client, don't hang around. This falls into the same category as standing outside a parked car leering at the sexual acrobatics going on inside. Strong as the urge to watch might be, no good can come of it. And as noted elsewhere, many johns strenuous-ly object to being watched—although it's hard to see the logic when they're sending the train into the tunnel in a public place, but it's true nonetheless.

L.A.

The face of robbery changes depending on where you are in Los Angeles, but anywhere you go, parking lots, ATMs, and gathering spots are dangerous. Unlike New Yorkers, who use snatch-and-run techniques or mob threat, most of L.A.'s robbers use weapons. It's a very direct proposition: he with gun = you with no money.

FOLLOW-HOME ROBBERIES

L.A. robberies aren't as elaborate as New York's either. In fact, the only really unique form of robbery that L.A. has come up with is the "follow-home" type. Oddly enough, this type of robbery is more likely in the San Fernando Valley than in South Central L.A. Not only are victims in the chichi sections of the valley more likely to have things worth stealing in their homes, but the perpetrators are less likely to get their brains blown into a fine, pink mist for badgering people at home.

Follow-home robberies have become extremely common ever since the robbers discovered that upper-middle-class people are even less aware while driving than when they are wandering the malls. The L.A. attitude about cars is they are protection, a safety zone where no one can touch us. Cars offer distance, hence safety, from others. In this safe spot, we let it all hang out. A well-known example of this is the mild-mannered person who suddenly becomes a red-eyed, profanity-spewing kamikaze when behind the safety of the steering wheel.

A more common reaction, however, is to zone out. In a safe environment people relax and go on autopilot. Since most accidents happen within two miles of the home—a person goes on automatic in familiar territory—a follow-home robbery is extremely effective. Someone who has been scrupulous about staying aware when out and about suddenly relaxes and shuts down his entire defense system when he turns down his street. Nearly home, however, does not home make. While I'm not recommending screaming paranoia, looking in the rearview mirror now and then doesn't hurt. A ratty looking car with two or more people in it cruising through a nice neighborhood is of interest to the police. Why shouldn't it attract your attention? Especially if it's behind you!

Always look in the rearview mirror after you've turned onto your street. This involves nothing more than a quick flick of your eyes. The longer a car has been behind you, the less likely it is to be innocent, especially when it turns onto your street. There are lots of streets in L.A.; the likelihood of that car needing to make the same turns as you goes down dramatically with every turn.

Often, when you've turned down your own street and started to park, the other vehicle will either slow down or sit in the middle of the street. Once you are in a position to be trapped easily, the stalker will accelerate toward you. If you see a car purposely hanging back, then you have every right to suspect that its occupants are up to no good. Subconsciously you know how fast cars normally drive in L.A., especially on your own street. If the guy is really just passing through, he should be going a certain speed, not crawling.

Even though many follow-home robberies originate in local minimall and supermarket parking lots, you can pick one up from a random drive by. For the most part, though, bad guys prefer watching people come out of stores. Not only is it more likely the person has money, but it gives them a chance to do a complete silent interview. Commonly, the car will pull out from the parking lot you've just come from, but occasionally it will just pop up out of nowhere. If you hadn't spotted the tail on your way home, the backward glance on your own street will do the trick. It is especially important that women practice this technique because they're more likely to be followed home.

Now here's an important safety tip: if a car that you don't like turns onto your street behind you, don't pull into your driveway! A key strategy in a follow-home crime is pulling in either immediately behind you and/or blocking your driveway. In either case, your car has suddenly become penned, and you are left on foot—which is exactly what you should use to get out of there. Leave your purse or wallet, throw your house/car keys in another direction, and head for the hills (not toward your house, but away from it).

The same thing applies with parking on the street. With simple placement of their car, the bad guys can snag you like a rabbit in a trap. How many times have you been accidentally parked in? That was by accident, and look how effective it was. It's easy to intentionally park someone in so he can't escape. Keep going; drive past your house and, as soon as possible, make another turn.

If you're blocked in, don't think that flooring it is going to help, either. From a nose-to-nose parked/blocked position you cannot shove another car out of the way. Once penned in, your vehicle is useless as a means of escape. All anyone has to do to get to you is smash the window, and window glass isn't going to stop a bullet.

Just getting into your garage is not going to help you against a follow-home. I know of one such attempt that was foiled when one of the robbers jumped out of the car and began to force open the closing automatic garage door. The owner had noticed the car following him and his wife. They also saw the car block their driveway and the criminal jump out and run to the door. The man slammed the car in reverse and drove through his own garage door. The criminal was thrown to the side, and the couple's car slammed into the car blocking their driveway. That car accelerated away, and the couple fled to the police station. The perp, who had been struck by the car and abandoned by his friends in hostile territory, disappeared.

While this may sound exciting, it really wasn't the best choice the couple could have made. Not only did they have damages to their home, but to their car as well—that amounted to more than a few thousand dollars. This couple was also extremely lucky that the crim decided to split. Had he been hurt enough not to escape, they could have faced criminal and civil charges. Remember, up to that moment the criminal had done nothing more severe than trespass. Technically, he could have been charged with attempted breaking and entering, but a slimy lawyer could make it look like the couple was overreacting. Legally, they attempted vehicular homicide on an innocent man. Had civil charges been brought against them by the criminal, they would have lost everything. They came up with a multithousand dollar solution to a problem that could have been avoided by not pulling into their driveway.

If you see someone tailing you, don't go home. Go to the police station. If you see a cop car, use your horn and point toward your pursuers. That alone will make most pursuers bolt. If they rabbit in front of a cop, that's their problem. Mr. Policeman is going to want to talk with these folks. If he nails them and you pull up and tell the officer that they were following you, those guys are going to the station.

BUMP AND ROBS

Another type of robbery that plagues L.A. is "bump and robs." This is where a carload of guys bump into the back of your car, and when you get out, they rob you. Their main targets are people in rented cars because tourists often have all their money and credit cards with them. Those little Zot's Rent-a-Car bumper stickers can get you ripped off faster than anything else. Rich matronly types in expensive cars are also considered buffet specials. If you ever get involved in this type of accident with folks whose looks you don't like, you should drive directly to a police station. The problem is that most folks don't know where the police stations are outside their local neighborhoods, and if you're from Duluth, you definitely won't know where the stations are in L.A. In that case, drive until you see a cop and flag him down.

One thing to watch for is the car pulling up next to you while you drive away. Don't let it get to the side of you; the passenger might just decide to take a shot at you. If you have to turn off the street you're on, this is usually made easier if you stay in the right lane after this sort of situation. If the pursuers try to get next to you and you see the passenger window open, hook a turn immediately! A few people will shoot through their own windows, but a rolled-down window is not a good sign. Bump and robs are more common around LAX (and the 405) and Burbank Airport since that's where tourists usually are, but they can happen anywhere. Be especially careful about getting out of your car if someone only taps your rear bumper. In fact, don't even turn off your car before you give whoever is in the other car a good look over.

SHOPPING MALLS

Let's talk about malls for a moment. A while ago, my lady and I were watching the news about a gang fight that broke out in a chic Westside mall. Two rival gangs had started their stupid shit at each other, and as these things happen, they ended up shooting at each other. What occurred can only be called a firefight in the loosest sense of the word. Bullets flew everywhere, and the only people hurt were innocent bystanders (this is typical in a gang fight). Naturally, the vultures at the news swooped down and started interviewing people. One outraged woman said that the security guards should have done something. My reaction to that was a combination of amusement and disgust, with disgust predominating. Unarmed security should have rushed right in and stopped a gunfight? Not at $5 an hour, honey. What really annoyed me was that the woman was determined to find someone to blame other than the criminals. *Someone* should have done something to stop the criminals from shooting up her nice mall.

I snarled a nasty riposte against people always trying to pass the responsibility of protecting themselves off onto others and followed it up with, "Wake up! This is L.A.! Malls are prime rip-off spots!"

My lady, however, brought up an interesting counterpoint: "People have the right to go to a mall without fear of it turning into a gun battle. You go to a mall to shop and relax, not to get in firefights."

I thought about that for a while before I agreed: "You *should* be able to relax in a mall . . . but once you hit the parking lot, you go back to awareness!"

Comparatively little crime actually occurs in the mall. Generally, it is more along the lines of two groups of "young, dumb, and fulla cum" butting heads. If they happen to be gangsters, a firefight will ensue. Otherwise, you have two kids kicking and gouging while rolling around on the floor. That's the kind of physical violence most likely to happen in a mall.

However, you're not the only one who goes shopping in malls; criminals do also. But they are shopping for victims. The more aggressive ones will go into the mall and select their victims and then follow them outside into the seclusion of the parking lot. Sometimes you'll pick up a tail in the mall; other times, the assailants loiter near an exit waiting for an appropriate victim. The rest of the time the bad guys are cruising the parking lot, sometimes on foot, sometimes in a car. Often, they'll hang out near the edges of the parking lot so they can escape into the street. Again, robbers usually run in packs, so if you see a group of young men in a parking lot, you should always steer clear of them. If they follow you, head toward the lights and noise, not to your car!

As you leave the mall, always check to see who's behind you or around the door. If some suspicious-looking people are heading in the same direction as you, turn around and go back into the mall. Do it while there are too many people about for the criminals to safely mug you. By staying away from your car, you can't be forced in and driven away. Reaching your car doesn't mean safety. How much distance can the muggers cover while you're fumbling for your keys, getting in, starting your car, pulling out, and driving away?

THE FRINGES

Robbery is a fringe crime. It's something that occurs on the fringes of crowds. The robber needs the crowd to supply his victim, but he can't get too close to the same. Too far away from the crowd and there's nobody to rob. Too close, and he can't do it safely. Criminals lurk on the fringes. Where there're light and noise, there're crowds; if you avoid the fringe, your chances of getting robbed decrease markedly.

You're not likely to be robbed on the Venice Boardwalk, in the Forum, or in Westwood Village proper. It's when you're walking away from these places and their attendant crowds to your car that you're most likely to meet a robber. It's the "to and from" that is the danger zone. Anytime you enter the fringe your awareness needs to go up.

When you're walking through a fringe area, you need to realize that the crim could be watching you come his way. It's obvious when you see someone watching you intently or coming your way. What's not so obvious are the guys sitting in the running car waiting for you. All they do is park on a street and wait for someone to come walking up to them. The passengers spring out, rob you or snatch your purse, hop back into the car, and then drive away. Cruising robbers also loiter in mall parking lots, so beware the carload of guys pulling up as you walk. If someone pulls up and opens the car door, immediately cut through the lanes of parked cars into another aisle and then run back to the lights and noise.

Where you are determines what you're going to be robbed with in L.A. Guns are real common all over, but knives hold their own Downtown, with crackheads, and in Hispanic neighborhoods. Fortunately, with knives if you're more than 10 feet away, you're functionally out of danger. Then again, considering the fact that most criminals are lousy shots beyond 10 feet, you're usually safe from gunfire too.

Skid row and heavy drug-use neighborhoods generally keep with knives, primarily because the residents pawned their guns a long time ago. Hollywood, Venice, San Pedro, and Van Nuys also have their share of strong-arm robberies. These are usually the haunts of slightly less psychotic gangs, who might just decide to rob you the old-fashioned way. A disturbing event is the number of strong-arm robberies committed by upper-middle-class white boys, more for kicks than monetary gain. They usually limit their predations to people near their own age, but sometimes they pick on others. These gangs are common in the San Fernando Valley, Riverside County, and parts of Orange County.

L.A. is the bank robbery capital of America. L.A.'s yearly bank robberies number in the thousands. A bank robbery can range anywhere from one guy quietly handing the teller a note to five guys kicking in the door and waving guns. While the former may happen without your ever knowing it, you'll know when the latter occurs.

Bank robbery is the jurisdiction of the feds and a pack of charming guys from the FBI. Many criminals are leery of messing with the feds for one simple reason: how many wrongful death or civil rights suits do you remember being brought against the FBI? FBI agents don't play around, and they don't care if the criminal gets hurt because they can't be sued. The feds don't give warning shots. Because of this, the full-blown armed bank robbers are generally considered one of the nastiest elements of the criminal world. Not only are they willing to buck the feds, but they're hitting a place with lots of people in it.

If you have the bad luck to be in a bank that is being robbed by this type, hit the floor with your hands out wide and freeze. Not only does this reduce height, getting you out of the way of most bullets, but it's harder to hit someone on the ground with a bullet. There're all sorts of reasons for this that shooters know and drone endlessly on about, but all you need to know is that you're safer on the ground from stray fire. Holding your hands out shows that you're not going for a weapon and that you aren't a threat. Covering your head also signals the same thing. The freeze part serves two purposes: 1) it shows you're not a threat, and 2) since the human eye targets motion better than shapes, becoming a frozen lump on the floor makes you less obvious than a person who is bolting across the room and hence less likely to draw fire.

Technically, if someone points a gun at you and tells you to cross the room, that's kidnapping. If anyone is killed during an armed robbery it is murder one. Don't think that criminals don't know about these legal ramifications. Because of this, it is common for the robbers to simply tell everyone to drop. By hitting the floor early, you avoid the rush. On your way down, you may want to take anyone you care about down with you. This reduces the risk of that person taking a stray bullet.

The problem with convenience stores, banks, gas stations, and liquor stores is that although they conform to the same five-step process of other crimes, the action happens away from where you can see it. Unless you see them coming, your first warning will be when they hit the door. This means you can suddenly find yourself in the middle of a shit storm with little or no warning. Liquor stores and 7-11s are choice targets in L.A. because of the available cash and the likelihood of fewer people in the store.

Often, what you're going to see is an extremely tense person walk in and immediately scan the place for customers. It's the combination of the batwaves and the more than casual scan of the people that signals that something is amiss. If he's alone and there are too many people in the place, he may wander down the aisles or leave. If he stays, he often is waiting for everyone to clear out. Don't disappoint the man; grab your stuff and split immediately. If he immediately beelines it to the cashier, hang back. Don't try to beat the guy to the cash register. You don't want to arrive there the same time that the gun makes its appearance. And, unlike street robberies, most commercial robberies involve weapons. Whereas 7-11 stores prohibit their employees from keeping guns behind the counter, employees in liquor stores, bars, and some gas stations often have them. This means the people who rob them have to be armed to get away with it. The guy is going to be amped up, scared, and willing to pull the trigger rather than risk getting hurt himself. You don't want to be noticed by this guy, nor do you want to be in the same area.

If there are two guys, they often will split up upon entering. This could unfold with one walking in while the other stays by the door, both approaching the cash register then splitting up, or them cruising to the back either separately or together and then floating up different isles. Anytime you see two guys do the split while watching people, you've got a problem.

Once you realize that something is about to go down, either get out of the store or get to the back of it. There are few things in a store that can effectively stop a 9mm slug (the shelves are made of tin), so get in position to beat feet out through the back door, hide in the walk-in refrigerator, or squeeze behind a stacked can display.

L.A.

New York

BURGLARY

New York

The authors' years of empirical evidence and testing have led us to the conclusion that the American brand of heavy padlock is one of the finest—if not the finest—on the market. One of us unindicted co-conspirators teamed up with a bonded locksmith to try and defeat an American padlock that used a barrel-type key. We tried a couple cans of automotive freon, big heavy hammers, bolt cutters, everything short of explosives with no damage to the lock at all. One of the authors has been chaining his motorcycles with an American lock—the same one—for almost 20 years. These heavy padlocks are also the universal choice of New York City merchants, who use them to secure the big steel night gates over their storefronts and their basement stairs.

Due to new federal environmental regulations, freon is far less accessible and portable than it was. For years, freon was available in small cans made to recharge automotive air conditioners. Since freon is so harmful to the ozone layer, it has been effectively taken out of the hands of amateur mechanics (and thieves) by packaging. It is only sold over the counter in 20-pound bulk containers now, which cost around $200. The small pocket-size cans that were formerly available are now sold only to repair garages with hard-to-get special licenses.

Supposedly, freon will chill the steel in a lock to such a low temperature that it will shatter on impact, like the petals of a flower that has been dipped in dry ice. For a couple of generations, this has been an amateur burglar's axiom, the kind of folk wisdom passed along from one class of high-school-age thieves to the next. As near as we can tell, it doesn't work—or if it does work, it only sort of worked a little bit and wouldn't have been any help at all to a serious thief, only to a high school kind of perp. I personally tried it on that hefty American lock, and it did nothing but ruin the concrete under the lock. Possibly, it will help defeat a cheap lock, but a solid hammer blow will also defeat a cheap lock, and it's a whole lot easier and faster. In applications like garage doors with sheet-metal hasps, you can just torque the hasp apart and it doesn't matter what kind of lock is on there. All in all, the freon threat is a thing of the past, if indeed it ever was a threat.

New York City, because of its stringent fire codes, pretty much demands steel doors these days on all apartment doors— either steel or fire-retardant hardwood, which is much more expensive. A well-mounted steel door and frame with a good deadbolt rimlock will take a hell of a beating before it gives up. And it requires a physical assault to defeat it—finesse won't do the job unless you're a lock-picking wizard locksmith. This system is the norm around town, and there are a number of very good, very cheap accessories to help beef it up.

There is a cylinder guard, an external panel, priced at about five bucks, that prevents the burglar from using a slam hammer to jerk the cylinder out of the door. Decent rimlocks have a small spring-loaded door inside that snaps shut in the event of the cylinder being torn out and creates another small line of defense, but it's not too tough. The heavy-steel cylinder guard just halts this whole song and dance before it gets started. The guard should be anchored with quality carriage bolts, which come with the kit. On the inside, many steel doors have had the rimlocks changed so often that the screw holes are loose. You can use a punch and hammer to swage the holes closed so they hold the screws better, but if it's shaky at all, I recommend installing a brace on the inside too. These gems are between five and ten bucks, and they're nothing more than a heavy steel band that fits on the inside of the same carriage bolts that hold the cylinder guard on the outside of the door. The brace hugs the rimlock body and clamps it down securely. You can even apply one of these in a situation where the screw holes in the door are so reamed out that they won't hold the lock in place at all. Really, a door in that rough a condition should be replaced, but in the real world where good steel doors cost a couple hundred dollars and either the landlord doesn't want to pay or actually forbids you to change doors (it's New York City, and they're soulless, scum-guzzling vampires), you can do well with the inside band.

Another alternative in these cases where landlords forbid you to have a secure door to your own home—because of possible fire violations if the new door isn't an approved unit, because the hallway paint won't match up, or because there's no reason, it's just policy—is to have a locksmith cut a whole new set of holes in a new location and plug up the old hole. Plugging hardware is available from any city locksmith. All this stuff is common, you see; at least it's common to locksmiths. The only piece you may have trouble finding is the inside band. I use the cylinder guard and inside band combination on all the rimlocks of people I care about. With both in place, you're going to need a battering ram, a hydraulic ram, or a halligan (fireman's pickax), and it's going to take time and make noise and all those fine preventive things—which maybe aren't all that preventive. As a point of personal reference, I have done surgery on my own doors in buildings I had just moved into, where I was not known, using power tools, hammers, and great thundering curses, and never once has any other tenant phoned the police. It's just one of those things to not count on.

There are great tongue-and-groove iron channels on the market that can be attached to doors near the locks to effectively prevent the insertion of a wedge or pry bar between the door and jamb. These are also very cheap, especially considering the protection they offer. Realize that New York is a city under constant siege, and these security devices have been field-tested by junkies and burglars and kids and found to be very effective. Effective enough that in 10-plus years in the Apple I have yet to hear of a contemporary case where a burglar came through the front steel door by defeating the lock or the door. These days, they do windows. The sole door job I remember happened because the large economy-sized mail slot gave the burglar enough room to snake his hand in and flip the rimlock open from inside. You can either make or buy a sheet-metal guard that will prevent this from happening or install a double-lock rimlock, which requires a key on the inside.

The big gun in New York door security is the Fox Police Lock. These babies come in two flavors: tough and double tough. Tough is the rugged bar-to-the-floor model, which wedges about four feet of steel bar at an angle between the door and the floor. It's like shoving an electric chair under the knob—except without the juice. Protectionwise, there's no downside to a Fox lock. Practically, that bar takes up a lot of floor space and most New York apartments don't have that much floor space to start with. Also, I busted my toe tripping on one once. They're great, but in close quarters that bar can be a hazard and a half. But, then, the bar can be a weapon and a half, too, if need be.

My personal favorite is the side-to-side double-bar Fox lock. This is big iron, people. With a turn of the key, which is located in the middle of the door, two huge steel bars slide into cleats on both jambs. For all practical purposes, this is just like welding the door shut. One of these in the middle of a steel door and the halligan punks out. You're safe from everything except battering rams and hydraulic apparatuses, and even that stuff is going to take some time. I've never seen more than one Fox bar lock on a door, but if you were to put one chest high and one thigh high, burglars would have to take the entire door area out of the wall to get in. They'd be better off attacking the wall, which is probably just what they'd do . . . unless they just decided to go elsewhere. I hear that it's tough to get Fox locks outside New York. If you live in a place where you think you need one, try ordering it from a New York locksmith. In this town, they all have them. There are a number of exotic pick-proof or heavily pick-resistant locks on the market, and they do offer peace of mind. But in New York, the most likely assault on a door will not be a pick, it'll be a hammer or some kind of ram. Might makes right, in this case.

Your New York window problems are also solved at the locksmith via window gates. They're ugly and they're expensive, but like door systems, they have been built, attacked, revised, and refined, and the models available today are the product of serious burglar immunity genes combined with quick-release devices for fire safety. Burglars often try to come in through the fire escapes, but if you lock a gate across the windows that access the fire escape, of course, you run the supremely dangerous risk of not being able to unlock it fast enough in case of fire. If you have to err in the window gate field, do so in the name of fire safety. My personal feeling is that there's nothing anyone could steal that would be worth your life or the life of your family.

L.A.

One bubble popping coming up. You can't make your house burglarproof—not in L.A. or anywhere else. The best you can do is to make it both noisy and slow for the criminal to break in. Often, this in itself will be enough to make the burglar veer off and head for the hills.

The noise attracts attention—just what the burglar doesn't want. It wakes you up if you're home and lets any neighbors know something is amiss when you're not. Waking up to a stranger crawling through your window is a sign that everything is not peachy-keen.

Making it slow to break in often causes the criminal to abort the process when it starts to take too long. His success depends on speed both getting in and getting out. Take that away and his chances of getting caught (or shot) increase dramatically. Speed and stealth are his tools. Slowing him down and calling attention to him are yours.

TYPES OF BURGLARS

L.A. has three basic categories of burglars: smashers, prowlers, and pros.

A *smasher* doesn't care how much damage he does getting into you house. He'll bust a window, kick in a door, or, in extreme cases, throw lawn furniture through a sliding door.

He's often your bottom-line addict or punk kid. This means he's only concerned with stealing enough to get his next high (if he's a heroin addict and hurting, that is a pretty pressing issue), or he's too scared to hang around long enough to do a thorough job. Unless you live in a pit of a neighborhood, where addicts roam the streets, these kind of jobs are most often done by kids. (The same type of burglary occurs in nice upper-class neighborhoods and is also done by kids.)

The bad news is that the smasher will bust a window, dash in, snatch your VCR, and split. This is seriously uncool news here folks: he can be in, out, and down the street in less than three minutes. This is why posting the "armed response" with Rent-a-Cop-R-Us is such a joke. Response within 10 minutes means the guy's seven minutes gone. The only good thing you can say about smashers is that the amount of damage they do is offset by the limited stuff they carry off.

The *prowler* is in many ways more destructive than a smasher. Often he'll enter in a quieter way or bust a window on the blind side of the house so as not to attract attention. Avoiding attention while breaking in means he's now got time to pick and choose what he's going to take. Often this type of burglar ransacks the houses he hits. You walk in to find your personal belongings tossed around the room because the burglar totaled your house looking for loot. Often these burglars have cars waiting or even shopping carts to haul away their booty. That's how much they're going to swipe. There is nothing shy of rape that can convey the sense of violation that a ransacked, burgled house does.

By the time a crim gets to this point, he's no longer a scared kid. He may be young, but he's got enough experience to be confident. More often than not, though, you'll be dealing with a full-grown adult here. Although prowlers generally strike during the day, you are most likely to encounter them in your house at night. Whereas all criminals can be dangerous, you should be most concerned about the night-working criminal who enters people's houses when they're home. He's taking a risk that most criminals shy away from, and often he's carrying something deadly and is gonzo enough to use it. It's a much more aggressive form of violation that he's committing, and these are the types that often turn from burglaries to rapes and assaults. Even a daytime prowler that you walk in on can turn as dangerous as a cornered rat.

Pros are an entirely different caliber of thief. People think of a pro as cat burglars or some such, like Robert Wagner in *To Catch a Thief* or Whoopie Goldberg in *Burglar*. These guys are few and far between. They do exist, but unless you have a six-figure income, you're not likely to get nailed by them. Often they choose their targets based on information supplied by informants or girlfriends working at insurance companies, brokerage houses, galleries, etc. It's not the brokers who will do you in; rather it's the clerks. The prestigious firm you're dealing with regularly hires young women at lousy wages and with shitty conditions. It's real common for these women to have scumbag boyfriends or be approached by a pro for information. A Xerox copy of an itemized insurance sheet slipped into a purse is what will set you up for a rip-off more than a car cruising down the street. Pros go after jewelry, art, and collections with a knowledge of the items' worth equal to, if not greater than, the owners'.

These information networks are like spider webs, and the criminals are the spiders. When you buy something, or insure it, they get a jiggle on their web and check into buyers. Once they know there's a market, they hit. Once something is taken, it is sold immediately to an agent. (When you're on this level, they aren't fences—they're agents. Hoity-toity, eh?) There the item is either sat on, shipped out of state, or, for specific collectibles, turned over to the person who authorized the job. It's rare that a burglar would have such items in his possession 24 hours later. With a professional ring, it's likely to be out of state inside a week.

This is not a common burglary. The pros could give a shit about your VCR; it's your diamond collection they're after. Unfortunately, you have about as much chance of stopping a typhoon as these guys. They're more up on alarms and locks than most people who are legitimately in the business, including how to get around those systems. They also know every common hiding spot. How many women have something hidden in their underwear drawers or on the upper shelf of the closet? That's the first place any burglar will look. They can do a thorough sweep of a room in less than five minutes. Figuring bedrooms, offices, and dens are the most likely rooms to contain the kind of valuables a pro is after, you can see how fast he's going to clean you out. Hiding a safe may work against prowlers and smashers, but many pros know how to get through combo safes in a New York—er, L.A.—second. If a pro has done his research, he knows what kind of safe you have and what your security system is.[1] The best way to be protect yourself from a pro is to keep anything small and valuable enough to insure—the kind of items they're are interested in— in a safe-deposit box at the bank.

As we said, most people think of pros as diamond thieves. The truth is, if you get hit by one, you're probably going to walk into your house and find it stripped bare. Bare walls and totally empty rooms are the the mark of a pro. These guys also work on an information network: friends or associates in insurance companies, the local newspaper's circulation department, house-cleaning companies, the local kennel, travel agents, etc., who will tell the criminal when you're going to be away from your home. While you're preparing to go on vacation, they're preparing to clean you out.

The most common dodge is for pros to show up as a moving company, sometimes even show up in coveralls. They walk in, roll everything up, and load it on the truck. To anyone passing by, it just looks like the people are moving.

Before taking trips, most people suspend newspaper delivery or have a friend come by and pick up the paper, tell the post office to hold delivery, and take other precautions to keep the house from looking deserted. That works against prowlers (though not against smashers, who don't care if you're gone a week or an hour). Unfortunately, this sort of precaution is the very thing that tips off pros.

AVOID LEAVING YOUR
HOUSE EMPTY AND UNWATCHED

The best defense against these kind of guys is to not leave your house empty. Find a house sitter so you don't have to board your animals or cancel your paper. If anyone asks you about going out of town, casually mention the fact that you've gotten a house sitter.

Enrolling in a Neighborhood Watch program is also a good bet (call your local police or sheriff's department to find out how to enroll or set one up in your area). Failing that, just being friendly with your neighbors helps. Once people know you, they're going to be aware that a moving van has no right to be there. When you go on vacation, tell your immediate neighbors where you're going and for how long. A retired person or couple is a great source to cultivate to keep an eye on the house. Most pros hit during working hours, so there are fewer people around to question them about what they're up to.

If you live in a nice suburb, where the cops aren't scraping up bodies every night, inform the local police when you're going to be gone and have them come out and check your property now and then. In the city you're not going to get much of a response, but out in the 'burbs where things aren't as hairy, the police still do care about break-ins. They will drive by a few times a night and have a look-see.

Never advertise your security secrets by posting "THIS HOUSE PROTECTED BY . . ." signs. Without that sign, a criminal doesn't know he has to do a smash and grab. All those signs do is tell the burglar how long he can spend tearing up your house. However, if he doesn't see that sign, one of two things will happen: 1) he's going to stay too long and get a rude surprise, or 2) when he realizes he's tripped an alarm, he's going to get the hell out of there. The latter is the sort of unpleasant surprise that prowlers hate. Unless he's blown your front door, he will have been in the house for a few minutes before he sees the alarm panel. The panic is usually enough to send him packing, often taking little or nothing with him. If a silent alarm has been tripped and he's seen pushing a shopping cart full of TV and stereo equipment, don't you think there are going to be some serious questions asked? He usually decides it's better if he cuts his losses and splits.

Unless you're in an apartment or condominium, the odds are that the criminal won't come in through your front door. He's going to come in through the side or the back to lessen the chances of being seen. By slipping around back, even a smasher increases his chances of success. One, the noise is pointed in a direction other than the street, thereby reducing the chances of someone hearing it. Two, even if someone does hear something, unless he is on that side of the house or can see into your backyard, he's not going to see anything when he looks. By the way, because of this, being adjacent to an apartment building with a view down into your backyard will lessen your chances of being ripped off by a prowler coming in through your backyard. The same applies to areas where the backyards are marked by low fences. A person in an upper-story unit can see down three or four houses, and it's just like being on the street.

LOCKED FENCES

Your first line of defense against a burglar is a locked fence. Even a small 4-foot locked fence or wall will slow a prowler down, if not force him to choose another unfenced target. The reason doesn't have to do with keeping him out, but rather making it hard for him to get back out. If the gate is locked he's got to schlep stuff over the wall/fence in order to get away. Try and imagine how easy it would be to carry your TV over a fence. This is why any fence that abuts an alley should be locked at all times as standard operating procedure. Also, someone jumping a fence is sort of obvious.

Admittedly, the lock may be a hassle. But remember the purpose of the fence is to keep a burglar from loading up his car or a shopping cart unobserved. He's not going to carry away as much if he's got to carry it by hand out the front door. Nor is he as likely to load up in plain view in your front yard. If you have a wide open driveway, the criminal can pull in to your backyard, load up his car, and drive away without attracting attention. Anyone in the neighborhood who isn't looking directly down your driveway won't see the crim.

WATCH DOG

The next good deterrent against a burglar is a dog. Not because Killer is a pit bull/Doberman trained attack dog that will eat the burglar in one gulp, but because he can bark. Remember what we said are the two things that will cause a burglar to veer off? Noise blows his stealth. Letting your dog roam around in your newly fenced yard lessens the chances of his becoming a yapper. Dogs that are tied up often bark a lot, so nobody listens—even when he's doing it for real. Incidentally, in case you haven't noticed, there's a distinct difference between a dog that's just woofing and one that's telling a person to back off. Anytime you hear the latter, take a look to see what has Spot's panties in such a wad.

Several studies have been done that question burglars about what they avoid when choosing a house to hit. Consistently, they list dogs as the top deterrent because of the noise they make. Burglars are less concerned about being bitten (unless it's a big dog) than about someone coming to investigate. If you can't afford to put in a home security system, then Bowser is the next best thing.

DEFENSIVE LANDSCAPING

Opinions vary about the value of bushes near your house. Some maintain that heavy bushes act as a screen to prevent people from seeing the guy as he tries to break in. Others argue that the hassle of wading through the bushes and trying to work in them acts as a deterrent. Personally, I vote for this option because crawling over a bush that is planted close to the house to get to a window that an intruder still has to get through is a real pain in the butt.

A hedge or bush (especially one with thorns or brambles) under a window keeps people from trying to come in through that way, especially along the side of your house. Walk around your house and look for the best place to break in, where the noise will be muffled or directed away and where nobody can see what the criminal is doing, and then plant a rose bush there. A blueberry patch works just as well except it has a habit of attracting kids and birds. If you live in the desert, a cactus patch is also loads of laughs. Naturally, you don't want to plant bushes near the doorway for someone to hide in, and you should keep the bushes near the windows trimmed down so they act as a deterrent rather than a screen for the burglar.

Animal found another interesting fact about bushes and leaves on the side of the house: they make noise when someone moves on or through them. Unless your intruder is a former Green Beret, the odds are he's not going to be good at moving through the bush quietly. The noise will alert you that someone is moving around outside your home.

WINDOW SCREENS

One thing that slows down burglars is the use of window

screens. Screens won't stop the guy, but they represent time spent getting through them that he can't afford. Most window break-ins are through windows that don't have screens. If you're inside the house, you're more likely to hear someone wrestling a screen off than if he comes through a screenless window. Incidentally, four or five small nails hammered along the base of the screen make it harder to get through than the single-loop-and-hook setup that holds most screens in.

The presence of a locked fence, a watch dog, and strategically placed bushes will often convince a crim to walk down the road a few more feet and hit an easier target. Though that isn't good news for your neighbor, it is for you.

MOTION SENSORS

Another thing that has become popular of late in L.A. is the use of motion sensors. But unless they are properly installed, they are of limited use. Many of these sensors operate in a field that resembles a flat spray. Any criminal worth his salt knows this and knows how to sneak under the field. To prevent this, get a double-headed unit and have the sensors covering the area at different angles. One of the most effective systems around is a three-sensor unit, with two units covering width and the third turned sideways to cover depth. Once you install the system, spend an hour or so trying to sneak past it. Once you find a hole, either adjust the sensor or add another.

The sensors should be placed away from where the criminal is likely to try to get in, so it will be activated before he reaches that spot. For example, if you have a motion sensor on the side of your house, it should be positioned toward the back and aiming toward the front. This covers the entire side of your house against approach and puts him in view of the sensor as he tries to get over the fence, not when he's next to your window. Also, by its being placed further back the criminal is less likely to see it until he actually trips it, and suddenly Chuckles is in the spotlight.

A motion sensor should be placed high enough so the crim can't reach it, or he'll just knock it to the side. A sensor shooting off in the air is pretty useless. Also, if you have invested in a sensor, buy lamp cages for it to keep the intruder from simply breaking the bulbs. Many attacks happen when people are getting in and out of their cars. If you have installed a sensor over your driveway (a good move), make sure it can be neither tampered with easily nor avoided. A rapist or robber will wait in the shadows, either avoiding the field or having disabled the sensor, and then move when a person shows up.

If your motion sensor suddenly doesn't work one night when you show up, *don't get out of your car!* Most systems these days have two lights, and it's highly unlikely that they both fritzed out at once. Back your car out of the driveway, turning so your lights shine on where an attacker would likely hide. If you don't see anyone,[2] park it on the street and watch for a minute or two. Your best bet is to go knock on the door of the neighbor you've befriended through Neighborhood Watch (subtle, ain't we?) and either have him or her (a him is better) accompany you home or call the police. If this is not an option and you see no movement, get your house keys out and ready. Skirt wide of the driveway and any hiding spaces as you approach the door. If you live in a state that allows you to carry a gun in the car and you do, take that too.

Once inside, if you live alone or nobody is home, lock the door behind you and stop and listen at your doorway for the sound of someone moving.[3] The waiting is important because the guy will probably have frozen when he heard you hit the door. Whoever moves first will be making the noise. If there is someone there, get out! Even if you have a gun, back off! If you don't hear anybody, continue on.

If you have a cat or a dog that normally greets you and it isn't there, something is wrong. Animals get uptight when some stranger is in the house. If, on the other hand, your pet is relaxed, the odds are that there is no problem. Nonetheless, a quick check of the house to make sure everything is secured is a good idea. Don't just walk into rooms; peek in first and look through the crack between the door and the frame to see if anyone is there. Check the entire house before you relax.

IDENTIFICATION NUMBERS

If you do get burglarized, one thing that makes recovery of stolen property easier is a list of serial and identification numbers (make/model and particular unit), so make one now. Also engrave your name on the back of TVs, stereo equipment, microwaves, and other appliances with an electric pencil. This not only makes it harder to sell the stolen goods, it also makes it harder for the thief to deny that they're stolen if he's caught. (He's a guy named Linda Swartz—right!) Every year millions of dollars of stolen property is recovered but not returned because the police can't find the owners. Which of the six exact-same model VCRs is yours? If you can't ID it, forget it. The serial numbers and engraving will increase your chances of recovery.

LOCKS

When it comes to locks everyone and his brother has an opinion about which is the best. There are locks that can't be picked, and even a locksmith has to bore out the door. Unfortunately, these locks cost up to $200. Remember, the guy at the locksmith's is trying to sell you the system that will make him the most money; he's not going to tell you the system's weaknesses unless you specifically ask, "How can someone get around this lock?" Also, the best lock in the world isn't going to do you any good if it's surrounded by flimsy materials that can be more easily broken than the lock.

Let's start with your basic padlock. First of all, picking a combination lock is much easier than many people would believe. Those long, three-cylinder bicycle locks are a joke that any kid in the street knows how to pick. A round combination lock is harder to pick, but it can still be done. The hardest locks to pick are normally key locks. Not only do they take special tools, but unlike what you see in the in the movies, picking them is a slow, laborious process.

Unfortunately, there are ways around almost any system. The first method actually has nothing to do with the lock itself; it involves the chain that most people use to keep something where it belongs or keep someone out of where he doesn't. A set of bolt cutters will walk right through most chains, except the case-hardened steel ones. Take a stroll over to the local hardware store and see how easy bolt cutters are to get. It's illegal to have lockpicking equipment unless you're a certified locksmith in most states, but anyone can carry a set of bolt cutters in his trunk. Few smashers or prowlers are actually this prepared, but it does happen—especially if the prowler is up to something besides burglary, or if the criminal knows ahead of time what he needs to get through your defenses. Motorcycles, boats, trailers, and equipment can all disappear PDQ when a pickup truck and a pair of bolt cutters show up.

Manufacturers proudly point out that your average padlock will take a bullet head on and not pop open and that the loop is case-hardened to make it harder to cut with bolt cutters (not impossible, mind you, just harder). But why bother shooting the lock or cutting it when all someone has to do is smash downward with a heavy hammer? A swipe with a heavy chisel and small sledge will wipe out most of the locks that you can buy in the local hardware store.

Whenever possible, position your lock away from the front of the gate. When you loop your case-hardened cable (not chain) around something, turn it so the lock is behind the item being chained down. The same goes for fences and gates. All you have to do is flip the lock up to unlock it, but the criminal cannot get a solid purchase with either bolt cutters or hammer. Swinging a hammer over a fence isn't an easy job nor is reaching behind a trailer wheel with bolt cutters.

If you have expensive cars, a workshop, or equipment in your garage, you should place a steel hood over the lock and hasp. This not only protects the lock against the weather, it also makes it hard for the crim to get in. To get to the lock the crim has to make lots of noise and lose time while tearing through the hood, and then he has to deal with the lock. If there is a smaller side door, installing either a couple of those expensive locks and a reinforced door frame or a drop bar across the inside will make getting in difficult.

Another simple thing you can do is to throw away the baby screws they give you with the hasp and use bigger ones. A 1/4-inch screw gives way against a solid kick real quickly; however, a 5/8-inch-long screw is much harder to kick out. Also whenever possible, replace weathered lumber that the hasp will screw into with fresh hardwood. If the wood is old and splintery or dry-rotted, it won't matter how long the screws are; a swift kick will blow through it. On the other hand, a fresh oak post with long screws will bust a foot before it lets go.

WINDOWS

When it comes to your house, your first concern should be the windows because it is easier, faster, and quieter to go through a window than it is to force a door. Even smashing a window is quieter than blasting through a door. Now the bad news: any lock you're going to put on a window can be bypassed by simply smashing the window. Even that sometimes isn't necessary because your average window lock can be bypassed with a hacksaw blade or a thin knife. The crim slips the blade up between the upper and lower window and simply taps the lock open. Prowlers, especially the rapist variety, commonly use this method so they can enter quietly.

For wooden-framed (double-hung) windows, you can purchase window stops. These are either screws that drive into the window frame directly or attach to the upper frame. When open, they allow the lower window to slide past, and when closed, they jam it at a certain point. You place these so the window can be opened enough to let air in but not allow a body to pass through. The former can't be bypassed from the outside. The latter require a special tool to get by, which most burglars don't carry. If the guy is a prowling rapist, he might have that wire tool, but the numbers are in your favor that this will work.

For aluminum-framed windows or any sort of side-sliding window/doors, a dowel is still your best bet. For aluminum-framed windows, you'll need to go to a hardware store and buy a 50-cent clamp. This clamp goes above the bottom window and secures the dowel in the groove by pushing it against the top of the window frame. This method is more secure, but if you want, you can just use two of these clamps on either side of the window frame.

Anytime you use a dowel on a side-sliding window, make sure that it is the exact length of the groove. If the crim can get the item even as much as 1/2-inch open, he can lift the entire window or door out of the frame. Lay a piece of ribbon or string across the groove before placing the dowel in it to help you pull the dowel out when you want to open the window.

Louver windows are a security nightmare. A burglar can break into your house, quietly, in less than a minute with these type of windows. If possible, replace them on all ground-floor windows and doors. If you can't afford to change them or your landlord won't let you, *glue the slats into the frame* so the crim will have to bust the slats.

The cousin of the "bushes outside the window" is a table with a lamp and other items on it placed just inside the window. Either the guy has to sweep everything aside (noisy) or spend the time picking everything off (delay and possible noise). Tall items that are easy to knock over or large items that are hard to move quietly make the best choices, with a combination of the two even better.

DOORS

Let's look at locks for doors now. There is an important point to be made about deadbolts. There are two basic kinds of deadbolts: single key and double key. The single-key ones have a key on one side and a knob on the other, while the double-key deadbolts are operated by keys on both sides. A single-key dead bolt is worse than useless in a door with a window near the lock. Both the smasher and the prowler will pop the window pane out and then simply reach in and turn the knob. If you have a solid door with no side windows or a door with small decorative windows beyond the reach of the lock, a single-key dead bolt is fine and dandy.

If you have a door with a window, you're between a rock and a hard place. During the day when you're not home, the double-key dead bolt will serve as a block against a burglar's entrance. Now instead of just popping a window, he has to kick the door in—a noisy and slow proposition, to say the least. However, at night, when you are home, a double-key dead bolt is a death trap if an emergency occurs. Not just fire, but earthquakes, hurricanes, and tornadoes can all require you to exit quickly. If the door is locked and you have to fumble around for the keys or if your children can't find the key, an emergency suddenly becomes lethal.

The solution is to get the double-key deadbolts for windowed doors but to leave the keys in them at night. If you have to get out quickly, the keys are there and ready to go. Unfortunately, by leaving your keys in the door you reduce the dead bolt effectively to a single-key version. The burglar can still smash a window and turn the key, but you are home to hear him coming in.

Now the real bad news about deadbolts: they can be blown through very easily. In fact, any lock you install is only as good as the wood it is set in. The door frame is the weakest point of the whole operation. If you look closely, you'll see that the faceplate sits over a hole. This hole is only about 1/4 inch in from the edge of the door frame. The second level of wood you see is a separate piece called molding and is normally very brittle and easy to break. Wood breaks more easily along the grain, and most door frames are grained up and down. That means if someone kicks the door open, the wood wouldn't blow out immediately behind the bolt, it'd crack up and down until it slivered out. It is easier to take out a foot-long piece along the grain of wood than it is to tear through 1/4 inch against the grain. This is how most back doors are blown through. When this happens, not only do you have to replace the molding, but the side of the door frame. This operation can run you a few hundred dollars to have a handyman do the job.

In apartment buildings (unless you live on the ground floor), the odds are the burglar is going to come through the front door. The worse the neighborhood, the more likely the guy is to bust your door down. Unless you're in an apartment building that is about to collapse or the builder was so cheap that he put in hollow-core doors instead of real ones, the intruder will probably use a tool rather than kick the door in. A $5.95 crowbar or sledgehammer will get the crim through the front door right quick. All the pressure is applied to that 1/4 inch of wood, and it just splinters out. Unlike trying to kick the door in, with a tool there's only one smash and the crim is out of the hallway and in your apartment. If he shuts the door behind him, anyone looking down the hall will not see anything unless he looks closely at every door. Watch these real-life cop shows sometime and see how the cops go through a door during a raid. That's how long it takes for a prepared person to blow through a locked door.

Once again, you have a choice of how to handle this situation. You can either place multiple locks on the door or you can reinforce the door frame. If you live in a real pit, you might want to consider both. The reason multiple locks work is that they defuse the impact of a kick or leverage over the entire door frame, thus making it harder for the wood to split. Someone can't easily kick your door in if locks are evenly spaced over it. Now, even with leverage applied by a crowbar or tire iron, the crim isn't pressing against just 1/4 inch of wood; rather, he is up against the entire door frame. That's a lot of work. With a hammer, an intruder must bust each lock individually. In either case, it takes longer and makes more noise.

To reinforce a door frame, you must find the studs. The door frame should be connected to one on either side.[4] If appearances matter, take the molding off the lock side of the door frame in one piece so that it can be put back on. But don't be too concerned about saving it if it's just regular molding because it is cheap and easy to find. Take a 4-foot strip of steel and drill holes in it.[5] Then, with long screws (or if you want to do the steroid version, short lag bolts), on the inside of the room where the molding was, bolt the steel over where the lock hasps are in the door frame. This strengthens the integrity of the entire door frame against impact. If you're using lag bolts and you want to make it pretty, you're going to have to drill out a countersink in the back of the molding for the bolt heads to fit into. Replace the molding with either nails (through the extra holes you drilled for them in the steel) or glue. Also if you're using lag bolts, don't forget to pilot hole into the door frame first! Slap some wood putty and touch-up paint on the whole thing and in one afternoon you've just created a nightmare for anyone trying to power through your door. If you're a handyman (or are friends with one), the whole operation shouldn't cost you more than $30 and a few hours of work. That's a small price to pay for the security this will give you against smashers. Even if the guys have a battering ram, it's going to take them some time to get through that. And you can be sure that most crackheads aren't wandering around with a police battering ram under their shirts.

Double doors also provide a security risk because they are easy to kick open. Make sure the bolt holes of the second door go at least 1/4 inch into the floor and the door frame. The top door jamb can be secured as described in the last paragraph. Place another strip of steel that has been specially drilled on the side of the second door. This strip can either replace the faceplate entirely, or it can be screwed back on. The new door alignment is tricky, and you have to prime the steel before you paint it. This can turn into a bigger job than it seems. If you're not a handyman and if you can afford to live in a place where you have double doors, you can probably handle paying someone to do it.

Another common problem with double doors is that their locks can be bypassed with a credit card. Since the doors open inward, the flat side of the lock's latch is on the inward side, leaving the beveled edge to the outward side. To see how this works, open the door and lock it. Although you can't turn the knob, on many locks the latch can still be pushed in. A crim with a credit card, knife, or screwdriver just has to rip through any molding and press against the bevel and ease the lock open. Someone who is good can be through a cheap lock this way in less than five seconds. Either buy a deadbolt or a lock that has a latch that can't be moved when the lock is engaged.

If your door has many panes of glass, the only way to be really safe is to replace it. Second best is to install a double-key deadbolt. The next best thing is to place at least four locks on it, and this also works on doors and French windows where a deadbolt won't. Place one each at the top and bottom, one at handle level, and one at about eye level. They don't have to be complicated; in fact, even the sliding-bolt type will do. This forces the burglar to smash out four different window panels to get in. If he pops the pane near the knob, he's going to fight the other three locks until he figures out what is going on. Then he has to smash and grope until he gets all the locks. All this means noise and time, which work in your favor. This multiple-lock system also works on any type of swinging window.

If you live in a second-story apartment with an entrance on the ground level or if your dwelling has an enclosed garden that leads to the front door, install a set of bells or chimes by the door or gate opening so that they ring when someone approaches. An unidentified thump below you is one thing, but the sound of your front door opening into chimes is a threat.

If you own a business with a back door or you don't care about the appearance of your house, the best way to stop a smasher is to put a crossbar across the door. Two braces lag-bolted to the studs and a 2x4 placed across the door will stop anything short of a tank. Animal worked in Hollywood with a setup like this. One night, criminals came down the alley and blew open every door on the businesses around them but were stopped cold by two deadbolts and a crossbar. They brought tools with them, yet the crossbar held.

Another common technique to keep burglars out is to place a long metal plate on the door over the door latch. This is usually reserved for garages or shops because it is ugly, but it is highly recommended if you have a large gap between the door and the frame. If you can see more than 1/8 inch of the latch when the door is closed, either get the door rehung or place this sort of protector on it. It is easy to slip a piece of wire or a screwdriver behind the latch and simply pull it back to open a conventional lock. Just as common, a hammer and a screwdriver will tear through the wood holding the faceplate and allow the screwdriver to lever open the latch. The plate prevents the criminal from reaching the latch with his tools. These plates should be held in place with round-headed bolts that go through the door so that the criminal can't unscrew the plate.

AN OCCUPIED HOME IS A SAFE HOUSE

Probably, your best bet to keep all the different types of burglars away is to keep an erratic schedule of comings and goings, thereby establishing the impression that someone is likely to be at home at any time. If you can afford services such as house cleaning, pool maintenance, and gardening, stagger them to come on different days. Even though it's more expensive, you should always try to go with bonded agencies. These agencies do a more thorough background check on their employees and give the hairy eyeball to scumball boyfriends.

If you have a large house and live alone, you might consider renting a room to a college student. A student's erratic schedule, combined with yours, will offer a stronger likelihood of someone being home. The next possibility is a roommate with a different work schedule from yours, especially if you have a busy schedule that takes you away from your home more than 12 hours at a time.

SECURITY BUILDINGS

Let us for a moment talk about "security" buildings, which are real popular in L.A. Putting it simply, there ain't no such animal. Animal has a running game with a longtime friend and his wife. No matter what security building they move into, he never buzzes to be let in. He always breaks in and then shows up at their door with comments about "people who believe in security buildings." The problem with most security buildings is that people who live in them really believe that they're safe, and they go on autopilot because of this. Once the criminal bypasses the initial security system, the people he's going to rob are even less aware than the people in the street.

Certain complexes and estate communities hire security guards, but before you get too comfortable, check to see when and what they've hired those guys for. A guard sitting at the shack isn't going to be much good against someone parking outside the wall and coming in over the fence. Nor is a night watchman going to do any good against midweek crime if the complex only has him on weekends. Finally, remember that regardless of what fee the company is charging, security guards are $5-an-hour employees. Although you do get the odd Rambo rent-a-cops, most of them aren't going to risk their asses for that kind of chump change.

Something that is becoming popular among L.A. residents, but has raised an outcry among the bleeding hearts, is the use of hired "protection." These are not guards; they are closer to bouncers and bounty hunters. This practice raises serious legal questions about civil-rights violations because, frankly, you can't hire someone to break a crackhead's jaw without violating a few laws. These protectors are expensive, often violent, and can cause the building owners to end up in serious trouble. Technically, all the crackhead is doing until he decides to bust a window or light up is trespassing. Trespassing is not something that keepers of the legal system feel warrants a person getting beat up. In the streets, however, that's the normal punishment for transgression.

A protector establishes the word in the street to leave his building alone because it's guarded by a big dog that bites. Word gets out, and the scum give that building a wide berth. This works for about three months before either a new batch of scum shows up or the old group decides to test if the boundaries are still up. Unfortunately, most residents can't afford to hire protection, so they have to risk being attacked in the hallways of their apartment buildings.

For those of you who believe in trying to simulate the presence of someone being home by installing a timer switch on your lights, allow me to add just one small note: a house with lights on and no noise is just an empty house with the lights on. If there isn't any noise or movement, it's not too convincing. Without sounding too woo-woo about it, there is a "feel" about a house when no one is home, and many burglars can sense this. It's a type of "silence" that an empty house projects or, to be more exact, doesn't project. Perhaps it's on a subconscious level, perhaps it's got something to do with the primal lifestyle they lead, but many criminals have a sixth sense about choosing safe targets. Something about the batwaves of a deserted house will tip the criminal off, despite the lights.

To this end, I recommend that you jam the criminal's radar. On the same circuit as the lights, attach either a radio or TV. Whatever you choose, make sure that it's just loud enough to be heard through the front door. Even a muted rumble will serve as a sign that someone is home. A talk-radio station or a TV is more effective than a music station. Music is too regular; the cadence of speech is more convincing. Although it is true that many criminals knock on the front door of a house they're about to hit as a final check to make sure nobody's home, most are basically cowardly, and this noise may be just enough to scare him off.

Another trick is to let someone park in your driveway when you're not there. A neighbor with two cars (or one who must park on the street) will often be glad to help out. A house with a car in the driveway looks like a house with someone home to a passing prowler.

This doesn't normally apply to L.A., but if you live in an area that gets snow, arrange with a neighbor or a local kid to clear your walk and driveway while you're gone. This includes a path from where you normally park your car to the front door if applicable. Tracks in the snow are a great indicator of whether someone is home or not.

Finally, you have to know that these are tricks. Like camouflage, they're designed to confuse, not stop, a burglar. They are not guaranteed to keep burglars from choosing your house, but rather to provide you a little edge to put you ahead of the game.

NOTES

1. If anyone from the insurance agency calls up and asks you questions about your security system (especially if you've upgraded it or changed it), don't answer any questions until after you've called the company back on the number you have and confirmed that the person works for the company and is in a position where he/she has a right to ask this kind of question. A simple "I'm busy now; can I call you

back?" will put them off. Listen to the response. If the person gets flaky, you've just been checked out.

2. Don't forget to look down near the ground for legs and feet. Someone's body may be hidden by a bush, but the white British Knights will stand out big time. So will those stupid flashing shoes.

3. You lock the door behind you to keep anyone else from coming through it. If you feel uncomfortable about locking it, jam the side of your foot against the bottom and take a wide stance.

4. However, we have seen some flimsy construction where the door frame is left floating by itself and is held in place only by cross braces. If this is the case, move because you're sitting in a rip-off trap, and the local criminals know it too.

5. If you want to save yourself some problems with warping, get a piece of steel the same length, shape, and width as the molding. It doesn't have to be thick; a 1/8-inch piece will do the job. The molding will seat better if the entire area is one level.

L.A.

New York

DRUGS

CHAPTER THREE

The Basics

With drugs, there's a world of difference between the casual user and the hard-core addict. It's not the guy who comes home from work and smokes a joint to unwind or the guy who does a few lines before he goes off to a party who is going to rob you. It's someone who is so torn up internally that he can't function normally enough to keep a job who's going to rip you off. As with all addicts, this guy is looking for the magic pill that will cut him out of the pain loop of his life. The fastest way to support that escape route is through crime.

One thing that provides us no end of amusement is the sanctimonious yo-yo who says such intelligent things as, "People who use drugs are trying to escape reality." No shit, Sherlock! If you had any idea of what kind of reality a hard-core street addict comes from, you'd hand him the drugs yourself! Take the worst scenario of child abuse you can think of and then triple it and you're getting close to what sort of reality these people are trying to escape. But it is no less a reality that the guy doesn't care how many people he stampedes over to escape.

Your average street addict grew up in a vicious, ignorant, bullying environment where the only constant was pain—either giving or taking it. It's what they know and what they do.[1] "Normal" reality is a state of constant internal pain, a spiritual toothache if you will. Drugs are the way to shut off the pain for these people. When they are high, the pain of their existence goes away. Nobody condemns someone who has a painful terminal disease for committing suicide, but they get upset about drug addicts. However, it is literally the same thing.

Although it is true with criminals in general, you should *really* consider a street addict as someone from an entirely different planet. You should remove any fantasy you have that when dealing with a street addict you're dealing with a middle-class person who's gone amiss. The so-called normal standards and values of personal boundaries and respect for one's fellow beings are not suppressed by this person's addiction. They were never there in the first place! We're talking someone who was conditioned from childhood that the way to get what he wants or needs is to batter and abuse the weak and take it from them. You are not a person to an addict; you are a source for what he needs.

For every run-of-the-mill addict who manages to pull out and get help, there are 50 who go down permanently. Before a person can begin to change, he has to "bottom out." He has to realize how far he has slipped and say, *"No more!"* Many never reach this point; most hard-core street addicts bottom out by dying. In order for the person to reform, he has to freely make the decision to straighten up. Even then it's likely the addict will slip. Alcoholics Anonymous (AA) has people who have been sober five, 10, even 20 years; if you go to a Narcotics Anonymous meeting, most old-timers have been clean about 18 months. That's with a support group and a sincere resolve to clean up!

Cleaning up is much harder than many people think it is because the source of the addiction is based in the person's concept of reality. There's a tongue-in-cheek AA slogan that might give you an idea of what it's like: "It's easy to quit drinking; all you have to do is change everything about your life." It's just as hard, if not harder, for an addict to quit. Most addicts can clean up pretty easily in jail or a forced rehab because life is structured there; however, once they must reface the pressures of the outside world, they slip back into old patterns. This cycle goes on until the addict "hits bottom" or dies. Whether from an overdose, AIDS, health complications, or murder, death is what normally "cures" an addict's drug problem. To a street person, an addict is at the bottom of the totem pole. He is the most despised and victimized of all street folk. We cannot accurately convey to you the casual ruthlessness directed at addicts. It is this mind-set that the addicts fear, because they know a street person will leave them beaten and bloody in an alley (if not dead) with the same lack of hesitation he'd have about killing a rat. A street person is always aware of the rats lurking in the shadows waiting for an opportunity to strike. They don't leave anything out that would be easy for the rats to snatch. When the rats get too bold, they get put back in their place. Because of this, addicts avoid ripping off the major league street people.

Unfortunately, this leaves the rest of us as the marks for the addicts. Awareness, willingness, and ruthlessness are what keep the addicts at bay. As a wharf rat is fearless of anything its size or smaller, a street addict has nothing to fear from a normal civilian who would hesitate to use violence. Liberal idealism is dinner on the hoof to these people. Fortunately for us, if addicts encounter any sign of physical danger, they will evaporate. That means that anyone willing to participate in violence is too dangerous for the addict to tackle.

Just because an addict doesn't think like the average person does not mean that there is no pattern or that the addict is unpredictable. Nor does it mean that he is omnipotent and unstoppable. It's when you fail to recognize that you are dealing with a truly alien thought pattern that you will become the victim.

Most street addicts are opportunistic. We hate to keep using the rat analogy, but it really fits. If there is a hole somewhere, a rat will find a way in. If you leave any holes in your defenses, an addict will eventually see it and go for the chance. In fact, it's more accurate to consider most street addicts as scavengers rather than criminals. Anything they see left out in the open will be scavenged. Just as rats will chew holes in a wall to get through it, an addict doesn't care how much damage he does getting in. They'll tear up a car's dashboard as fast as they'll pry a garage door open. Like their four-footed counterparts, they will strike and slip away between the cracks.

Also, like rats, they excel in hanging back and watching. You may not be watching their actions, but you can bet they're watching yours. An addict knows the second you walk away from your car and where you're heading. He knows the exact second you shift your bags into your strong hand, leaving either your wallet or purse exposed. He knows when someone leaves for the day and how long that person usually is gone. Remember, he doesn't have a job; he's got nothing to do except get high and watch for ways to get his drug money. In a real sense, his profession is being an addict and a thief. That's what he does best.

In their own areas, addicts are an overwhelming force with which to contend. Drug neighborhoods are hotbeds of rip-offs for a simple reason: there're just too many addicts. There is no way a single person can prevent getting ripped off in a full-blown drug neighborhood. A strike can come from too many different areas. You don't survive on the street without a solid knowledge of breaking and entering; addicts know it and use it on a constant basis. I know convicted felons who have been ripped off by addicts. Whether you have street smarts or not, there are just too many addicts to prevent being ripped off.

Also on their own turf, addicts' full dysfunction come out. In their world there are no boundaries except those enforced by violence and obnoxious behavior. Screaming obscenities is all in a day's work for an addict. From violent language, the next step is physical violence—maybe not done competently, but done nonetheless. For people who aren't afraid of jail, that works fine. The only people who aren't targeted by the addicts are the dealers and suppliers. That is because both of them will kill an addict in a heartbeat if challenged, and the addict knows that.

Addicts know they have nothing to fear from the average person. Unless you're willing to break the guy's jaw, pepper spray him, or shoot him like a dealer would, there's nothing that you can do to intimidate him. He may move away for the moment, but he will be back. If you're not around at the time, he's going to rip you off if he gets a chance. He knows there's very little you can do about it. Unfortunately, if you use physical violence on an addict for the crime of larceny, you have committed a bigger offense in the eyes of the law than he has. Can you afford a few days in jail and the subsequent hassles? He doesn't care if he ends up in jail except as an inconvenience; on the other hand, you have a life to live.

Understand, the best the police can do is contain the problem. They can push the local flotsam and jetsam into a particular area and then nail them when they leave. This is more true in L.A. than in New York. There's a difference between a bad neighborhood and a drug neighborhood. A hard-core drug neighborhood is the lowest of the low, rejected even by the run-of-the-mill street person: an area may be run down and have drugs, but a drug area looks like skid row.

The only good news about a deep drug neighborhood is that normally the only people who have guns are the dealers and gang members. Your hard-core addict will have pawned his gun for drugs to some budding psychopath a while ago. Unfortunately, the lower you go along the socioeconomic level, the more likely you are to encounter knives and razors. What this means to you is that without the enforcement of a gun, most addicts end up resorting to "safer" crimes of burglary, theft, and nonconfrontational types of robbery. This is why the rat analogy is so applicable.

It's relatively easy to spot when you're in a drug neighborhood: the area is run-down and dirty, and small, scattered groups loiter—usually around bagged bottles.[2] Although the condition of street people in general is not high, in a drug neighborhood the people look worse than normal. Pale skin, drawn features, dirty clothes, discolored or splotchy skin, and glassy or bloodshot eyes all add up to an impression of unhealthiness.[3] While there are homeless all over, if you find yourself in an area that looks like they're having a convention, you'll know you've wandered into the wrong neighborhood (or skid row in Downtown L.A. . . . hmm, same difference).

A crack house is nothing but trouble. The crackheads will fan out into the neighborhood, committing petty crimes to support their habit—like stealing a car radio down the street and then swap it for drugs at the house. The addict only has to walk a short distance with hot property. Look for a constant flow of unhealthy-looking people—many without cars—in and around a particular house. These people will be coming and going at all hours. That and an increase in petty crimes are the two signs of a drug house. Cops love it when you ID the crack houses for them. They know they're there, but unless they get confirmation or a complaint from the neighbors, there's not much they can do about it. It's not that they don't want to; it's just that they don't have "probable cause" that would stand up in court.

How smart the operator is (and how respectable a neighborhood it is in general) will determine if he lets people hang around outside the house. Some houses are merely supply houses, while others are smoke houses (where the person both buys and smokes his drugs). Often, nearby parks are the addicts' hangout when they are not actively high. (A crack high lasts about 20 minutes, but heroin goes for a few hours.) Watch where the main flow of park sitters go to and from and you'll usually find your supply house. Alleys are also popular for lighting up. If your property abuts an alley and you're finding burned matches, toilet paper rolls, and scraps of Brillo pads, your back area is being used as a smoking spot. Call the cops and ask that they patrol the alley more, and the crackheads will move on.

Heroin addicts are more prone to go off somewhere and

become gelatinous masses. Speed freaks are roamers. It's any-body's guess with hopheads (they do PCP). Crackheads tend to roam when they can't find a safe place to light up, but they do like to zone out. The glassy-eyed shuffling zombie often isn't a mental patient, but someone high on drugs.

The street dealers are a breed unto themselves, and they are dangerous. Generally, they have a staked-out territory, and they will defend this area ferociously, against both intruders and locals who try to push them away. This could be a corner, a park bench, or even an entire block. They, unlike your average addict, are usually armed to protect the large amounts of cash they carry. Even though they do occasionally keep the drugs on their persons, they generally cache their drugs nearby in case a cop searches them. They have certain ways of advertising their wares from the calls of "Yo-yo" and "What's up?" to wagging their hand in a thumb-up gesture (western United States). These signals change from area to area and from year to year. About 10 years ago, the way to spot a street dealer was by the stethoscope he wore.

Dealers often hang out on corners and approach likely looking people. If you suspect that a corner drug dealer has moved into your neighborhood, call the narcotics division of the local police department and ask what the current dealer flag is. If you see the person doing it, tell the local beat police and have them deal with it. If you have a video camera (or access to one) that has the time and date option, taping drug deals and turning the tape over to police is even better than just telling them about it. It's not going to stop the guy, but if he gets hassled too much he's going to move on. You can't really stop him, but with the help of the police, you can hassle him out of your neighborhood and back into the pit.

Something else that is becoming real common everywhere is the drive-up drug buy. If you see someone regularly walking up to cars, and either reaching into his pocket and then passing something into the car or walking away and coming back to the same car and reaching in, or regularly jumping into cars and going around the corner only to be back a few minutes later, you're witnessing a drug deal. Identify the guy for the local PD. Again, videotapes work wonders, and with them you can also get license tag numbers.

Here, we'd like to infuse a little reality into the myth of the mugger on drugs and the resultant "war on drugs" that it has spawned and continues to fuel. We cannot tell you the number of times we've heard someone say, "You don't know what he might do! He could be on drugs!" This perspective is supposedly backed up by the oft-cited statistic that claims that approximately 80 percent of all crimes are committed under the influence of drugs or alcohol. This statistic is a little misleading and requires some explanation.

1) It's hard to get a drunk-driving rap when you're sober. And this offense greatly affects the alcohol-related crime statistics since there are nearly two million driving-under-the influence (DUI) arrests every year. Drunk-and-disorderly and under-the-influence citations add another million arrests to the totals. So these "crimes" skew the overall statistics.

2) Nearly 70 percent of all violent crimes are committed by people who know each other. What this means, more often than not, is that, in the middle of a drunken quarrel, someone pulls out a gun and blows someone else away or launches himself across the table. This is the true nature of most violent crimes, and, yes, the alcohol/drug connection does apply but that's not the same as the crazed mugger jumping out of the bushes and threatening to blow your brains out.

3) There is a big difference between being "under the influence" and giving a dirty test. Crack cocaine remains in the system and is easily detected for more than 72 hours, and THC can be detected for up to a week. If you were to test most criminals for drugs/alcohol, you'd get some sort of positive reading. The issue isn't that he had residue in

his system, but whether or not he was high at the time.

4) Committing a premeditated crime is scary: it is not uncommon for a criminal to take a hit of a joint or a drink to screw up his courage and calm his nerves. But for his own self-preservation, the crim is not going to do any substance that would impede his reflexes. Speed freaks are still around, and, yes, they could decide to rob someone for their drug money, but unless you live in a meth neighborhood, it is really much rarer than people think.

For addicts, drugs are the escape. The heavier drugs like heroin, crack, and PCP (angel dust) leave the user incapable of thinking coherently enough to tie his shoe, much less organize a robbery. Under their influence, the addict is free from the pain of this world—literally, he's on vacation. When you're on vacation you don't go out and work! If you're robbed by someone on drugs, it's going to be weed, speed, or alcohol, not heroin! Calm down, the criminal isn't likely to be a total werewolf.

5) Ever since PCP came to the forefront of America's attention span, a lot of behavior has been misdiagnosed as drug freakouts. It doesn't take PCP to put someone into a superhuman state that the media have hyped so. The proper term for this condition is a "manic state." A manic state is when someone blows a gasket or a diagnosed manic-depressive is having a bad-hair day. Every horror story you've heard about a PCP freakout is possible with a person who is simply manic. PCP does appear to trigger an episode with people who have this mental condition, but it is not the source of the condition; no more than a match flipped into a pile of gunpowder is the source of the explosion—although it does start the ball rolling. Certain people and certain drugs combine badly.

The reason we mention this PCP myth is to point out that unless you are a cop or a hospital orderly or are related to someone who uses PCP, you are not likely to be targeted by someone on a PCP freakout. Both cops and orderlies have the unpleasant job of having to subdue a situation involving someone in a manic state, PCP or not. That means that when everyone else is running away, they have to run toward the problem. When you hear a story about Mace not working on someone, this is a special situation where a lead pipe across the forehead wouldn't work either.

Drugs or no, manic freakouts are dangerous and difficult to control without harming the person who is experiencing it. We know of an orderly in a mental ward who got his nose bitten off by a young guy who suddenly and unexpectedly flashed into a manic state. The guy was standing there talking one second and the next he tore the guy's nose off. Afterward, the biter had no memory of the event. He had no drugs in his system, yet he exhibited the blind rage and superhuman strength so often ascribed to a PCP freakout.

When you hear about police officers shooting someone they thought was on PCP, you're hearing the PR machinery at work. The officers who decided they were dealing with a manic state also decided that they didn't want to try wrestling with the Incredible Hulk.[4] The general public doesn't understand that a manic state can present the kind of threat that might warrant shooting someone, but they do understand a "PCP freakout." Even if later it is shown that the person didn't have PCP in his system, the perception still remains. Rodney King, for example, showed symptoms of someone who was in a manic state. Nearly incoherent, he had taken two Taser hits and continued to attempt to rise despite the blows being inflicted on him. That is someone you don't want to have standing in a confrontation—whether he has PCP in his system or not.

NOTES

1. Incidentally, we consider early abuse and trauma to be motivations, not excuses.

2. This is not to be confused with the casual-labor workforce. Usually, you can see the casual laborers around paint stores, lumber yards, and other areas of construction. This is an established gathering spot that is active in the morning but dwindles as the day progresses. There is little or no booze visible until the late afternoon. Nobody is going to hire a drunk, and the laborers know that. Although they often bring their own problems, most aren't addicts or criminals. If you hire a painter, many of his hombres are from this workforce.

3. Concentrations of toothless people indicate proximity to a methadone clinic. Methadone rots teeth. It is also commonly sold to recreational users to get money for heroin . . . so you might as well consider yourself in a drug location.

4. These days, police are loathe to go to the ground with someone because of the likelihood of AIDS, and among drug users AIDS is epidemic. It is impossible to go to the ground with someone and not get open cuts and scrapes; blood flows freely in fights like this. Taking a suspect to the ground can be a death sentence to the officer.

New York

Parts of the city—many parts—are open-air drug markets. Being in a drug area increases your risk of being injured because violence happens around drugs, and bullets don't care whom they hit. Innocent bystanders are shot in New York at the rate of about one a day (the exact count in the first 190 days of 1993 was 171 innocent victims). In the really bad sections of New York, like Brooklyn housing projects, they call innocent victims of drug shootings "mushrooms."

Sidewalk drug trade is done mainly by the seller just quietly saying what he has. You'll walk past and hear something like "poison," "sence," "vees," "gold top" (or purple top, or any other color top), "D.O.A.," "lucky seven," "the unknown," or "works." Often, there are a lot of guys loitering around the same corner saying more or less the same thing.

To translate, "sence" is short for sensemilla, a high grade of marijuana. Chances are that it's just dirt weed, but sence is the buzzword. Vees are valiums. Gold (or any color) top is crack cocaine, and the reference is to the color of the crack vial cap, which is like a brand name to crackheads. Places where there are lots of crack addicts look like a scene out of *Night of the Living Dead*, with zombies staggering around or stumbling forward with their eyes ablaze. If you find yourself in a crack neighborhood, leave immediately. Crack addicts will steal anything, absolutely anything. Crack is so cheap, $2 to $5, that addicts can get high through stealing inconsequentials like radio knobs and hair brushes. In some parts of the city crack prostitutes will turn tricks for $5 or less—the communicable AIDS they have is like a free gift.

A lot of the most pathetic-looking individuals in the city are crackheads—they lose their clothes, stay awake until they drop in the streets, never bathe, become skeletal. A whole lot of them are insane—with or without crack. The social workers have a cutesy name for them: MICAs, which, as we stated earlier, stands for mental ill, chemically addicted. Make no mistake—these people can be dangerous, and they are totally unpredictable. The Upper West Side has become home for many of the best-known MICAs, and one resident recently said, "We live in an open asylum above 96th Street." Many MICAs are violent. Others are verbally abusive and unpleasant—they shout curses, snarl, and spit, and a good percentage specifically target children and scare hell out of them. They scare hell out of most people. Recently they have been getting heavy press and have achieved a kind of Public Menace status in the papers. They are a public menace, for sure, and the smart thing is to stay well clear of them. Cross the street, move down the subway platform, change cars, go into a store—just get away as gracefully as possible. A show of fear is not advisable, since they will pick up on that very quickly. The women are just as dangerous as the men. It doesn't take much to shove someone in front of a train—as one MICA woman recently did to two unwary citizens.

Anybody saying "poison," "D.O.A.," or "the unknown" is a heroin dealer. Dope is sold with brand names, and it's currently the vogue drug, so there's plenty of it around. A lot of the little neighborhood convenience stores, *bodegas*, in drug zones like the Lower East Side, sell junk under the counter. In many areas it's easier to get heroin than a diet cola. Anyone talking about "works" is selling hypodermic syringes.

One of my friends was strong-armed for $5 by two assholes

after buying a dime ($10) bag of weed in Washington Square Park. They saw that he had some money in his sock (he was wearing jogging clothes with no pockets), and they waited until he left the park and made him kneel down and give up a five. Crack was just coming in then, and five bucks was the lucky get-high number. Washington Square Park is a big tourist attraction and very safe in general. Here is where all the folk singers like Bob Dylan and Joan Baez had their hootenannies and sing-ins. It is surrounded by the New York University campus. Nonetheless, most of the black guys (I'm not being racist, they just all happen to be black) hanging around the western end of the park are pot dealers. Early in 1993, *New York Post* columnist Jack Newfield reported that one of them had been arrested like 44 times for dealing reefer in the same location. He once got 60 days but walked on the other 43 cases. Others had arrest records that are nearly as impressive, and jail terms that were nearly as puny. And that's in a wealthy neighborhood with a lively interest in keeping crime down to maintain the tourist business in picturesque old Greenwich Village. Given that kind of pathetic criminal justice system, imagine how hard it is to get dope dealers of a poor area with nothing special going for it.

Another guy I knew made a hilarious mistake while trying to buy weed. The location this time was a storefront pot emporium (believe me, they exist) in Brooklyn. They wouldn't sell to him, and since they had sold to him before, he stood around out front trying to figure out what was wrong. A guy walked up and said, "They won't sell to you because they think you're a cop."

"I'm not a cop."

"You look like a cop," the guy said.

"But I'm not." That went on for about 10 minutes, and finally the guy I knew convinced his new acquaintance that he was not the law. So the street dude pulled out a gun and robbed him.

I'm not going to tell you where to score for drugs in the city.

If you come to town and you're looking, you'll find what you're after. It's a risky business, though, and it might end up costing you a lot more than you think. There are vast and efficient webs in place designed to serve the narcotics and recreational drug needs of New York and the tri-state area. There is also an efficient army of opportunistic con artists afoot in New York, ready to separate you from your money in a second. Street smarts in Keokuk don't equal street smarts in the Bad Apple. If you march up to the first smiling cat you meet on 42nd Street and tell him you're interested in some King Heroin, he'll for sure sell you something—but it probably won't be what you want. You have already demonstrated that you don't know the game, don't know the players, and can't find the field. You also probably don't know prices or packaging or quantities. You are a wide-open mark, and you will get massively burned, I promise. In this case, as with so many things in the big city, what you don't know will really hurt you.

One last thing—don't get snoopy if you see what looks like a drug deal going down that you'd like to participate in. A Texan I know had a pistol barrel poked in his nose when he looked too closely at the goings-on inside a parked car. This also goes for sex. In areas where prostitution is rampant, a lot of sex happens pretty openly in the back seats of cars and cabs parked at curbside. It's impolite to stop and stare hungrily through the windows. In case you don't know it, interrupting people who are in the middle of sex or who are actively injecting drugs is likely to result in bodily injury. It's one thing if you live on the block and have an ongoing problem with this kind of activity. It's quite another matter to kick up a fuss just because you happen to be walking by and the monkeyshines bug you. Part of staying safe on these mean streets is minding your own business in matters of the groin and the mainline. Live and let live.

L.A.

Unfortunately when it comes to bragging about the scummy conditions of one's hometown, L.A. falls woefully short in the drug scene when compared to Miami or New York. Then again Dead Horse, Alaska, has a ratio of 30 men to every woman, so there are worse places to live.

This is not to say that L.A. is a shiny example of drug-free America. Some of the local pits are in South Central L.A., Compton, Downtown L.A., Hollywood, Inglewood, Venice, Echo Park, East L.A., Sunland, Pacomia, etc. Moving south there're such social attractions as Garbage Grove . . . er, excuse me, Garden Grove, and sections of Santa Ana behind the Orange Curtain. Looking east, Pomona is no picnic; however, it acts as a springboard to points in that direction. Now that San Bernardino County is becoming a suburb of L.A. (ooh, that pisses them off!), you have such charming sites as San Bernardino itself. In Riverside County you have Rubidoux, parts of Riverside, and Lake Perris. Charming places all. Do yourself a favor and don't invest heavily in property in these areas.

There's a difference between a bad neighborhood and a drug neighborhood. A city drug neighborhood is the lowest of the low, rejected even by the run-of-the-mill street person. There are pits in Downtown that no self-respecting druggie from Hollywood would even go to (at least not yet). On the main drags, a lack of banks and small businesses—in comparison to lots of dirty liquor stores, cheap fast-food joints, bars, and check-cashing places—means you should lean on the gas pedal because you're in a bad neighborhood, probably infested with druggies. Long stretches of abandoned warehouses that have people hanging out anyway or abandoned gas stations with zombie-eyed loiterers indicate that you've found yourself a druggie graveyard.

Out in the 'burbs, trash and cars permanently parked on dead lawns overseen by packs of unhealthy lowlifes present a pretty good indication that you're someplace you shouldn't be. It's the loiterers in yards and parking lots who start walking toward you that should really tip you off more than just people being around an area. In L.A., other than robbers and drug dealers, only fools approach strange cars.

While not as rampant as in New York, the "strawberries" (female addicts who prostitute themselves for drugs) do provide a floor show for passersby. But, as in New York, that old bobbin' head in the front seat is something you shouldn't come too close to inspect. Also as a point of etiquette, if you are called into such an area on business, don't get bent out of shape when someone says something as appealing as, "Hey there's a broad over there who'll blow you for five bucks." It's their way of being neighborly. Gosh, how quaint. Aside from the standing offer for free a case of AIDS if one partakes, one should avoid strawberries for the simple reason that the vacuum isn't limited to their mouths; things have a habit of sticking to their hands as well. Funny how you don't feel someone pick your pocket when your eyes are crossed.

There are crack dealers in the streets and parks in L.A., but crack houses provide the main flow of that drug by supplying the street dealers. Usually these houses are not kept up, but, more important, the windows are often blocked by cardboard or aluminum foil. This is to prevent the cops from saying that they "saw the drugs through open blinds or drapes." Crack houses pop up anywhere, not just in lousy neighborhoods. I know of several in the nicer areas of the valley and West L.A. Watch for scuzzy-looking traffic coming and going at all hours, as well as people wandering out looking dazed. Of course, the screaming fights that often occur at these places are a pretty good indication: addicts don't know how to behave, and they bring their bad behavior with them wherever they go. Furthermore, the dealer, all too often, has dipped into his own supplies, so he's no Prince Charming.

While crack is the drug of choice, heroin and PCP still have their disciples in South Central, Compton, and Downtown. Methadone and speed seem to be more popular in East L.A. and the Sunland areas. The Drug Enforcement Agency (DEA) reports that heroin use is increasing, with purer forms no longer having to be injected—it is becoming more popular to snort it. A bumper crop overseas resulted in lower street prices, and as odd as this may sound, with the upswing of quality, there is now greater use among the middle and upper classes.

Although not as popular as in New York, drug stores do exist. I've seen gas stations, fast-food stores, and even lunch trucks that are actually fronts for drug dealing. Something else that is real common in L.A. is the drive-up drug buy. There are certain streets that you can drive slowly up and down and know that someone will walk up to the car and ask, "What you want?" or "What's up?" You respond with the appropriate drug for that street. That way the dealer knows you're not a cop, and he walks away from the car or reaches into his pocket for the score. The all too familiar call of "yo-yo" also echoes through the L.A. night. If you're thinking I'm giving you a rundown on how to buy drugs here, I'd also like to point out to you that in L.A., letting someone approach your car is a great way to get robbed or carjacked, if not shot.

Now, the basic truth is that if you aren't of the right race for a drug neighborhood or you don't look right, you are a target. The ethnic part is obvious, but by looking right I mean either being a trucker, construction worker, mechanic, or biker, someone who spends a lot of time in society's underbelly. These are people who know the rules and will nail someone who tries to rip them off; anyone who doesn't have that look will get screwed either by buying God knows what or simply robbed. It's as simple as that.

Incidentally, if you are a casual user who is interested in scoring, do yourself a favor and avoid buying from the street dealers. Not only are they dangerous, but the quality is minimal. To top it all off, the guy may be a police sting. The drug business is considered America's number four industry. There's got to be someone in pocket without going to the corner. If you work in an office building, the odds are that someone in the company or on the building's staff supplements his/her income by dealing on the side. Even asking the guy who's snuffing and sniffing in the bathroom of the local chichi meat market/fern bar is better than going to the corner.(By the way, if all you want is to use the facilities, another point of drug etiquette is to ignore the "snow" in the bathroom. Unless the guy's snorting right there in the open, the signs are usually pretty subtle—until you know what to look for. Then they might as well hold up a sign: five people bouncing around a sink with glazed eyes and sniffing uncontrollably or, especially in the women's room—don't ask how I know—people leaving the stalls in threes.) These people are safer to buy from than the animal on the corner. Getting yourself shot and your date raped is not a good way to have a good time.

Aside from the obvious danger just mentioned, if a cop sees your bright, shiny face in certain neighborhoods, he knows what you're there for. It's sort of obvious what's going on when three young guys in a car are driving around at night in a particular ethnic neighborhood. The cops know it, you know it, and if they pop you . . . well, thems the beans. Oh yeah, by the way, if you're in a vehicle that's stopped, if nobody cops to owning something found in it, everyone in the car is guilty of possession.

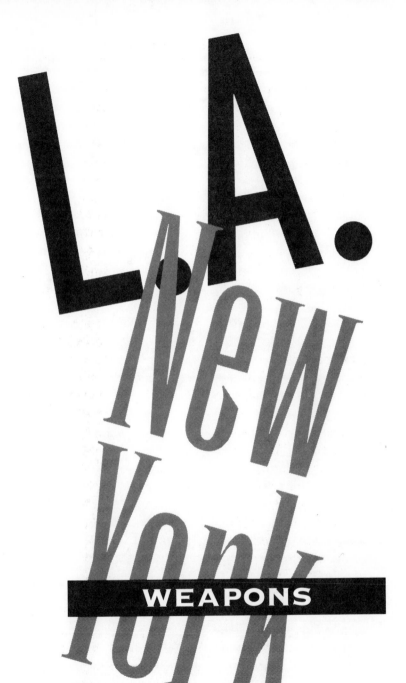

L.A.

New York

WEAPONS

Legalities

Before allowing you to proceed further in this chapter, we have to emphasize that we are not lawyers. Truth be told, any advice about the use of weapons not told to you by a lawyer on your retainer is suspect. This is why it's not a good idea to take as gospel any legal advice given by the guy in the gunshop. He's neither qualified nor unbiased. As with anything, you should check out the information in this chapter as it pertains to your own state, both what is written in the books and the precedents that determine its interpretation. Gather your sources from local qualified lawyers, specialists (instructors) in the field, National Rifle Association guidelines, and personal research. But be very careful because, although it's not supposed to happen, interpretations vary from county to county.

In spite of the fact that we are not lawyers, we'd like to introduce you to some of the basic concepts that will help you understand what you will encounter when you do your own research into weapons use.

What you need to understand is that if you use a weapon to defend yourself, you're going to be dealing with the cops and courts—bottom line. Unless you drop your victim and leave him lying in the street and then manage to make a clean getaway, this is how it is going to be.[1] In fact, if you shoot someone you can expect it to cost you at least $3,000 just to start with, and it's likely to be much more when you consider lawyers' fees, impound costs, 10 percent of whatever bail is, and a host of other smaller costs. To say nothing of the hassle you're going to have to put your family and friends through. If there is any doubt about your action being self-defense (this means unless you have multiple witnesses saying the guy, brandishing a weapon, attacked you), you will probably be arrested and your weapon confiscated. And depending on which state and city you're in, good luck getting it back. Getting something back from police impoundment is like pulling teeth from a wolverine on steroids. Even if it was self-defense, you're still going down to the police station to give an affidavit. One thing many people don't realize is you can be taken to the station without being arrested. That means the police don't have to read you your rights. A piece of advice: if you go to the station, you can and should have a lawyer with you. If the police feel there is insufficient evidence to support your claim of self-defense, you will be charged, and that is when your Miranda rights must be read to you. By that time, if you don't have your lawyer with you advising you to be quiet, you may have put your foot into it already.

One of the main factors to consider when looking at the legal use of weapons is to realize that, as with anything, there are two ways the legal system works: the way it is supposed to and the way it really does. And any discussion of the legal system (and how it actually works or doesn't work) has to begin with lawyers.

There have been many disparaging remarks and jokes made about lawyers over the years.[2] Much of the hostility is based on the belief that lawyers apparently lose sight of the issue of guilt and innocence and instead focus on winning. Basically if a lawyer loses, especially in a criminal case, the odds are he won't get paid! Face it, people don't become lawyers in spite of the money. Dead presidents are mighty powerful motivators for lawyers to win, as are lawyers' reputations. If a lawyer gets a reputation for losing too many cases, the big money is going to pass him by and go to someone with a better track record. When you dealing with the legal system, forget any idea of right or wrong, guilt or innocence, and accept the fact that everyone is going to do anything and everything to win. Justice takes a back seat to coming out on top when you're in court.

The bottom line is to prevent the situation from reaching the police and, certainly, from going beyond them into the courts. Fortunately, there is a lot you can do to prevent that from happening. Most of this has to do with being prepared beforehand and keeping a cool head during and afterward. Most important is for you to understand what constitutes legal self-defense and excessive force, which are nowhere near as clear-cut as you might think.

The laws are specifically written in such a way as to give life a higher priority than property and to emphasize *reasonable* force. To start with, a gun is classified as deadly force. Most states categorize the use of force into two categories: deadly and nondeadly. But to complicate the situation, there are all sorts of fun terms that define the acceptable use of deadly force: *immediate threat, grave and serious injury, aggressor, felony,* and *intent*. All these help determine when it is acceptable to pull the trigger. The general gist is that if you are not immediately confronted with the application of deadly force, you cannot pull the trigger. If you do so, you are using deadly force in a nondeadly situation, and that puts you in the wrong.

If you pick up any gun magazine, you'll see more than a few ads based on the gun owner valiantly defending his home. He heroically stands there lantern-jawed and steely-eyed, facing a horrible unknown with his weapon clutched boldly in his hand. (Actually, the one we like is where the guy is doing all the posing and the wife is the smart one on the phone calling for help.) In a similar vein, there's also the one of our hero Bruce Lee-ing a horde of villainous attackers while protecting a wide-eyed, adoring female. Before we tear these portraits of

John Wayne manliness apart, let's take a moment to admire them for their macho fantasy content. Okay, all done? Right, let's get on with it.

In a practical interpretation, if the person is not threatening you with physical violence, you cannot respond with physical violence even though he is trespassing or in the act of stealing from you. In many states there is a general opinion that if someone breaks into your house at night, he deserves what he gets, but the law usually doesn't see it that way. Somebody's breaking into your home isn't enough reason to use deadly force, and this is one of the more clear-cut situations involving the use of deadly force. If you point a gun at him and say, "Freeze," and he boogies to the door carrying everything, you can't shoot. You legally have to stand there and watch your possessions go bye-bye instead of using lethal force on the guy. This is what screws up most homeowners in shooting burglars: they shoot when the guy isn't attacking.

In the most absurd sense, if you had a Rolls Royce and you were getting out of it and a criminal jumped in and tried to drive away, you could not legally physically attack that person because he was not offering you the threat of physical violence or trying to take something from you by force. (By jumping in, he's not threatening or attacking you.) If he tried to knock you down first, *then* you could strike him because that would be robbery rather than larceny.[3]

Technically, you can use enough force to prevent your items from being stolen or to eject a trespasser, but unless you're a trained martial artist or law enforcement officer, the odds of your applying just the right amount of force is nearly impossible. The ideal is to use just enough physical force to prevent the person from stealing from you, but not enough to hurt him. If you can magically detain him without hurting him or striking him, then you've managed to not use excessive force on him. If you're a master of judo, you just whip a quick armlock on the guy and (without hurting him) hold him for the police.

However, if you punch him (rather than retaliate after he punches you for trying to stop him), you've technically crossed the line into excessive force. Sound unrealistic? Basically it is. Regardless of what the law says, stopping a violent crime isn't Goldilocks and the Three Criminals: "This force is too much, this force is too little, but this force is *juusst* right!"

Somehow the term *vigilante justice* developed a bad reputation in this country (probably because of the book *The Oxbow Incident*). It's brutal, vicious, and reactionary. Unfortunately, it seems that immediate vigilante retaliation does work, at least on the street level. In fact, it's well-known street protocol that leaving a torn-up burglar or addict lying in the street is one of the best deterrents against a particular property being targeted for crime. The criminals know someone else isn't playing by the rules, and if they cross that person they will be hurt for it—ergo, leave him alone! Unfortunately, this is strictly illegal and, unless done properly, is guaranteed to get the property owner in trouble.

Basically, it's a delicate balance between the self-defense statutes and assault and battery statutes, with anything beyond your preventing the criminal from stealing your property considered excessive force. Naturally, however, when you ask the nice crackhead to stop what he's doing and give you back your car stereo, he's going to willingly comply. Yeah, right, and pigs wearing aviator goggles will be zooming around your ears any second now. The law, though well meaning and intentioned, ends up protecting the criminal from retribution over his actions. A petty theft will maybe land him in jail for a week, max, if he's caught by a cop, and more than likely he'll walk with time served.

If you chase after the guy, maybe he'll throw what he's stolen and keep on booking, a common trick to get someone to stop the chase. If you catch him, you've probably already committed excessive force against him just by stopping him. How do you effectively stop someone at a dead run without hurting him? The scene in *Crocodile Dundee* where he nails the purse snatcher by throwing a can is heartwarming, but it would have landed Dundee in jail on an assault with a deadly weapon (ADW) charge.

Besides the legal considerations, you also have to be careful about chasing criminals because you never know when the guy might suddenly turn around with a knife in his hand and attack or lead you down a dark alley. Realistically, if someone does a snatch and dash on you (or runs away when you discover him ripping you off), you have to just let him go. Remember: life over property, especially your own life.

Putting it simply, if you are not in fear for your life, the use of deadly force is not justified. The standard that is used is what a "reasonable person would deem as a threat to your life." In some circumstances it's pretty easy to determine this. An unarmed guy 10 feet away is not deemed a threat; however, that same guy with a knife charging at you is a threat. That particular situation makes sense.

It gets complicated, however, when you consider the gray areas. Unless you have all sorts of specialized training, you are not going to be able to differentiate between when the guy is going for a weapon or dropping cargo and splitting. When he made the wrong move and you shot him, it sure made sense at the time. However, in the courtroom when the lawyer asks, "Did you actually see a gun?" and you answer, "No," it's going to look like you overreacted and murdered the guy. Even if he really was going for a piece, you are not an expert nor are you consciously aware of the real danger signs. All of those subtle signs your subconscious saw are going to seem pretty weak under cross examination by the prosecuting attorney.

Unfortunately, most real-life situations during which someone would use a weapon on another person land squarely in a gray area. If someone is in the middle of an enraged state and is roaming around your house screaming and destroying it, you can't shoot him, even if he's verbally threatening to kill you.

Likewise with the guy who says he's going to kill you later. Laughing boy may have multiple murder raps, assaults, and rapes on his record and be dead serious about his intention and be able to carry it out, but you cannot take him out with a preemptive strike. According to the law, you now have time to run to the police and tell them a threat has been made against your life. Of course, the cops can't do anything until he strikes you or you get a restraining order put on him, but you still have time to notify the authorities. Saying that he's going to kill you at a later date does not constitute an immediate threat. Until he actually strikes, he hasn't done anything wrong.

An even more confusing ambiguity occurs when someone is physically assaulting you. Basically, if the guy isn't using a weapon, you can't use one on him. He is committing battery; you, however, are committing assault with a deadly weapon, excessive force to that being used against you. The one major exception to this is a woman who is in danger of being raped (at least in some states). Sexism does have pluses when it allows a woman more latitude with what she can use in self-defense.[4] A male, however, basically ends up having to meet a barehanded attacker nose to nose. The occasional exception is when the attacker is significantly larger than his victim, a trained martial artist, or has partners, but those are determined on a case-by-case basis.

Let's take a little reality break here. By the time someone is normally in danger of dying due to a bare-handed attack, he is so badly damaged that he is not capable of using a weapon effectively. Watch the tape of the Reginald Denny beating during the L.A. riots and you'll see this. There was no way he could have defended himself in that situation even with a weapon. It is here that the clause of "or great bodily injury or harm" comes into play. This is the other justification to use a weapon on someone. Unfortunately, the same situation applies as with fear of death. When it's gotten to the point in a bare-handed conflict where the victim is in danger of great bodily injury, he is usually too messed up to fight back, much less draw and operate a weapon. What you are left with is a Catch-22, whereby you can't use a weapon against an unarmed attacker until it's too late for you to use it!

Realistically, however, these things happen too fast to make a legally perfect decision. Look how fast Reginald Denny went down when attacked. He had no time to react from the moment there was a threat of great bodily injury to when it became a reality against which he was helpless. It is this reality that motivates people to pull weapons when they sense that they are beginning to lose a fight. However, by acting at that time instead of when they are lying on the ground being beaten, they become the ones who are guilty of excessive force in the eyes of the law. Complicated, isn't it?

Some states maintain that before you have the right to use deadly force, you have to retreat first in an attempt to prevent it. This means if you shoot someone, you have to be able to prove that you could not retreat because of 1) the imminence of the threat, 2) the attacker's ability to maintain a threat at a distance, 3) it was physically impossible, or 4) you were protecting someone else. Although there is more latitude given if you are attacked in your home, you are expected to retreat rather than use a weapon in almost every other situation. The long and short of it is that the only time you can legally shoot someone in self-defense is if you or a loved one can't get away from the attacker. If the guy is all over you and you can't run, that's self-defense; if you're cornered and up against a wall, that's self-defense; if he's got a gun and will shoot you if you flee, that's self-defense. If you could have run away or escaped through a window, that's not self-defense—that's ADW.

In the more granola states,[5] some bright boy came up with the idea that you have to warn the criminal that you're armed. This is so he can make an informed decision whether to attack you or not. So in the middle of a life-threatening situation, you basically have to read the criminal his rights:

Criminal, you have the right to roam freely around my house looting and pillaging as you will. The law says I cannot shoot you for this. However I have a gun and am prepared to use it if you attempt to offer me bodily harm. I must warn you that any approach toward my person will be considered a threat upon my person, and I will use lethal force. Having informed you of my armed status, I will be obliged to shoot you if you choose to attack me. Do you understand these rights I have explained to you?

Supposedly, you say all this calmly and loudly during a crisis before you shoot, as well as remaining clearheaded enough to remember that "if he's not immediately attacking with life-threatening force" you can't do anything. It's either that or you must remember to lie on your statement and tell the cops that you did warn the guy.[6]

Of course, if the guy happens to live, he's naturally going to refute everything you say. He's going to say you didn't tell him nothing, he wasn't attacking, he didn't intend you any harm, he wasn't committing a felony—you jes shot 'im in cold blood! He was just standing there in your front room, minding his own business, and you attacked him!

How progressive (read: dim-witted) your state is determines how strictly it adheres to these ideals. In some areas where the attitude is "ye jes don' do sumthin' like that and *not* expect to git shot," police officers aren't going to be real sticklers for some of these details. On the other hand, where laws have deviated from the general opinion of the majority (e.g., California and New York), law officials do care about these details, a lot! As odd as it may seem, the larger the city, the more they seem to care. There's more crime in the city, yet officials seem to get more bent out of shape about you defending yourself in the city than they do in the rural areas.

Also, if you live in a big city, the authorities might even get upset if you fire a warning shot. In many cities it is illegal to

SAFE IN THE CITY

discharge a firearm within city limits. Even out in the boonies, it is often illegal to discharge a firearm within 150 yards of a habitation or road. Many people would think that a warning shot would be ideal to prevent the criminal from either trying to flee or choosing to attack. This is not a bad assumption; however, again it's property over life. What the cops worry about is where that bullet went. Bullets have a nasty habit of traveling and finding innocent bystanders.

Animal was sitting in a house when a .357 magnum bullet originating in a bedroom passed between him and his friend in the front room, pierced the duplex's outer wall, crossed a breezeway, and entered another person's home. By peering through the bullet hole, they could see that it had struck the far wall of the neighbor's bedroom. A .22 LR round shot out of a rifle, if given the correct trajectory, can carry a mile. Bullets will go until they run out of energy.

Shooting into your ceiling is not the solution, either. Even those who don't live in apartments, condos, or high-rises with other dwellings above them have to worry about where the bullet will go after it exits the roof. What goes up must come down, and essentially at the same speed at which it went up. This is why it is often illegal to shoot guns off into the air, a popular habit among Hispanics to celebrate New Year's.

If you live in a city where there are lots of people closely packed together and the houses aren't made of bricks, the odds are that the cops will get more upset about your firing a warning shot than they will about the guy in your home. If you fire a gun in self-defense and hit an innocent party, *you are liable*! That bullet is your responsibility. This is why certain states don't have "fleeing-felon laws." They don't want bullets flying around in crowded areas, even if someone just got robbed. Even in states that have fleeing-felon laws, this principle applies, so you had better be damn sure of your target before you pull the trigger. Just a friendly warning on that one.

Now, another little tidbit about your home and what a reasonable person might or might not do. In many states and counties across this nation, the precedent is that a person who willingly gets up and goes through his house looking for a burglar is not doing what a *reasonable person in fear for his life* would do. Do you hear the warning bells ringing? We hope so. The contention is that by arming yourself and going to where the criminal is, you are willingly putting yourself into the situation. In short, instead of being in fear for your life, you are being a cowboy. Therefore, if you end up encountering someone and having to shoot him, you were not being reasonable and are therefore the aggressor. This also applies in nonfleeing-felon states when someone shoots into your house. If you go out of your house and shoot at the first party, you are now the aggressor. Lawyers throw around the terms *Dodge City, gunslinger, vigilante,* and *showdown* to make it look as though your getting up, arming yourself, and investigating the noise you heard prove that you intended to murder someone. Unfortunately, this ploy has proven to be extremely effective with juries in granola states.[7]

More realistically, though, it is flat-out impossible for just one person to effectively secure a house, gun or no. S.W.A.T. and elite military personnel have known this for years. Hollywood is totally off the mark on this one. The lone Hollywood hero cautiously checking out a building full of bad guys waiting for him would be dead in real life. You simply can't do it safely for a number of reasons.

1) *You're going to make noise.* Most people aren't trained to move silently, and a walking human being has a distinct rhythm. Creaking floors, scuffling feet or slippers, opening doors, and bumbling pursuers all alert whoever is there that he's not alone. If he's got a weapon, you're in trouble. As an experiment, try moving through your home quietly in the dark and then listen while someone else tries.

2) *There is no way a single person can cover the entire area of a room immediately upon entering it.* An intruder could be

anywhere in a room, and there is simply no time to inspect all the possibilities before he has a chance to strike. If you have multiple people enter the room, they can divide it into sections and immediately detect the intruder's position.

3) *Most specific techniques developed for survival in such situations are counterinstinctive.* They are based on thousands of hours of experience and research and, as such, are not likely to be accidentally stumbled upon by the average person. For example, holding a flashlight out at arm's length to draw the intruders fire two feet to the left of the flashlight holder's actual position is not something most people would normally do. Without knowledge of such techniques, a person will make mistakes, such as accidentally drawing fire to his position, making himself an enlarged target for the intruder, giving his location away by shadows, or attempting to take cover behind an object that will not stop a bullet. This is why in the burglary chapter we advised that, if someone is in your house when you enter, you get out! As a training exercise, one combat shooting school has people, armed with fake guns, go alone through a "house." During the 10 years this school has been open, it has had a 0-percent survival rate of its defenders. The school's owner is one of America's top police instructors, and he uses this demonstration to prove the point.

When it comes to home defense, according to lawyers, the safest answer is for you to get behind your bed and point the gun at the door. When you hear the intruder at the door, proclaim loudly that you are armed and in fear for your life and if he enters he will be shot. If the intruder enters after being warned, then it is assumed that he intended you bodily harm.[8] This is especially applicable if your bedroom is not on the ground floor and you cannot escape out a window. If you have children or other people in the house whom you cannot leave, position yourself at a strategic location to prevent the criminal from approaching them or you and then get down on the floor and make the same announcement.

In some states the prevailing attitude is "if you shoot, kill him." Animal's old partner shot an intruder in the leg, and the officer who came looked at the criminal and said point-blank, "You should have killed him." Sure enough, the guy sued, claiming he wasn't attacked, and won! The raw truth is as long as he is around to tell a different story, you're in jeopardy. It doesn't matter if you claim you were only trying to "wound" a criminal, thinking that this will give you brownie points. Using a gun still constitutes deadly force. If the guy was only enough of a threat to make you think of wounding him, you weren't in fear for your life, now were you? You've just opened yourself up for everything from assault with a deadly weapon to attempted murder. Remember, when push comes to shove, these cases are decided on a case-by-case basis!

If you live in a state that is more tolerant of home defense, you may be able to get away with just shooting to wound, but for the most part, don't pull that trigger unless you are in the gravest danger.

When the police ask why you shot him, *always* answer, "I was in fear for my life." When they ask if you were you trying to kill him or wound him, answer, "I was trying to stop him." You never say you were trying to kill or wound him—you were always trying to stop him. This is critical. When they ask why you shot him more than once (if you did), answer, "I was trying to stop him, and he was still attacking after the first shot." These are the pat answers to the most dangerous questions that you will be asked by the authorities. But you should double-check these responses with a local attorney before you find yourself in this situation, since local variations will affect what else you need to say Also, have your lawyer present when you make a statement.

Another critical point to consider is children and weapons. There is always the fear of young children accidentally shooting themselves or others. More realistically, however, teenagers are a bigger problem. Inner-city high school problems are often solved with guns these days. You can thank the media for glorifying gangs enough so that they are now moving out into affluent areas, smaller cities, and even towns. These kids are armed and dangerous, and they terrorize others with real threats of extreme violence and murder. Gone are the halcyon days of high school where problems were resolved with a fistfight in the locker room.

A few years ago a local television program on kids and guns reported that approximately 70 percent of all the arms that kids carry actually belong to their parents.[9] In light of statistics such as this, certain states proceeded to enact legislation that said, in effect, that if your kid shot someone with your gun, you were not only liable as a parent but guilty of a felony as well. Theoretically, this law was to get the parents to keep the guns out of kids' hands; practically, though, it's another example of good intentions potentially becoming a monster.

If you have a gun in the home, you must secure it from your children. This is easy for rifles, shotguns, and spare guns because simple trigger guards will suffice to keep the guns from being used. You keep the keys, and there is little chance of misuse. Also, this prevents your guns from being turned on you if you have the bad luck to walk in on a burglar.

It is the pistol you keep handy for home defense that will be the real problem. With some pistols, a trigger guard can be bypassed by simply pulling back the hammer and releasing it. Additionally, if you lock it down against your children, you're not going to have time to get it, prepare it, and use it if you ever need it in a hurry. If you leave it ready to use, your kids can get hold of it, and God help you if something happens. You can try to hide it (or the ammo) and hope for the best. Unfortunately that doesn't work too well in real life with older kids. (Remember going through your parents' room as a kid? They still do it.)

Probably, the best thing you can do is invest in a safety vault. The best type of gunsafe is keyboard controlled: in the dark, you punch the combination into the glowing keypad, and the door pops open, revealing a loaded and ready weapon. More important, though, unless your kid is a professional lockpicker, he won't be able to get to your gun. Some of the vaults even have security devices so that if the wrong number is dialed in three times, it locks and won't open until reset. There are two kinds: one that is set into the wall (for home owners) and another that bolts to the wall (for renters). These safes run about $250 at the local locksmith store and are well worth the investment.

If your job takes you into areas of high crime, if you're in a high-risk profession, or if you own property or a business that might be targeted, you need to take steps to protect yourself from both criminal and civil proceedings. Find a good criminal lawyer right now and give him a retainer—especially if you own a business. It may sound absurd to give a lawyer a thousand dollars for nothing at this moment, but if you ever have to defend yourself, you make a phone call and get that attorney's ass down there before you make a statement. If you don't own your own business but work in a high-risk industry and can't afford an attorney or get your boss to spring for a retainer, get together with some of your co-workers and have everyone pitch in. This isn't to bail someone out of a drunk-driving rap; it's to save someone's ass from a murder charge. This way, if it ever goes down, that attorney gets off his butt and waddles down to the station to help you with your statement. That kind of help can and will keep you out prison. Face it, this is insurance nobody likes to pay, but when it hits the fan, man, oh man, are you glad you did.

Up to this point we've been just talking criminal charges; now let's consider civil charges. If by some miracle the guy survives (you'll be sorry) and you live in a granola state, even if you are cleared of criminal charges, you're likely to be hit with a lawsuit. And if the guy dies, it's possible that you'll get nailed with a "wrongful death" suit from his survivors.

Civil proceedings make criminal charges look like the

height of common sense. These are the cases you hear about where a burglar trips on the windowsill and breaks his leg while escaping and sues the owner of the house he just burglarized. Or the child throwing lit matches down a car's gas tank, and the owner of the car being held liable. Or the people who jumped two fences, ignored warning signs, stood in a dangerous curve area of a raceway, and when a crash occurred and injured them, sued the promoters for negligence for not supplying enough security to keep them out. Or the all-time favorite, the woman who suffered toxic shock from wearing a tampon for a ludicrously long time and sued the manufacturer for having a dangerous product. Or in this case, the homeowner/private person who shoots someone in self-defense and loses everything. In all of these suits, the plaintiffs were trying to avoid the responsibility of having to maintain a level of common sense above that of an eggplant.

Complicating this, of course, is the fact that most of the people on juries for civil cases are on eggplant status themselves (the rest of us have jobs). The plaintiff's lawyer is going to be trying to fill that jury with as many eggplants as he can.

Someone once wrote that the weakness of democracy was that the masses would eventually realize they could vote themselves more and more perks. A jury full of eggplants won't see the long-term effects of their actions in real or economic terms. They only see cash. Then they see who has it and who doesn't, and they want to take from those who have and give it to a fellow have-not.

Remember the comment about jury trials being about placing blame? That's what you're up against in a civil case. The victim, his lawyer, and the law enforcement officers want to blame someone for his getting hurt. In the eggplant mentality, anyone who would use a weapon on someone is a bad person. Never mind that you both were armed and he was attacking; you used the weapon more effectively. Do you begin to see an ugly picture emerging? When combined with a lawyer who doesn't care about justice, you get some ludicrous court results and settlements.

It's that excessive-force clause that lawyers love so much. Suddenly the crackhead who attempted to rob you was a brilliant young neurosurgeon who was financing his way through med school by robbery, and your unprovoked assault on him cut short his promising career. His lawyer is going to go for damages against what the guy could have made (if he was a CEO) while he was recovering from his injuries, not what he would have made. Another speciality is the lawyer going after you to pick up the guy's hospital tab. Any bets as to the hospital ever seeing any of that cash? The lawyer's going to take up to half the settlement in fees, and the lowlife is going to stiff the hospital. As I said, from crackhead to upstanding pillar in the community until he gets the money, then he reverts to form.

If you don't believe me, look at Rodney King. Aside from being a multiple offender, he was not only committing felony reckless and drunk driving, but also violating parole (for armed robbery no less) by being drunk. Suddenly, in spite of all this, he was miraculously changed to innocent-sounding "motorist." Surprise, surprise, as of this writing, motorist Rodney King has been busted four more times![10] At the time of this writing he still has his lawsuit pending against the city. The $64-million demand has been reduced, but it is still outrageously high.

These personal-injury suits have proliferated because lawyers often take them on a contingency basis for part of the settlement. Scratch away the veneer of public spirit and you'll find a shyster who stands to make up to half of whatever settlement he gets as a fee! He's gambling on his ability to win, not on his client's ability to pay. If the client was hard up enough for money to be out committing a crime, how would he pay for a lawyer?

Before Sam the Shark takes a case like this he's going to do a thing called an asset search. This means he is going to find out how much you're worth before he decides to go after you.

We live in a world of information, and getting someone's net worth is not hard. Once he sees what size of target you are is when he'll decide whether to pursue the case or not. It's the size of your holdings that will get you sued faster than anything else. Except in places like Colorado, if you use a weapon against someone, expect to go to civil court if you have anything resembling money. As the old joke goes, a pessimist is seldom surprised.

Even if you are cleared of criminal charges after using a weapon to defend yourself, the minute you walk out of the police station you call a civil lawyer and batten down the hatches against a suit. This means either having a civil lawyer on retainer already or going out and getting one. Remember how we mentioned that shooting someone is expensive? This is just another aspect.

There are two things you can do to protect yourself long before you ever have to defend yourself with a weapon. One is to hide your assets. This is something that will take lots of time and fancy dancing on paperwork, but it's worth it. The other is to put all of your money and belongings into a trust. You can be sued for damages resulting from an assault, but your trust can't. Even if the guy wins, all of your money and belongings are safely stored away from attachment in the trust. Talk to a lawyer and protect yourself up front. The reason most criminals aren't sued is they are "judgment proof." That means they ain't got nothing. Even if you win, you can't get blood from a stone. Do the same back to 'em.

A new technique that originated in California turns the eggplant mentality against itself. Immediately after the shooting has been cleared from a criminal standpoint, sic your civil lawyer on the criminal and his survivors first. That's right, you sue first! Try something like this: the survivors were aware of what the deceased was doing and were therefore liable because they didn't turn him in. Whatever, the purpose isn't to win any money, it's to establish another legal ruling on the case before they bring suit, make their attorney work for free without any chance of payment on the first case, and put them on the defensive. For that lawyer to get any money, he has to win not just one but two cases. If he loses the first one, the chances of him winning the second are looking pretty weak. Sneaky, huh?

You are legally required to notify the police in the event of any type of violence. However, in a purely hypothetical situation, if someone wanted to avoid any problems arising from an assault in which the attacked was forced to resort to nonlethal action, he would behave in a certain manner that, while illegal, would improve his chances of avoiding any legal entanglements. If one were not of the mind, say, to wait and discover what the authorities' interpretation of the justification of one's action would be, knowing full well that such course of action would be illegal, how would one go about doing such? The would-be victim simply departs the area quickly. If this event happened near said person's car, instead of phoning the police, the person would (illegally, of course) phone a friend or relative to drive over and meet him somewhere away from the scene, preferably in some sort of establishment. If necessary, that person would request a change of clothes be brought. They would exchange cars, and the newly arrived person would go pick up the first person's car and drive it to that person's home.

In many cases, the defeated attacker would have vacated the area under his own power and not called the police. However, if his injuries were severe enough, the presence of the police is almost a certainty. The severity of the wounds determines how seriously the police would check into the cause of his injuries. If the police find the individual who left the scene, there is a good chance of being charged with leaving the scene of the crime even if proven innocent of any other charges because it is highly unlikely that the person's behavior would be simply written off to shock due to its organized nature. This, of course, is to be weighed against the severity of the attacker's injuries and the caseload of the local police.

Oddly enough, in large metropolitan areas, nonlethal use of force against someone under questionable circumstances is not assigned high priority.

The above is, of course, only a hypothetical scenario for *information purposes only* and in no way advocates that the reader should break the law.

In a similar vein—and, like the first, totally illegal and in no way endorsed or recommended by either of the authors—the following hypothetical scenario could be used in a home-defense situation that involves lethal force. An unregistered handgun (illegal in and of itself) would be kept in the house. This gun and any bullets would be wiped of fingerprints before being put away. Stored with this device would be a pair of surgical gloves. If an intruder is killed and it is discovered that he had no weapon, the new gun is immediately placed in the dead man's hand or printed. The rubber gloves would be then flushed down the toilet, and the police called. This ruse would not fool an intensive investigation; however, it could pass a cursory investigation. Again this is *for information purposes only*, and we in no way recommend that the reader break the law.

NOTES

1. Besides the fact that this action is exceedingly illegal, most people don't have either the fortitude to do this or the training to make an effective getaway. Their most common mistake is to jump into their cars and drive away, allowing everyone to see their license plate numbers, or they immediately go directly home.

2. Incidentally, Animal collects lawyer jokes, so if you have any good ones, feel free to send them to him in care of Paladin Press.

3. Larceny is theft, where something is simply stolen. Robbery is where something is taken through force

or the threat of force and is treated as a more severe crime by the courts.

4. In cases like this, *prosecute!* Go after the attempted rape conviction. If the guy doesn't get that on his legal record, he can sue.

5. Those states that are legislated by nuts, fruits, and flakes.

6. But that would be dishonest, and we'd *neeeever* recommend you do something like that.

7. A good point to remember about juries was brought up in the movie *A Few Good Men*: "The purpose of a jury trial isn't just to prove right or wrong; it's to place blame!" One of the major pastimes of granola-eaters is blaming someone for something, usually the politically incorrect non-granola-eaters.

8. That is, of course, unless you live in Colorado, which has a "make my day" law (18-1-704.5), thus making it the intruder's problem. If you want to cut out a lot of this nonsense regarding weapons use, go after your state lawmakers to pass a similar law.

9. It's probably safe to assume that this number is way off, not because of mistakes by the reporters, but because of the source of the numbers. If it came from the police, that's only the number of guns they actually caught. If it came from the kids themselves, they were probably lying.

10. Associated Press, August 22, 1993.

Realities

When it comes to self-defense, up to this point everything available has been either extremist or watered down. The American public has been left with either fanaticism or inefficiency, and all too often a terrible combination of both. The practical options have either been outlawed (like pepper spray in California) or have political ramifications hanging on them like anchors. There is no realistic middle ground for the average person. The macho gung-ho attitudes are too far afield for sane people, while the remaining options flat-out don't work. People aren't interested in extreme measures that would cause them more trouble than the original crime, nor are they looking for something that will turn them into supermen five years down the line.

One extreme is exemplified by the martial arts world. The viewpoint that most American martial art schools promote is that self-defense is synonymous with fighting. The martial arts world has been taken over by an adolescent macho attitude reminiscent of that high school terrorist club commonly called "jocks." They've turned self-defense into a sport, and their idea of fun is to go out and beat each other up at these tournaments. Gosh, we bet that's exactly what you want to do for fun.

Most martial artists insist that knowing how to fight barehanded is "self-defense"—despite the fact that 80 percent of all violent crimes are committed with a weapon and, as you've seen by now, the professional criminal has no interest in fighting you. If he sees the standard karate machismo, he's going to bust a trash can over your head and be done with it. There is a type of attitude you need to be safe, but macho isn't it.

The other extreme is the gun world. Although there are varying degrees within the group, the ones that scare most people are the penis-replacing wannabe soldiers of fortune who spout endless statistics on stopping power, rounds per minute, incapacitation indexes, and muzzle velocity. Often, folks like this aren't exactly tightly wrapped to begin with, but when you combine their rhetoric with their physical appearance, it gets spooky, sort of like Laurel and Hardy armed with Uzis coming off an amphetamine binge. Scary! With these guys, you're right to be uneasy. Unfortunately, with the help of the media, the extremists draw more attention than the calmer, more rational voices in that community.

More realistically, though, the average person has some serious hesitation about shooting someone. He really doesn't want to kill anyone, and shooting someone is a real good way to kill him—but, oddly enough, not the way you might think from watching TV. A bullet is a wild card, and even a big one can take up to two minutes before it has the desired effect of stopping someone. The hesitation over shooting someone, combined with the necessary time for the bullet to work, leaves the criminal all sorts of time to do damage if he's attacking! It's critical to realize that, despite what the gun nuts say, a gun doesn't make you invincible; nor will it do you any good if you can't get to it in time.

Karate and guns become useful only if you know you're in danger in the first place, and if you misuse them they are more trouble than they're worth. Without an early-warning system to allow you time to prepare, you're not going to be able to use these options or justify their use later. If you don't have time to bring these systems on line, it's safer not to have them! If the criminals have the drop on you and you try to go into superman mode, you're going to get hurt. To be safe, you have to be ahead of the game, not in the middle or bringing up the rear.

Here's a free safety tip from a street veteran: you don't survive on the streets by allowing the other guy to get the upper hand. Nor do you survive the aftermath by acting entirely in good faith with the authorities. It's cover your ass on all fronts when it comes to defending yourself. You don't let the crim control what's happening, because if he does, he'll attack. With the authorities you choose your words carefully and use predetermined answers to the questions. The authorities aren't necessarily the problem; it's the lawyers that use the cops' reports afterward who will nail you.

Let's first talk about the physical realities of having to defend yourself: realities that are far different from what you see on TV or in a movie. Number one, when it comes to the effects a bullet or knife really have on a person, if the only information you have comes from TV (or the aforementioned sources), then the joke of "everything you know is wrong" comes into play. Bullets are the ultimate wild card. If you think that someone has actually sat down and figured everything out about how bullets affect the human body, we have some bad news. Bullets are like Chaos theory; you can have the finest minds in the world working on it, and they can't tell you specifically what is going to happen, just generalities. There is no way to predict how someone is going to react to being shot until after it's over. If you're relying on someone to simply fall down as they do on TV, you could be in for a rude surprise.

In their excellent book, *Handgun Stopping Power* (available from Paladin Press), Evan Marshall and Edwin Sanow provided the best practical evaluation of ammunition stopping power available today. They realized that there was a serious discrepancy between wound ballistic studies, relative stopping power theories, and manufacturers' claims about how the bullets should work and how they actually performed in real situations. These two police officers went out and gathered data from actual shootings about how people reacted when shot, how long the bullet took to have an effect, and what the actual damage was to living—rather than dead or simulated—tissue. What they discovered was something that will bring you to a screeching halt when relying on a handgun to stop an attack.

They discovered that a critical, yet often ignored, factor in how a bullet affects a shooting victim is his mind-set. If the victim has watched too much TV and believes that when he's shot he simply falls down, that is what he usually does. There are even reports of people dying from what amounts to a flesh wound from excessive fear. They didn't die from the effects of the bullet but from the conviction that if you get shot you die! On the other hand, some people are knocked unconscious and immediately drop to the ground when shot.

Unfortunately, if the person shot is in an altered state of consciousness, it may take between 10 and 90 seconds for a bullet to incapacitate him, even if he is fatally wounded. An altered state doesn't necessarily derive from drugs; anger, fear, mania, or an adrenaline rush all affect how quickly a person succumbs. You might even be able to say sheer stubbornness affects how long the guy is going to be able to stay up and moving. With a bullet in his heart, the guy can still remain hostile for 10 to 15 seconds! If you're lucky he may fall immediately, but to be safe you should expect at least a 10-second delay time for the bullet to work. Now you begin to understand why people get shot by the police more than once.[1]

Also, there is a difference between fatal and incapacitated. Someone can be shot and die later from loss of blood or other complications, but that's still a fatal wound. Note the number of people who survive long enough to die in the hospital, sometimes hours after the actual shooting. Those who receive a sufficient shock to the reticular activating system (RAS) to faint immediately are incapacitated. How that shock is conveyed depends on both shot placement and the mind-set of the person shot. It doesn't mean he's dead or even fatally shot, just that his nervous system overloaded. He went "Tilt!"

In a more practical vein, if the guy is shot but not in an immediately fatal way, he may not go down for two or more minutes. There are more than a few examples of people with lead in them continuing to attack or escaping at high speed—or in some cases slow speed. Chris still managed to get down the street, up a flight of stairs, through a locked door, and then make two phone calls after being shot. If the guy is of hostile intent and isn't fatally wounded, he can stay up for a long time, until blood loss and adrenaline wear off. If he's attacking you, that means he can still continue his attack and that you're both going to the hospital with wounds.

If you hit a supporting bone, the physical collapse will be of a mechanical nature, but that doesn't mean the person is incapacitated. The guy can still shoot back from the floor. When shooting someone, you want to incapacitate him, to stop him from continuing his attack. Taking it back to the legal mumbo jumbo, you want to stop your attacker, not necessarily hurt him.

Many people don't realize the danger of a knife attack against a gun. A standard police procedure when confronted with a knife-wielding suspect is to not allow that person closer than *21 feet*. This may sound extreme until you realize this is the distance someone in a manic state can cover before an officer can draw, aim, and fire his pistol. The bad news is that this is not taking into consideration how long the bullet will take to incapacitate the attacker. The guy with the knife can be up close and slashing all that time. Yes, the attacker may die, but someone in a manic and/or altered state doesn't care. Another real common thing you should know about is "suicide by police." This is when the guy decides to check out by attacking a cop; he won't pull the trigger himself, but it's still suicide. It happens more than you'd believe. Next time you hear someone getting upset about the police shooting a guy with a knife, remember these little facts; then you can begin to understand why the officer pulled the trigger.

The next tidbit that you should know is that there is a world of difference between range shooting and combat shooting. Most of the differences have to do with our physiological reactions, the way our bodies react in combat: we human animals have predetermined programs that affect our fight-or-flight reactions. There are entire systems based on physiological responses under combat; e.g., the Israeli combat system of both hand-to-hand and gun combat is designed to work based on the way the body reacts to the stress of combat. There are indications that the Israelis have designed systems to win against trained fighters by turning their reflexive reactions against them. The U.S. Army Special Forces have also done extensive research and training into this phenomenon. In America, Massad Ayoob brought this concept to the public's awareness with his book *Stress Fire*.

Basically, the way your body will react under the stress of an actual situation is often at odds with what your training on weapons use indicates. Your muscles will cramp up, your time perception might warp out, your hands will tremble with adrenaline, you will often void your bladder and sphincter—in short, you will be as jumpy as a long-tailed cat in a room full of rocking chairs. Unless you are trained to operate under these conditions, you ain't going to be able to hit shit. All that time down at the range is just out the window during an actual situation.

For this reason, if you are serious about using a gun for self-defense, don't just buy a gun and think that will take care of it. In states where there is required training, that is fine and dandy—but it won't teach you how to use a gun in a real situation. All those classes do is show you enough to not shoot your own foot off during normal operations. We're not going to talk about combat-shooting tactics, but we highly recommend that you take a class before you need to know how to react in a stressful situation. If you don't think you need this, go out and try surviving a paintball game.

It's worth mentioning that by living in a gang-infested city you might find yourself in a firefight at any time and in any place. Gangs roam and no longer limit their fights to their own neighborhoods. If you find yourself in a place where the bullets are flying, do everything you can to get behind something concrete or put a car engine between you and the shooters. A simple household wall will not stop a stray round, and if the guy is shooting "hardball" rounds, neither will a car door.

For some reason, the 9mm seems to be the weapon of choice of the gangs. It may have to do with the number of rounds that the nine has (up to 21 in a pistol). A long-standing joke is that most gang members are such lousy shots that they try to make up for it with volume. Gone are the days of the six-bullet revolver as the weapon of choice. Full-size automatics generally hold eight bullets and are faster to reload than revolvers. (The good news is most punks don't carry a second magazine.) The nine is a nasty fast bullet that will punch through the outside of a car (whereas a .38 will often bounce off). This is another reason gangsters began to favor it. A common attack technique among gangs for revenge killings is to pull up beside a car containing a rival gang's member and rip the car with bullets.

A more terrifying aspect of the 9mm is that it will slice through a stucco or wood wall. Unless it hits a stud (one every 16 inches per code), a 9mm bullet fired inside the house will often travel completely through two or three rooms. Incidentally, this is why having someone hiding behind a wall during a movie shoot-out is incorrect. Much of the punching power of guns depends not on the caliber, but on the load (bullet) itself. There are bullets out there that basically self-destruct on impact, transferring all the shock to the target and stop right there; there are also bullets that travel forever, through whatever gets in their way until they run out of energy.

It is bad enough when a few bullets are flying from a pistol, but having 30 coming out of an AK-47 or Uzi with a banana clip is a horror story. If you ever hear the roar of an assault weapon, *hit the dirt and stay there.* It means you have walked into something beyond serious.

Fortunately, unless you're in a gang, have a gang member living with you, or live next door to a gang member, the odds are unlikely that you're going to get involved in situation involving a machine gun or semiautomatic rifle. Normally, the gangs only pull these weapons out for serious problems with each other, like drug wars or vendetta raids. They do have them, and they like to play with them in their homes, but they don't bring them out too often because it's hard to explain to the cop who pulls them over why they have an assault rifle under the seat of the car.

If you're in your home and shooting starts outside, get to the back of the house, keeping as many walls and metal objects (like stoves) between you and the shooting, and get down on the floor. In fact, walk around your house now and look for the best hiding place with the most walls, furniture, and closets between it and the street. Even though no one item will stop a bullet, collectively they will either stop or deflect it. If you hear the shooting start down the way, head for the hiding place. Train everyone in your house to do the same.

This is especially important if you live in an area where brick and concrete are not the basis for outer-wall construction. Except for the serious desert, the lower latitudes and suburbs don't build houses that will stop a bullet. A house in California may survive an earthquake, and a house in the South may be cool during the summer, but neither will stop a slug.

Whatever you do, *don't look out the window*! Keep away from the windows. Even if you miss being hit by a wild round, flying glass can carve you. And people will shoot at anything in the heat of the moment. This doesn't mean that you are accidentally hit by a flying round; this is them shooting at you for attracting their attention. Animal knew a man who was shot during a gang fight when a gang member took refuge in a liquor store where the man worked. The kid was there to reload during a running firefight that was coming down the street. The man said, "You can't come in here" to the kid, and the kid shot him dead. Face it, when people are shooting there is no reason for you to look. In fact there is no reason for you to do anything but get out of there. It may sound obvious, but you'd be amazed.

A firefight in the street may start out with an ambush, but it takes time for it to come up to full force. Often, firefights will travel down a street with both sides shooting while fleeing or advancing. When you hear shooting down the road, get to the back of the house immediately. If, however, the shooting erupts immediately outside your door, hit the deck and crawl to the back of the house. On the floor of the front room, your chances of getting hit are the same as when stationary or crawling. If the shooting turns out to be prolonged, getting to the back reduces your chances of being hit.

It is critical to realize that with gangs it doesn't matter if you are a member yourself. The presence of a single gang member can be enough to draw fire from a rival gang. Although a great many of the so-called innocent victims of gang shootings are actually girlfriends, family members, or (in the case of babies being shot) the actual children of gang members, just as many are simply people who had the bad luck to have a gang member living in the neighborhood. These are the folks who take a round while sitting in their front room or pushing a shopping cart across a the parking lot. Gang members call innocent victims of their shootings "mushrooms" because, like mushrooms just pop up in the yard, these innocent victims just popped up in the way of the shooting.

If you're the target, it could be considered good news that most gang members are lousy shots; however, in another sense, it means that more noncombatants get hit in the crossfire. The audience laughed about the scene in the movie *Falling Down* where Michael Douglas is unhurt in the telephone booth while bullets spray wildly, wreaking havoc all around him, but that scene isn't that far from the truth. There is a thing called "wild fire," which means that bullets fly the wrong way as often as they do in the general direction of the target. Animal once walked onto a scene where a firefight had broken out in a Hollywood parking lot the previous night. To start with, the police had estimated that about 300 rounds had been exchanged, yet no combatant had been hit. The firefight had been on an east-west alignment and had riddled cars and businesses in both directions. However, standing on the other side of Sunset Boulevard north of the parking lot, a four-lane street with a turn lane in the middle between him and the lot, he glanced down at a bullet hole in a store window that was 90 degrees off from the alignment of the firefight.

Now something else that people don't realize about the realities of violence: it is messy. Unlike what you see on TV, people bleed, defecate, and urinate when they are get involved in violence. And the real bad news is nobody but you is going to clean it up! This is especially true in your home. Even if you are totally cleared of all charges and no civil suit is brought against you, you're going to be the one with the scrub bucket getting the blood off the walls and tearing up the carpet. No professional cleaning service is going to touch that mess at all.

It is also expensive. Often you have to replace the carpet to get rid of the stink. Blood stains cloth and carpet and is difficult to get out. Before you have a chance to scrub up the mess, the police are going to want to talk to you and make a report. If it goes to that extreme, they're going to have to wait until the coroner gets there, all of which allows the blood more time to soak in and permanently stain. Human blood has a special smell that, once you smell it, will probably gross you out anytime you encounter it in the future. That's not an odor you want left in your home.

NOTES

1. A grisly joke is to answer the question "Why'd you shoot him six times?" by saying, "I ran out of bullets." Realistically, that's how long it took for the guy to go down.

New York

irst things first: nearly everything generally recognized as a weapon is illegal to carry in New York City. Having said that, a great number of pocket weapons are sold over the counter. Pepper spray, the most effective defense spray (a cop we know who had to get hosed in the face with it as part of his training said it was much worse than the tear gas he had to take in Ranger school), is technically illegal but sold in many places. Blackjacks and saps in all the popular styles are on sale in the "martial arts supply" stores in the Times Square area. Knives are all over the place.

In drug areas, you often see people walking around with things like golf clubs, pipes, canes, and boards. If you were to do this regularly, it would be broadcasting the message that you're terrified all the time. To be effective, carrying an item like that has to be coupled with the right general attitude. When it is, it clears the sidewalks like the parting of the Red Sea. Billy Joel has a nostalgic kind of sad song about being in a "New York state of mind." In many ways, the true New York state of mind is when you're stalking along the sidewalk with four feet of water pipe on your shoulder, ready to bust the jaw off the first person who looks at you funny. It's not nearly as insane as it sounds. Hang around Fun City long enough, and it'll start to feel pretty normal.

Many old standby streetfighter weapons are not available in

New York. Trash can lids, for example, are all either chained to something or else they're missing. But many places in the city still have the heavy wire-mesh steel trash cans on the corners. If you're strong enough to pick one up, they hold another person off quite well. If you're not, they roll great.

Heavy electrical cable or multistrand wire, which goes by the local moniker "mungo," is both prized and feared as a weapon in the streets. A foot or 18 inches of mungo is a real bonebreaker, and though hard to explain, it is legal.

Another fun fact about New York City is that, like the French Quarter of New Orleans, drinking in the streets is permitted. It's an amazingly civilized facet of street life, and it's super fun when you're with friends on a pub crawl. But in some people it breeds this "the world is my lounge" attitude, which in turn means that you can find yourself in the wrong bar just by walking down the sidewalk. It's no fun at all to run up against some big malcontent who's skidding through the last nasty turn into a serious bender.

Should you find yourself suddenly walking through a dicey neighborhood, you can use New York's cavalier liquor situation to good advantage simply by (calmly) cruising into the first bodega (mom and pop grocery/convenience store) you see and buying a quart bottle of beer. Uncap that baby and swill freely as you proceed down the sidewalk toward safer turf. Or use the opportunity to make a U-turn, as if you were headed to the store all the time. In bad neighborhoods, the quart beer bottle is a well-recognized weapon. No special training is required. Rest assured that just about everyone in less affluent and more volatile areas has seen some big dude laid out bloody and unconscious by a sparrow-sized woman swinging a 32- or 40-ounce beer jug. The 32 is preferable from a handling standpoint because it has a longer neck and is easier to grip. When carrying one for deterrent effect, don't handle it like a club and don't get all cocky with it. Just drink and enjoy that fine glow, and walk toward a safer area.

By buying the beer you let everyone know that the odds just changed regarding you as a potential victim, and better yet, you let them know, without ever formally acknowledging it, that you knew you were being scoped by the whole street. Subtlety and shading. Also, you get points just for drinking from a quart, which is not something you see much of around Sutton Place, but a very common practice in working- and thieving-class zones. It's a sort of instant street chops.

Concealing weapons on your person is tricky. It's also illegal, as we mentioned, and naturally we wouldn't advocate that. But, from personal experience, I can tell you that a fanny pack that looks too heavy will draw police attention, to the point where plainclothes officers will "accidentally" bump into you and feel the bag for a pistol. They have other tactics if they think you're carrying a gun. Once two transit cops in uniform come up to me, one on each side, and never actually speaking to me, but clearly meaning me, one said to the other, "I bet he's carrying a gun." The idea was to get me to panic or break out in a sweat. Customs inspectors do the same thing—they ask innocent, silly questions while watching your face and fondling your luggage, the idea being that you'll flinch if they move toward hidden contraband. You can also forget about those bogus beepers that conceal a derringer—everybody in the street, slimeball or police, knows about them.

Carrying an unregistered firearm in the city draws a mandatory one-year jail sentence. In practice, it often gets bargained down to something like spitting on the sidewalk and draws probation, but that's usually only for poor underprivileged types. However, the cops in New York are more pragmatic than their L.A. counterparts and have been known to unofficially ignore a variety of hardware in the aftermath of a citizen successfully defending him- or herself against a mugging. In cases where Good Samaritans come to the aid of someone else, even up to the point of lethal force, one gathers that the police investigations are not overly vigorous. Public pressure in several well-publicized court cases has also led to community-service-type sentences for citizens convicted of using an unlicensed, unregistered pistol to protect themselves against an attacker.

Politics aside, New York City vividly demonstrates that gun control laws will not work in America. The city has the most stringent controls in the United States, yet according to the police commissioner himself, one in 10 New Yorkers has a firearm. My personal guess goes a little higher than that—I estimate that one person in 10 is carrying a pistol at any given moment, not to mention the pistols that stay home, and the rifles and the shotguns. For a great many law-abiding New Yorkers, a pistol is just as essential as money, keys, or makeup.

The bad part of illegal pistols under the current system is that it tends to escalate every confrontation right to the top. I know a guy who was singled out for a heap of verbal abuse on the subway while he had a revolver in his coat pocket. The clown with the mouth was drunk and clearly wanted a fistfight with this man. And the man was willing, except that fights draw police, and there's this pistol—and the mouth definitely was not worth shooting. In the end, the guy swallowed a lot of bitter pride and worse abuse from someone he could easily have handled, while the whole subway car watched.

L.A.

New York

PHONES

CHAPTER FIVE

New York

The public ones don't work. Even at Kennedy Airport, you often have to try as many as six coin phones to find a working unit. Small-time thieves and junkies jimmy the coin returns to retain the change instead of delivering it, and citizens—angry about being ripped off yet again—often disable the rest of the mechanism. Other times the units just crap out, and this is true of Bell and gypsy phones alike.

To double the jeopardy, the same brains at Bell who can't keep the coin phones working have replaced about a third of them in Manhattan with coinless units that require you to make a calling card or collect call—which, of course, means more money for them. Future futilities will include card-operated telephones, like those in Paris and London. Card phones use debit cards, which the user buys in advance. You insert the card into the phone, and it nibbles away at your balance as you talk. What this means is that the same mental midgets who can't keep simple coin phones operating are now going to bring advanced technology to the streets. And, this being New York and not Paris or London, the bums and wretched street refuse will jam the card slots with gum, feces, Popsicle sticks, used condoms, and whatever else they can stuff in there. It's a failure before it begins.

If you use a calling card for long-distance calls from a pay phone, shield the numbers when you punch them in. Stealing phone card numbers is a big business in New York, and the most popular places to do it are in Grand Central Station, Penn Station, the Port Authority, and the airports. Thieves look over your shoulder or peep with scopes. Your card number will then be beeped to street corner salesmen in, say, the Bronx or Chinatown. Salesmen then sell calls at a flat rate to their customers.

Your card will be used to finance hour-long calls to Yemen, China, Zaire, Botswana, Sweden, Greenland, and other far-flung locales. People who want to call around the world pay a flat rate to the salesmen, like 10 or 15 bucks. It's common in Chinatown at night to see lines around pay phones—customers lining up to call home and say hi to the family on a hot card number. Hot card numbers are networked around the country sometimes, so you can simultaneously have someone in Chicago calling Tibet, someone in L.A. phoning England, and somebody in New York chatting with Tierra Del Fuego—all on your bill, and all because you weren't secretive enough with your number. Guard it like you were James Bond and it was the secret code. And, sadly, because of all the deceased coin phones, you are often forced to use a card whether you like it or not.

I think that the inability of Nynex to keep coin phones working is part of a long-range conspiracy to force everyone to buy and use cellular phones, which again means more loot for the phone company. If you think that's jumping at shadows, you don't know the history of high-level conspiracies in the Empire State. A simple plan to let all the public phones collapse and force consumers to the next level of technology would be kid's stuff compared to the grand schemes that have been worked around here before.

How does it affect your safety? When I was shot, my first acts were directed at getting help. Mainly, I wanted someone to dial 911—and I had no faith in the 30 or so people who saw me get shot. I was right, too. No one lifted a dialing finger. The people in the street couldn't have even if they wanted to—there wasn't a working pay phone for three blocks in any direction. If you have a dire situation, such as a down-and-injured loved one in the streets, you may well be faced with the question of leaving to find a working telephone or staying with the victim. Stay with the victim and try to get someone else to go for help. Often, cabbies will either radio their dispatcher to call or go themselves. Whatever the other problems are with cabbies, they know that one day they may need that same help from a stranger and that it's a good idea to stack karma in that direction. Be aware that a nicely dressed unconscious person in the street will very likely be robbed, and that the crowd (there will be a crowd, you can just about make book on that) won't stop the thieves. Also, you will want to know what hospital the victim's being been taken to, which you won't learn if you're out looking for one of the elusive working pay phones.

An alternative is to try and get a cab to take you and the victim to a hospital. This is very tricky, but it may be the best route if there's no phone or it looks like the incident might continue. The problem will be getting the cab. I once tried to get a friend with a bleeding head wound into a cab. The first driver sped off with the victim half in the car and just about threw the guy into the street. Other cabbies decked it when they saw the blood. Finally one did stop, but it took a while.

I once saw four guys fighting at midnight on Crosby Street, which looks like a cobblestoned alley (by the way, there are very few actual alleys in Manhattan—the land is far too valuable to waste like that). Two of the guys were deploying pieces of 2x4 and getting the best of the other two. It wasn't actually much of a fight, more like a beating. The unarmed pair ran and swarmed a cab. The driver tried to get rid of them, but the dudes with sticks were closing in fast and the driver reluctantly decked it and zoomed out of there. Most cabbies strive for noninvolvement. To make money, the cabbie has to drive fares around. He or she cannot do that if they get involved in folk's personal tragedies and spend their time tapping their toes in emergency rooms. Nonetheless, some will help. (See the section on taxis in the chapter on transportation for more on how cabbies operate above and below the board.)

If you have a cellular telephone, by all means carry it with you. Even if you and your party don't need it, you might be able to save someone else's bacon by having the only phone around. But be sure to hang up your cellular phone when you're driving on the Cross Bronx Expressway or past high-crime areas. Thieves can eavesdrop on conversations from passing cars and read the telephone number and matching serial number by using a $200 scanner found in electronics stores or catalogs. That information is sold to an underground programmer, who incorporates it into the chip of another cellular (usually stolen) phone, and it is used to make calls all over the world. And you won't know about the theft until you receive a bill for thousands of dollars.

Should you be involved in a violent incident in the subways, or if you witness one and want to report it, make the call yourself or have someone nearby do so, even if you can see the token clerk inside the booth calling it in. Token clerks are required to call their office and have the call relayed from there to 911, which causes delays and garbled messages. Don't rely on token clerks unless you have to. Surprisingly, almost all the coin phones in the subways are functional. Don't ask why, it's just a freak of nature. (For more on token clerks and their role in emergencies, see the subways section in the transportation chapter.)

The bottom line on phones in New York is that they are not dependable and some are flat-out rip-offs. I know one cluster of phones that never accepts the nickel to extend the call. They ask for it then cut you off with a recorded message to "please try again"—for another quarter. These are the kinds of phones that otherwise normal citizens will destroy, and with good reason. The straw on the camel's back and all that.

If you have an emergency, try the pay phone. Maybe you'll get lucky. Try stores and bars and see if they'll call. But do your best to make the call yourself, so you'll know that it has been done and done right, then make yourself easy for the cops to locate.

L.A.

The good news about telephones in L.A. is they usually work. The bad news is they can be nearly impossible to find or that they are way over there while you're in trouble here. Generally, you can find a phone somewhere on one of the corners of major streets. There's usually one near a 7-11 store or corner mall, but don't rely on it if you're bleeding.

The further you go into the pits, the fewer phones you'll discover. Those you do find either don't work or have a bag lady set up next to them so she can make screaming phone calls to imaginary demons. In the real ooze neighborhoods, these phones are often located off the main drag. For some reason, phones don't last on Hollywood Boulevard, but they do on the smaller streets. Those small streets are where the wolves run, so you may want to reconsider making calls from them. If it's not an emergency, you'll probably have to go into a food joint and order some food to make your call. The call is 25 cents, but the Coke will cost you a buck. If it's an emergency, the odds are that they'll call for you. That is, until you hit the real pit areas of downtown where you're on your own. There the businesses have pulled up behind wood and walls. A blank wall isn't going to help you no matter how badly you need it to make a phone call for you.

The bad news with getting robbed in L.A. is often you're left without your calling card, and who carries change? So, you'll be able to call 911 because it's free but no one else. (Incidentally, that's something else you need to cancel if you get robbed, especially if you wrote the access number on it. Tsk tsk.) And you may end up walking a half a mile to get to the nearest phone.

The good thing about California life is that if you stand in the street long enough someone with a car phone will come cruising by. Often, people will drop 45 cents a minute to call 911 for someone in trouble, as long as they can keep driving. Most of the communication is going to have to be either mimed or shouted because only the foolhardy open windows in those areas. If you see a Mercedes or Beamer rolling down the road, you know you're looking at a car phone.

If you or your spouse travels a lot, consider looking into car phones. Prices have dropped, and with a little bit of self-control it won't bankrupt you—especially if you only use it for emergency calls. By having one, you can save yourself all sorts of time and trouble looking for a phone if something happens.

CAR CRIMES

CHAPTER SIX

The Basics

America seems to have carjacking on the brain, so let's get right to it. Carjackings are like any other violent crime in that they conform to the five basic steps of criminal violence. The criminal has decided what he's going to do, he's looking for a safe victim/opportunity, and he has to get into position to attack: intent, interview, and positioning.

Basically, there are two types of carjacking. One is where the attacker walks up, sticks a gun up your nose, and demands your keys as you're getting in or out of your car. Then he hops in and drives away. The second kind is where he walks up to your running car and drags you out and hops in. This latter type can be accomplished with or without a gun.

The first type is a basic robbery, and it has a simple rule: if he gets the drop on you, give him what he wants without fuss. Unless he tries to turn it into a kidnapping, it's not worth getting shot over. Again parking lots are where carjackings happen most often: anytime you pull into a parking lot, you should not only be looking for a parking space, but also at *who is in the parking lot and looking at you*. People generally tend to ignore each other in the city. Anyone who's looking at you should be checked right back. If you don't like what you see, don't put yourself into a position that would give your adversary the upper hand if he is up to no good.

The first type of carjacking conforms to normal robbery protocol. Unlike suicidal self-defense classes that recommend carrying keys in your hand to claw any attacker, we recommend you use your keys differently: throw them! The second you see someone make a sudden move for a weapon or charge you, hurl those keys, not at the attacker but 180 degrees away from the direction you intend to start running! If the criminal is only after the car, what he wants just went flying in the direction opposite from yours.[1] If you've kept him at five feet, by the time he can pull a weapon, you've just added to your lead and should be hot-footin' it away. If he pursues, drop your wallet/purse/money and keep on going. By doing this, you've just removed 95 percent of the reasons a criminal has for pursuing you.[2]

The other type of carjacking is harder to protect against yet easy to prevent. As with any other crime, your objective isn't to stop him, just to slow him down long enough to alert you. The first thing you need to do is lock your doors. With the windows up, a locked door is not something that is easily gotten past without alerting whoever is in the car that something is wrong. Even with the window down, it's going to slow him down for a second. Most car doors can't be opened and unlocked simultaneously. It can happen quickly, but the door needs to be unlocked first, then opened. It may not seem like much, but you do have time to react under these conditions.

The second thing you need to do is something that even if you don't run into a carjacker will save you $75 the next time you talk with a traffic cop: fasten your seat belt! Carjackers know how hard it is to pull someone out of a seat belt. And, though shooting may take care of a resisting driver, it will not undo a fastened seat belt. It's a pain in the ass, and it slows them down. A panicked person can't get out of a seat belt, and most hijackers are unwilling to reach in and unhook it for you. All a carjacker has to do is see the shoulder strap to know if you're wearing it or not. If a cop can see you putting one on at 50 feet, you can bet a would-be carjacker is going to spot it at 10 feet. Those are the two things that will not only buy you time but might discourage the carjacker altogether.

Something else you should know is that an alarming number of carjackings happen while the driver is on the car phone. As anyone who's been nearly kamikazed by a yuppie knows, people on car phones aren't paying attention! If you have a car phone, make sure you take those two safety precautions and pay attention to what's happening around you.

There is one obvious point to consider about foiling carjackers. In fact, it's so obvious that people are amazed when they realize it. Your best tool for stopping a carjacking is your right foot. A successful carjacker needs an escape route. That means there has to be an open space in front of your car that he can immediately drive into. The same route that he was intending to use can be used by you to escape. Your right foot applied to the gas pedal can get you out of there! It's not the second car waiting at a light, but the first one that is going to be carjacked. In a similar sense, the car waiting for a parking space is going to be nabbed faster than one that is already parked. Why? Because there's a quicker escape route.

There are two points to be considered here. Number one is the speed of your reaction. The reason most carjackings are successful is that the victim doesn't react in time. This isn't based on reflexes so much as failing to identify the danger fast enough. Ninety-nine times out of a hundred the person just sits there in shock, either wondering what is going on or stunned that someone should be acting in such a manner. In the movie *Grand Canyon*, the young secretary's response to the window smasher is, unfortunately, extremely accurate. If you haven't seen that movie, we recommend you go watch it and keep what you're about to read in mind.

The time to react to a carjacking isn't when the guy has opened the door and is reaching for you, but when someone suddenly materializes out of your blind spot by your car door. There is no reason why someone should be that close to your car or facing you in that position. Watch people in parking lots.

How close do they come to the cars going down the aisle? How close to parked cars? Unless you want to risk ending up on someone's bumper, that's how much space you give cars, and that is how close someone else should be—not popping out of nowhere next to your door. If that isn't enough justification to floor it, when you hear the door latch being grabbed put the pedal to the metal. If you wait until the door is open and he's grabbing for you, it's too late.

Here's an exercise to practice with a young, quick friend: put your car in the middle of the street, and with the engine running, pretend you are waiting for a traffic light/parking space. From your blind side have your young, nimble friend pop up and grab the door handle. The second he appears at your car door, scream to yourself, "Danger!" and floor it. Do this about five or six times until you don't have to scream anymore; instead, your body should react as if threatened when someone unexpectedly appears at that point. While it may sound silly, if you are not accustomed to physical danger, the shout is critical to conditioning your reflexes. This trains your subconscious to recognize the preliminary steps of a carjacking and in time for you to react. After you have the reaction down to where you don't need to shout danger, do the exercise again. This time, as you drive away shout, " Down!" as you hunch down in the driver's seat. Do this 7 to 10 times until you get the hang of it.

With this sudden acceleration you can buy yourself distance between yourself and the carjacker. Two things occur at this point: 1) the criminal suddenly has to deal with the fact that if he doesn't get out of there he could get run over;[3] and 2) something has gone seriously wrong! Criminals are humans; they react like anyone else when something unexpectedly fucks up. They sit there and go, "Huh?" Usually that period of confusion and shock will be enough for you to get away.[4]

The second point to consider about escaping carjackers has to do with where any bullets might end up. As mentioned elsewhere, most criminals are lousy shots. Anything beyond 10 feet has a good chance of being missed entirely by a criminal's bullet. A moving target is also something that is real hard to hit without specific training. When it comes to being in cars, another factor comes into play: unless he manages to fire as he's leaping away, the odds are that any bullet coming near you will be coming through the back window. Something most people don't realize about windshields is that they are not only safety glass, which makes them harder to punch through, but they are also sloped. A bullet hitting a windshield deflects upward. If you were to shoot at someone in an oncoming car, you'd aim at the top of the dashboard to compensate for the window. Therefore, if you find yourself in a situation where you have to escape, hunch down and tell anyone else in the car to do the same. Any bullet of .38 caliber or below will usually bounce off the car's body, while larger calibers will be slowed or deflected.

Although there is no way to guarantee that this technique will work, these two factors will combine to give you the best chances of escaping safely. In this situation, the odds are in your favor, 80 to 20 if he comes at you in an open space and if he 1) does not have a gun, 2) does not have it aimed and ready, or 3) is a lousy shot. With every second that you're moving away, your chances increase as his accuracy and willingness to shoot decrease. Think about it. Is he going to shoot when what was to be his escape is driving away?

Here, though, is a disturbing little fact about many people who are shot by carjackers: they're shot after the carjacker has succeeded in getting them out of the car. This often isn't unprovoked brutality on the criminal's part, however. The criminal climbs into the car and is trying to get away, and the victim then stands up and bare-handedly charges the crim, yelling and trying to drag the guy out. Important safety tip here, folks: if you're not willing to risk trying to drive away from an attempted carjacking, don't brace someone who's already succeeded. Also, realistically, if the guy flat-out gets the drop on you, let him have the car. It's not worth dying over. Nothing I have said can be done faster than a shooter pulling the trigger of an aimed gun.

Although carjacking has most of the headlines, plain old car theft is alive and well. Anywhere you can find a nice new car, you're going to find car thieves. If you're driving a '78 Impala, you don't have to worry. Who's going to steal it? There's no market for it. Basically, the only time a car like that is going to be stolen is if you live near the border and you're on an illegal alien highway. Older cars are ripped off for the sole purpose of transport to and from the border, not for profit.

Professional car thieves go after cars that are new enough so that the only supply of parts is from the dealers.[5] There is no aftermarket supplier manufacturing the parts or an abundance of them in the junkyards. The car is "parted out," and the stolen parts are either sold to an agent, who in turn sells them to an auto body shop, or sold directly to the shops. Avarice is the name of the game when it comes to hot parts. Often, the mechanic/supplier is buying cheap and selling high, using the same markup he would with the dealer price, or he's offering a special deal.[6] This is also why older cars aren't often targeted by professional car-theft rings: you can go to the junkyard and part a car out yourself. But a fender from a new Mercedes isn't something that is easy to come by cheaply.

A difference between a professional car ring and a pack of amateurs is where they take the car. Pros will take the car to a "chop shop." A chop shop is a body shop gone wrong. Big ones have all the tools to disassemble a car into a stack of parts in less than an hour. The odds are that if your car goes to a chop shop it will never be found. Just as a meat processing plant uses every part of the cow except the moo, a professional chop shop can handle every car part.

The rinky-dink brigade normally will take your car out to some deserted part of the world and strip it out there. Nearby wilderness areas, back roads, and industrial areas are popular because there are few witnesses at night. In bad neighborhoods the thieves will strip it right there in the street. A group of five guys with a truck and/or another car can strip a vehicle clean in a few minutes, although not as thoroughly as a chop shop. Anything that doesn't require heavy machinery is torn out and tossed in the back of the truck. A stripped out car is a total insurance write-off. When the cops call and say they've recovered your car off Mulholland Drive, don't call your insurance company and cancel your claim until you've seen the car.

Another professional variation is stealing enough of a certain model of car to create new composite cars from the parts. The vehicle identification numbers (VIN) are filed off and a bogus one stamped on, and several hot cars are jumbled up. These cars are then either sold directly to someone for a greatly reduced price (e.g., a new Mercedes for $25,000), or they are peddled off to a connection in another state or country. This takes lots of forgery and paperwork to make the car legitimate, but for a less than $10,000 investment someone can turn a $15,000 profit on each car.

If a pro wants your car, he's going to get it, bottom line. Most car alarms can be disabled in a matter of seconds. An object called a lock-pick gun can pick any lock in a matter of seconds. The same device works in the ignition, but so does a screwdriver and a hammer. The screwdriver and a swing of the hammer destroys the wheel-locking mechanism and starts the car. Even a determined amateur can get into a car faster than you can. Smash the window and pop the ignition and the car is gone. Hot-wiring is still popular with cars that don't have locking steering wheels, but it takes longer.

There is little you can do to stop a real car thief once he has decided on your vehicle. You either need to convince him not to try in the first place or try to nail him after he's gotten away. Just as with a house burglar, if it looks like it will take too long to steal your car, a car thief will choose another target. A criminal can't spend too much time hanging around trying to get in.

The first deterrent is a steering wheel clamp, often known as a "club."[7] It has a lock that is a mother to pick and will usually deter an amateur. Contrary to what the advertisements tell you, however, these won't stop a well-prepared thief. The clones especially are susceptible to being cut off: a pair of bolt cutters is all a guy needs, and he's past the club. So much for invincibility. But unless the guy is prepared, it's still too much trouble to mess with. However, if you get rovers (two or more in a car) they'll often have the tools. They pull up, one hops out, zap! and they're gone. You can also defeat a "club" by sawing through the steering wheel.

Recently, in L.A. police raided a chopshop that had more than 150 steering wheels with the clubs still on them. The crooks were bringing their own steering wheels with them and popping the old ones off. Also remember that car thieves sometimes destroy things out of frustration or spite. Animal knows of one woman whose BMW was the only car in a lot not stolen, but the crooks broke into it and slashed her upholstery just to show her that they could.

The second system is currently only available in the larger metropolitan areas like New York and L.A. These are car trackers, like the Lojak system. Here, you install a transmitter widget in your car, and if it gets stolen, you alert the police and they zero in and go giddum. Pfouts knows a guy who's in jail because he stole a Lojaked car. The cops found it right away and then just sat around to see if El Estupido would come back for it. He did. So the system does work. Chalk up one for the good guys. But it's expensive, and eventually the crims will discover a way around it. It won't stop your car from being stolen, but it will help in its recovery. If it nails a chop shop, all the better.

Of course, the other option is theft insurance, which will neither stop your car from being stolen nor aid in its recovery, but it will aid in yours.

Incidentally, something that Animal feels strongly about is

security system warning labels: don't put them on! This applies to both cars and homes. What most people think of as a deterrent is information to a criminal. You don't tell someone your defenses, because that also tells him what he needs to bring to get around them. It's like telling someone you're a black belt in karate; all you've done is told the person that in order to win he has to hit you with a chair instead of his fist. If you stick a label on your car that says it's protected by this or that, the crim now knows what type of system he's dealing with. That knowledge tells him what he needs to get around it. The same thing about those flashing red alarm lights; now the crim knows he has to disable a system, which is no biggie if he brought the proper tools. Hide the light! That way the guy is surprised to run unexpectedly into a system; that'll get him out of there.[8] The only people who veer away from car alarms are stereo thieves, and even they don't do so too often in the inner city.

Although car theft rings seldom steal near where they live, they can pop up anywhere. True professionals are few and far between, so you'll usually begin to see signs around a car ring. If you see a house where there's a group of people who are always coming and going at all hours and changing cars as often as you get a haircut, something is wrong. I'm sorry, but most young guys in their twenties and thirties can't legally afford to drive a Porsche one month, a BMW the next, and a Mercedes the third. Even with "dealer plates," something is squirrely there.[9] Give the boys at the local auto theft division a call and see what they think.

Now, it is nearly ridiculous to have to mention it, but because nearly 40 percent of all car thefts are opportunity crimes, we have to include it: *don't leave your keys in the car!* You'd be amazed at how often cops filling out a stolen vehicle report hear, "Of course not! My keys are right ... uh ...." If you leave your car running "just for a second while [I] dash over to ..." you deserve to get ripped off by the guy who jumps in. It's easier to turn the key and carry it while you dash than it is to fill out a stolen-car report—especially with the cop laughing at you. Also, don't leave a spare key in the bumper or wheel well. That's the first place the criminal checks.

Car theft is often a young person's crime; 62 percent of 1990 arrestees were under 21, and 43 percent were under 18. Incidentally, car theft is one of the few crimes where the majority of offenders are white (59 percent). Many of these are joyrides where a group of kids see a set of keys in the ignition and—ZAP! Then they drive around in the hot car getting drunk and throwing up on your upholstery. Upper-middle-class white kids, just like other kids, do this as a ha-ha fun game. Realistically, though, the police are only getting a 15-percent arrest rate on stolen cars, so the people getting busted are the joyriders and retards rather than the hard-core car thieves.

Another more common vein of car crime is the window smasher. Where you are determines if the sucker will have the courtesy to wait until you're out of the car before he smashes the window. Protecting your car from smashers can be accomplished by storing everything under the seats or, even better, in the trunk. In the more despondent parts of town, you don't even want to leave clothing visible to tempt smashers. A street addict or homeless person will bust your window to get a jacket on a cold winter's day. Crack is cheap, so anything of value can be ripped off to sell.

A rather unnerving fact is that theft from cars makes up 22 percent of all thefts, the largest of all types of larceny (purse snatching covers 1 percent). Theft of motor vehicle accessories (tires, hubcaps, etc.) makes up an additional 15 percent, which is only 1 percent less than shoplifting! Larceny accounts for more than half the crime in America, and 37 percent of all rip-offs are related to your car.

The best deterrent to criminals is to make it look as if you have nothing they want. If everything worth stealing is hidden away in the trunk, the roaming window smasher is going to move on to another car. Your average window smasher is either a kid or a street addict. Neither one cares that he's going to cost you $100 for a new window plus whatever it is that he takes. Take a walk through a parking lot and you'll be amazed at the incredible array of things that people leave sitting out in plain sight.[10]

The worse the neighborhood, the more stringent you should be about not leaving anything visible. Although it's always wiser to take things into the house or lock them in the trunk, if you're going to leave them in the car, cover them up. A blanket (which is always a good thing to have in your car anyway), an article of clothing, or a newspaper can be used to discourage window smashers. A lot of stuff can be set on the floor and then covered with newspaper.

The next of kin to the window smasher is the stereo thief. Even though most window smashers are simply snatching something out of the car, a stereo thief goes into the car and has to work the radio out. This takes time and increases the crim's risk of getting popped, so stereo swiping is largely a nighttime job. But large parking lots are also primo day targets because nobody is around to see. An astounding number of stereo rip-offs result from the car owner leaving the door unlocked (oops). However, a good number of them are basic window smashers on steroids. In the middle of the night the guy smashes the window, gets in, and lifts the stereo.

The new pop-out stereos are great: even if you just squirrel it under the seat, anyone looking in doesn't see anything worth stealing. A stereo thief is usually seriously destructive: you can end up paying nearly a grand to fix the damage that one does while getting your stereo out. He doesn't care how much damage he does ripping your radio out of the dashboard. He's going for speed, not efficiency.[11] Although you shouldn't expect a car alarm to keep your car from getting stolen or keeping out the window smashers, it does sort of work against stereo thieves because of the time necessary to pry the radio out of the dash.

If you have a convertible, you should live by the "don't

leave anything inside" rule. In fact, you'll need to get one of those pop-out stereo units because you're going to do something that shocks the shit out of people. You're going to leave your car unlocked. Yes, rather than having the guy slice open your roof to have a look-see, you're just going to leave it open. Anything you need will be stored in the trunk or carried with you. Unfortunately, there are assholes out there who will just slice your roof for fun and games. This is why sunroofs have mostly replaced convertible tops.

A sister problem to car theft is motorcycle theft. What's bad about this is that the best tool for motorcycle theft is a truck. It doesn't matter if the bike is chained; they just pick it up and toss it in. A rented cube van can hold about six motorcycles (don't ask how we know this). Three guys can usually pick up any bike and worry about chains or locks later in the safety of their chop shop. If you're going to chain your bike (which is a good idea), chain it to something! Something that a bolt cutter can't work its way through. And chain it through the frame, not a wheel. Otherwise, you'll come back and find just a wheel . . .

Harleys are more expensive and have a higher resale value, but most motorcycle heists are aimed at Japanese muscle bikes. The thieves are less likely to get shot during the actual rip-off, and a hard-core biker will hunt down and kill whoever ripped him off. This does sort of complicate the thief's life. There's also a bigger market for hot Japanese parts. This is in part because more kids are willing to buy a hot Jap bike, and the parts market for motorcycles is even more limited than for cars. But it's also because bikers are touchy about their bikes, and having a bike ripped off is like having a family member kidnapped. Drug dealer, hitman, embezzler—all of those are acceptable occupations in the outlaw community, but not bike thief. Someone trying to sell hot Harley parts is like someone who deals in white slavery. It does happen, but it's frowned upon even by the outlaws.

NOTES

1. Women: if he's after a kidnap/rape, he's now got a problem. By intending to use your car to get away, he's left himself flapping in the breeze. On the other hand, if you throw the keys at him, all you're going to do is hurt him and piss him off. In situations like that, a carjacking could turn into an attack or rape.

2. If your attacker doesn't back off, either you have a rapist, or, truth be told, you've been messing in something you shouldn't have; these kind of attacks just don't happen for no reason. If you have been messing where you don't belong, you're on your own, buckaroo.

3. This is why your friend who does the exercise with you must be nimble.

4. As screwed up as laws are in some states (especially California and New York), you may or may not want to report this to the police. Technically, until you see the gun or the person lays hands on you, it is not yet a crime. Of course, by that time, it's too late. If you hit someone with your car, you are liable—if not criminally then in a civil case. If you drive away, the odds are the carjacker wouldn't have had time to get your license plate number; if he did, however, suddenly his halo goes on overdrive, and you are guilty of a hit and run. Of course, if you drive to the police station and in the report filed you mention the fact that you were sure you saw a gun in the man's hand, it puts another spin on it. Going to the police and filing a report takes away the hit-and-run charge. If he tries to file a civil suit against you, you could press criminal charges of attempted robbery.

5. The prices the dealers charge make robber barons look like Mother Teresa.

6. When a body shop says it can save you $200 on the

panels to fix your car but you need to pony up now, the odds are you're dealing with hot parts.

7. Sort of like the brand names Tampon or Kleenexes.

8. In the case of home security systems, a well-informed crim knows how long the normal response time is for a particular model. That means he knows how long he's got in the house from the time he trips the alarm.

9. These are special plates that car dealers put on cars they drive around. The car isn't registered to them, but the plates give them exception. The only problem is that dealers usually stick with only one brand of car.

10. Not to mention the number of unlocked cars and keys left in the ignition.

11. This includes damaging what he's stealing. A lot of hot stereos don't work because they were damaged while being stolen. It comes as a rude surprise to the buyer of hot merchandise that he got ripped off as well as the original owner. Heh, heh, heh.

New York

New York City, Manhattan especially, is hell for cars. It's the last place in America where it's illegal to turn right on a red light. The road surface is rough as a jeep track. There are kamikaze cabbies and homicidal delivery van operators, and a subhuman species, the Traffic Enforcement Agents (vernacular: *brownies*), who slouch through the streets eating donuts and slapping monumentally expensive tickets on anything within reach, whether it's actually violating an ordinance or not. Brownies are like an annoying rectal itch with a quota to meet, ambulatory human roadkill with a sheaf of blank tickets. And, on top of all this pleasure and joy, leaving a car or truck on the street is an invitation to thieves.

Hundreds of cars are broken into, vandalized, and stripped each day in New York. The *Daily News* recently put the figure at around 90,000 such incidents a year in New York City—and those are just the ones that get reported. Just before Halloween 1993, the *News* bought a 1985 Honda Civic and parked it in upper Manhattan. From the balcony of a hospital, photographers and reporters watched as about 20 separate operators stripped the car and then stole the carcass over a two-day period. Almost immediately after that, the *News* watched someone's stolen van get stripped in the same spot—and they watched the cops watch too. Cops drove by the strippers, and one stripper, it was reported, removed a van seat, hoisted it onto his head, and walked past the patrol car with it. So much for the thin blue line.

In the area of burglary, looking at one particular story will help illuminate the situation. In all respects this was a plain old auto burglary New York style, but it got into the newspaper because it happened to a man with some clout. He was victimized just before the 1992 elections, and he used the newspaper story as a way of trying to bash his political opponents.

The victim was a state Republican party honcho from somewhere up near Buffalo, as I recall. He drove his car into Manhattan and stopped to see someone at the corner of 34th Street and Park Avenue. There were two expensive suitcases in the car. He went upstairs "for a few minutes" and asked the doorman to watch his car. When he came back the window was smashed out, and the suitcases were gone.

In his newspaper story he recounted the incident and blamed the Democratic mayor for the incident—literally, he all but accused the mayor of stealing the suitcases. Much as I don't like to blame the victim for crimes, this guy did everything in the book wrong and was shocked when he got stung. If there ever was a time when you could say that a guy asked for it, this is it.

First, he was an upstate Republican appleknocker with an overdose of arrogance—arrogance that slipped over the line into flaming stupidity. I wouldn't call his political party into account, except that he was so chesty about it. Okay, so he lives upstate and comes into New York. He brings along his "I am special and you won't dare accost me" frame of mind. Big mistake. People in the streets dare. They don't care how much senatorial juice you have.

You are fully entitled to be offended that the curbside thieves in the city will steal the shit from under a squatting dog, but don't be so offended that you don't take even simple precautions, like stowing your bags in the trunk. In that neighborhood, which is quite ritzy, thieves don't do exploratory surgery on car trunks. Too many cops and people with telephone fingers. The simple expedient of stashing his suitcases would have prevented the dastardly Democrats from perpetrating this heinous crime in the first place. It won't work on the Lower East Side, where thieves habitually punch out trunk locks to have a look-see, but it would have done the trick on that stretch of Park Avenue.

Number two mistake—packed with arrogance, he leaves his car in the street and asks the doorman to look after it. There is a parking garage on that corner. For 6 or 10 bucks he could have parked his wheels safe. Instead he was cheap. I'm always amazed at people that will drop 30 grand on some turbo convertible and balk at spending 10 bucks to put it in a lot. More about parking lots later, but here again, in this case, putting it in the lot would have prevented the crime by moving the goods out of range.

Combining these two simple steps—stowing the bags in the trunk and paying to park the wheels—and he would still have his luggage and his windows. And asking the doorman to watch his car—what a goddamn insult. I wouldn't be surprised if the doorman heisted the bags himself, actually. Doormen work for the building, to maintain order as well as they can and to make complex city life easier on the tenants in small ways, like signing for deliveries and holding them, announcing visitors, that sort of thing. They get paid chump-change wages and they often have to take shit all day long from the snippy rich people in their building who blame them for everything from the elevator not working to the mail being late and the coffee getting cold. They are not there to serve the whims and desires of self-important out-of-town cheapskates, and they are certainly not there to provide auto security. That's what the parking garage is for. If the Republican had been a tenant, the doorman might have been vigilant. But for some visitor to breeze in, presumably without slipping the guy some money, and expect this underpaid monkey-suited working man to put his ass on the line is arrogance at stupidity level. Your car burglar carries some tool—a piece of pipe, a hammer, a rock—heavy enough to break a car window. That same weapon will handily break a head. You cannot expect the doorman to put his health, health that is probably not insured by the people he works for, between some hammer-swinging crackhead and a tightwad stranger's Samsonite.

If this sounds harsh, it is. But it is how the game goes in New York. In your town, maybe it would be unthinkable for a citizen to stand idly by and watch a crime being committed. I hear there are places like that in America. New York is not one of them. Expect nothing except grief from strangers in this town, and you won't be disappointed. Certainly, you have no reason to expect a total stranger to guard your property when you are not willing to take any steps to guard it yourself.

The Republican could also have carried his bags inside with him. It looks stupid, maybe even paranoid, and it's a pain in the ass. But it's another way this guy could have held onto his valises.

In short, this guy's mistake was coming into a town that's famous for crime and totally ignoring the local rules. At his country club, I'm sure the doorman would have guarded the luggage. But the streets of the Apple are different, and failing to recognize and adapt to that difference gets expensive fast. On top of our Republican's basic attitude maladjustment, he made a number of practical errors. He cheaped out when there was a garage handy. If there hadn't been a garage nearby, he should have either looked for one or dropped some green on the doorman. Money talks. But if the doorman is a feeble retiree, go back to the garage plan. He didn't even try to hide his gear. In short, he did nothing to help himself—which just means that he acted stupidly. Stupid in this case is thinking "It'll never happen to me," or mistakenly believing that you are so gosh-darned important and powerful that no guttersnipe would dare choose you as a target.

The result is crime. Completely predictable. The thief needs no imagination, no brains, no skill. Not even any balls, really. If you present an opportunity like that one, you will only be spared if the scumbags with hammers are eating lunch during their window of opportunity.

Years back, car burglars finessed their way inside the vehicle. Today they just smash the window. And if they are after your radio (if you have a radio, they are after it), they will not disassemble your dash with a screwdriver. They'll bust it out with a crowbar. If you insist on parking in the streets of New York, remove your radio. Do it yourself, or someone will do it for you, I promise. Here again, investing in a parking lot space eases the problem.

My basic advice is that you don't bring a car to New York unless you absolutely have to. If you do, clean it out and put it in a parking garage. There are garages that are very secure and safe, and in fact most are. But don't push temptation too far. Don't leave a trunk key if you can avoid it, and don't get stupid and leave a camera on the seat. Also, whole cars occasionally vanish from garages, but only real luxury machines—Rolls, big Benzes, Jags, Beamers, and so on. Sometimes holdup men take the cars at gunpoint, and sometimes they just (oops!) seem to vanish. They are almost certainly shipped overseas before the engine cools. On the good side, I know a rockabilly band that routinely leaves the van with all the instruments and stage gear aboard in a garage and has no trouble at all.

As with other kinds of street crime in New York, expect help from no one, and don't anticipate a police presence. Auto B&E and even car theft are common crimes and don't rate high on the police priority list. The cops will be there in an instant if you're shot, but they really don't give a good goddam if someone bags the radio you have been warned not to leave in the car. And the thieving scum will steal anything they find if they pop your trunk—the jack, the flares, the tools, every little thing. In the downtown area, look for your stolen gear at the nightly thieves' market on the west side of 2nd Avenue just below St. Mark's Place (8th Street), from about 10 P.M. on until the cops come and break it up. On Sunday mornings, there is a grander version of the thieves market on Broadway just above Canal Street—look there for quality electronics and cameras, tools, leather jackets, and so on.

Should your entire car disappear from the street, call the Department of Transportation's Towed Vehicle information line first. The city operates a fleet of despised tow trucks that are empowered to ticket cars and then immediately tow them away and hold them for ransom. To some eyes, this appears to be government confiscation of personal property without due process. To me, it's another Gotham horror, and it's done only so the city can make even more money off the breaking backs of the citizens. It costs about $250 at present to retrieve your car from the tow lot. Rumors of pilfering by city tow employees are common.

If you're a victim of this outrage, expect no mercy, no courtesy, and no help. Just shell out and shut up. Tellers at the impound lot work behind thick plastic shields, and there are signs on the wall imploring you not to revile, abuse, scream at, or otherwise heap contumely on these filthy jackals. I understand that tow victims often try to spit on the tellers. They were successful until the shields went up. This, if you haven't already figured it out, is still another reason not to park on the street. They cannot tow or ticket you in a parking lot. (Actually, if you have outstanding tickets, they can, in theory, haul your wheels out of a lot, and even right out from under you—can and do. Manhattan is New York County, and there is a sheriff, and he's a miserable mother. One often sees traveling schools of tow trucks operating under this stinking sheriff's auspices, especially in the poorer neighborhoods where folk are less likely to have garages or the resources to pay the city's back-breaking parking fines—here again, issued whether or not you're guilty of anything because they've got a goddamned quota to fill and donuts to eat. They spot a plate with tickets, and off baby goes to the pound. Your ticket dollars then go for political graft and chiseling. In recent years, the Parking Violations Bureau has been a teeming field of theft, mobbed-up contracts, scams, patronage, hustles, lies, and carpetbagging. The only crime we're certain they didn't commit is the Lindbergh kidnapping. They are worse scum than crackheads and more injurious to society. And I'll waggle the old middle digit at the sheriff anytime.

One trip to the impound lot will tell you the sad truth—a significant number of the towed cars are from out of state. They didn't believe the signs and parked where they shouldn't have and are now royally screwed. An especially vulnerable area is the west side of Manhattan, along the Hudson River, from the Fifties on down to Battery Park. The Manhattan tow lot, you see, is at 38th Street and the Hudson River. To meet their quota, the slime with the hooks (this is brownie slime, not sheriff scum) tend to stay close to home base. It's just easier that way. Any routine parking violation in this area, especially the West Village, can become a heartbreaking tow in a second.

As an aside, brownies are often assaulted in the streets by irate motorists, and they are so universally despised that passersby will often jump in to deliver a few good licks when they can. To the local citizens, you see, traffic enforcement is the only arm of city government that you can unfailingly depend on—that, and the fire department. New York cops are pretty good, and unless there's something more pressing, they'll come when you call. The fire department will for sure come when called. And believe me, if you get cute with parking, the brownies will show up, either with or without a tow truck. They're as common as the cockroaches they resemble.

At this writing, it is still only a misdemeanor to assault a brownie. Although we certainly do not advocate violence, you can easily see how it comes about. The fine for parking at a hydrant is $55. For parking at the wrong place on the wrong day, it's $40 to $45. If the sign says 11 A.M., the tickets will fly at 11:01. Plus, many brownies have been caught making up tickets while sitting in donut shops—creating whole fictions that end up involving real car owners who are, of course, quite innocent, and who have to take time off from work and go through the ring of hell that is the parking adjudication system, where the burden of proof rests entirely on the hapless motorist. The ticket says you were on 42nd Street. How to prove that your car was elsewhere? Not to harp, but a receipt from a garage is one good way.

If you see this as it is, that the city government really doesn't give a damn about your car being burglarized or stolen, but cares passionately if you park in the wrong place because it can make money, then you're that much closer to understanding why so many New Yorkers are pissed off all the time, and why the city is rapidly becoming unlivable. Then there's that old story about how cops and insurance companies don't get all weepy when your vehicular pride and joy comes up missing because 25 percent of car thefts involve the owner just dumping his or her wheels to get the insurance bread.

And if you believe that, I got a bridge to sell you. Or even more profitable, an insurance policy to sell you. Where does that 25 percent statistic come from? Yup, an insurance industry source. And somehow, insurance companies feel that if they weep and moan about how they're getting (allegedly) reamed by a full 25 percent of their customers, then us working joes and checkout janes won't mind the annual Rate Increase Jamboree. Bullshit. I used to know a guy in the insurance business who pointed out that there is no law on the books requiring you to lock your car, install antitheft devices, park in a safe place (assuming you could find one), or even check on the thing every few days. Stolen is stolen. If they find out you left it unlocked and running in Times Square, for example, they might not be too quick to pay off—but then, they aren't going to be quick about that anyway, as you know if you've ever tried to get any of your hard-earned dough back from an insurance company. Stalling is part of the game. If they wait long enough, maybe you'll shut up and go away frustrated half to death.

That 25-percent figure is pure gas. If it's true, then why aren't they prosecuting 25 percent of auto claims for fraud? Because they can't—and they can't back up that bullshit statistic, either. It's not a crime to be stupid or trusting; it only makes you more likely to become a victim of a crime. Should you become one and have your car stolen, the last thing you should put up with is the damn insurance company trying to blame you for it. One cop from the Auto Crimes Division recently said about this particular subject, "People will park their car in a place where they know it'll be stolen—the side of a road, a shopping mall. They'll wait a couple of days, wait until they see it's been taken or stripped, then report it stolen." Like, if you don't park on the side of the road, where you gonna park? And what about if you want to go to the mall? This just points up the lack of police teeth in this area of crime, not owner culpability. Sure, some car owners have their vehicles stolen on purpose, but with all the sleazy characters I know I can only recall one bona fide case of this, and that guy later returned the car, as I recall. And when you have a situation like the one at the beginning of this chapter, where the patrolling police drive right by car strippers and do nothing, you can really see this 25 percent thing as the contemptible, scurvy lie it is.

OTHER CAR CRIMES

Number one auto mistake, especially for women: getting a vanity license plate with your name on it. All a mugger or rapist has to do is see a plate that says "Mindy" and he knows, number one, that the car belongs to a woman, and number two, her name is Mindy. Huge error. You return to your car, and here comes a guy smiling real wide calling your name. This can also work with guys, a mugger getting the drop on you by knowing your name in advance. If you have to get a vanity plate, choose something other than your name.

There are very few drive-by shootings or carjackings in the New York metro area. Traffic is so thick almost everywhere that trying to flee on wheels is hazardous—you might not get very far very fast. But some thieves use traffic to their advantage. Kids, either alone or in gangs, have been known to run up to commuters stuck in traffic—always lone women—and break their windows with big rocks. Before the woman can react, a hand snakes in and grabs the purse, and the kids run away. This was happening on the West Side Highway and near the 96th Street approach to the Harlem River Drive.

It's hard to defend against that, short of keeping your purse in the trunk or under the seat. At many lights around the city, window washers stand around trying to squeeze a few bucks out of the stopped motorists. They will come up to the car and slop soap or shoot window cleaner all over the windshield and then wipe or squeegee it off and try and get fifty cents or a buck from you. Sometimes, if they're really far gone, they will just mop at the glass with a greasy old rag and hold out their hand.

Intimidation is a big factor here. Most of these guys are toothless, dirty, scabby specimens who will bully a wimpy milquetoast kind of man and threaten a woman. It's often a form of small-time extortion. If you see a window washer, a common tactic is to stop well back from the intersection—like half a block. If he's hubba-hubba enough to walk to your car, pull around him and drive ahead to the limit line. Most likely the light will have changed by then and you can proceed. Turning on your wipers is another well-understood signal that you are not interested—but planting yourself right in the guy's face with the wipers flicking will probably not stop him from trying for some change.

When frustrated, washers will often hit the car with a squeegee. The situation can now develop in all sorts of directions. If you get out of the car, he'll either run or stand, depending on how loaded he is, if he thinks he can take you, if he doesn't like your face—whatever his motive is at the moment. Before you John Wayne it, ask yourself if you really want to roll around in the brake dust and oil and cigarette butts with a filthy homeless skel. Do you want his blood on you? Do you want to mess up your clothes? Basically, how far do you want to take this situation? Bear in mind that a lot of these guys don't give a damn if they go to jail or not.

You can also give the guy a little change or a buck and forget the incident.

Through experience, window washers know to avoid vans with big guys at the wheel, since a lot of deliverymen think nothing of taking a bat to these bums. They avoid cars full of young men. They generally do not annoy motorcyclists, since this is another group of people that will happily stuff an offending squeegee into some window-washer orifice or another.

Always, in New York, keep your doors locked and your windows up. Use the air conditioner or the heater.

Because of the nature of the city, you can find yourself in the wrong neighborhood very quickly. Most people define the wrong neighborhood as being one where you are not part of the prevailing racial persuasion. New York is a city with a lot of racial tension, and that tension is right on the surface. If you're white and not streetwise, your knees might start knocking under the steering wheel in Harlem, Bed-Stuy (Bedford-Stuyvesant in Brooklyn), or East Tremont in the Bronx. If you're black, you will feel hugely unwelcome in Howard Beach, Bensonhurst, or Cross Bay. No matter what color or shape you are, someone on Staten Island will hate your guts. Oddly, you don't really find a lot of attacks on cars in these situations. Far Rockaway is a racially mixed area, and the only way to get there by car is through Howard Beach and Cross Bay. Harlem's famed 125th Street is a major crosstown thoroughfare. Traveling around and about Brooklyn often takes you right through East New York or Bed-Stuy. Just keep driving, avoid local entanglements, don't hit other cars, and you should be fine. The black neighborhoods, for sure, are plenty used to white faces rolling through. Be advised, though, that in the real ghetto areas there are no traffic laws. Young kids rip around on unlicensed motorcycles, people ignore signals, drive a hundred miles an hour, race up and down on ATVs. That's no exaggeration. Mind yourself and keep rolling with all available dispatch. If things look really ugly and your car is positioned for it, go ahead and run a red light and get the hell out of there. The very worst thing that'll happen is a ticket, and more than likely you'll be able to tell the cop—if there is one—that you panicked and had to go. It won't be the first time he's heard that.

Car alarms sometimes work. I have actually witnessed a car alarm scaring off a thief. Once. I have also come up on a car that was picked clean while the alarm whooped away. Do not park and alarm your car blocks from where you will be, especially at night. People have to sleep, and they can't do that while a car alarm is wailing on hour after hour. In many neighborhoods, after a certain hour and duration, folk will gather around the offending vehicle and pretty much destroy it. A lot of normal working people are right at the edge in New York, and any pain-in-the-ass annoyance like that sends them over. They'll bust out the windows, the lights, flatten the tires, cut up the seats, spring the trunk. It only takes a couple of minutes. Then if the vehicle is at all desirable, car strippers will descend on it like buzzards, and by morning your dream machine is history. Possibly barbecued history, if there's a firebug in the neighborhood. That one car I saw that had been picked clean while the alarm raged impotently away—I was out there specifically to cut the guy's tires. It was one in the morning, and I'd been listening to his friggin' alarm for an hour. When it's keeping you awake, that sound worms into your mind like a damn snake, and after while you would murder to shut it off. Remember that. Nobody in New York is going to run outside to save your CB—but otherwise honest people will, with grim determination, smash hell out of the whole car if the alarm impedes their pursuit of happiness.

Another thing: people tend to touch-park rather robustly in New York. Touch-parking means backing into a parallel spot until you hit the car behind you, then turning in and pulling forward until you smack that car—and repeating until you're snug in your spot. People touch-park hard enough that it would be considered hit and run anywhere else.

If a car is taking up a space and a half, it's common for other cars to force it forward or back, as necessary, with just brute horsepower and their bumpers. Is it necessary to point out that touch-parking will set off your car alarm? Is it necessary to point out that none of this happens in a parking garage? Need we mention shattered headlights and smashed expensive taillight lenses? Loud motorcycles and fireworks will also set off car alarms, as will thunderclaps. Many bikers, me included, think that triggering car alarms with my loud pipes is great sport. I really hate them, and if you have to get dressed and come downstairs in the rain to reset it every 15 minutes all night, I don't have a problem with that. Every damn $100 behemoth Oldsmobile in New York now says "chirp" when its minimum-wage owner walks up. Like anyone else wants the damn thing.

And here's a hot tip you won't find anywhere else: some new automobiles with fuel injection have electric fuel pumps located at the tank, in the rear of the car. There is an impact-sensitive cutoff switch in the system, designed to stop the fuel pump from spewing gas all over in case there's an accident and the fuel line gets cut. Hard touch-parking will sometimes trigger this cut-off—which means you come out to your car, and it won't start. There is a reset button, a little red thing, usually mounted inside the trunk on the rear side. Push that and you're on your way. But if you don't know the trick, you're at the mercy of cutthroat tow truck drivers, who will happily whack you for an $80 tow (it's

$50 just to hook up) and soak you for whatever else they can get. They know about this reset button, believe me. And here again, what you don't know can hurt you bad.

One interesting local wrinkle we had involved Cadillac and Lincoln front bumpers. These bumpers come off with four bolts that are quickly and quietly removed, and cost about $800 new from the dealers. Local thieves created an artificial (and very brisk) market in hot ones by stealing them off every parked Cad and Abraham they could find. They could pull down like $400 or $500 from spinning four lousy bolts. It's kind of passé now, but it shows you the level of local ingenuity. Smart luxury car owners, when they replaced their stolen bumpers, learned to have the four bolts tack-welded on. So the thieves had to move back a few inches and unbolt the isolators too. Same effect, still four bolts.

Some of the malls in the New York suburbs—especially Staten Island—are plagued by car thefts. Cars are stolen from the lots with tow trucks or flatbeds. There have been gang fights between groups of trolling car-thieving dirtbags working the same turf. Here's how the tow truck deal works. Hiring organizations, whoever they might be, look for specific makes and models—and maybe even colors—of cars, luxury jobs, of course. They will offer a tow truck driver $500 for the pull, which is good money for a relatively low-risk job. They guarantee the trucker maybe three minutes of safe time—no cops and no irate owners (you really don't want to know about that part)—and they will presteal any cars in the way of a clear shot at the target vehicle. The time limit is rigid—if the driver can't make the hookup before the deadline, he's strictly on his own. This is a situation that's very hard to defend against, and it's the upper limit in car theft. When people tell you, "If they really want it, they'll get it," this is the what they do when they really want it. A garage is a big help here. These people do this as a business, and they pay for information on the location of certain cars. A garage goes some distance toward concealing the car. You're vulnerable coming in or out, but if you follow Animal's advice on watching your mirrors when headed home, you'll eliminate 99 percent of that problem.

If you have an accident that disables your car, and you're not hospitalized, stay with the car and have the cops call a tow truck. Leaving a disabled car is just like abandoning it, and it'll be skeletonized by morning. Not long ago I saw a major one-car accident outside my window—a near worthless old Delta 88 wrapped around a light standard on the sidewalk. The driver ran, and before he got to the corner, a bum snatched his jacket off the seat. Then the cops came, dragged the heap off the curb into the street, and left. An hour later there were—no lie—20 body snatchers and carrion pickers working over that junk GM carcass like it was pure gold. By morning it was minus doors, most of the engine, wheels, lamps. Anything of even marginal value was gone. This was absolutely typical.

If you break down on a major highway in a rough neighborhood, wait for a cop or a tow truck and get towed to a secure area. The Cross Bronx Expressway is part of Interstate 95, the major East Coast north-south route, and a lot of it is very rough territory. A recent three-mile tow off the Cross Bronx to Webster Avenue cost one motorist $80. But for the $80, the car was removed and safely stored until it could be towed to a less piratical repair shop—which was better than leaving it on the Cross Bronx, where it was certain to be stripped. I also knew a guy whose expensive motor home swallowed its ignition system in the South Bronx. The garage charged him a lot of money, but they did fix it, and they did keep it safe. Mostly, you will not be in a position to comparison shop, so grit your teeth and do the best you can.

If you're on a surface street in a bad section of town, look for a pay phone and hope the sucker works. Tow truck companies often put advertising stickers in phone booth shells. If not, you should know to ask information for all the usual names— AAAAAble (all spellings), Reliable, Triangle, etc., etc.

Information operators can't pick a company out of the yellow pages; you've got to have a name for them. I don't know if these tow companies exist, but it's a good place to start, in New York, or Anytown USA. That and a little fast talking will get you a number. If there was ever a place for fast talking, this is it.

L.A.

If you live by the car, you die by the car. And people in L.A. *definitely* live by the car.

Since carjacking is on everyone's mind—including Angelenos'—let's start our discussion of L.A. car crime off with that. To tell the truth, you're more likely to be carjacked in L.A. than you are in New York for a very simple reason: New York gridlock. L.A. may have serious traffic problems, but you still can drive at least a block and turn down a residential street. Not necessarily so in the Big Kumquat . . . er . . . Apple.

In fact, L.A. is a carjacker's dream.Once on a side street, there's no way in hell anyone not immediately following in a car is going to catch you. One turn puts a carjacker in a position to reach a minimum of three major streets. In parking lots (where it's most likely to happen), the criminal has usually selected one with more than one entrance/exit. The car he hits is going to be pointing toward an exit. This means that once the perp has succeeded in tossing you out, he's got a clear shot to escape. One quick dash and he's on the street and gone.

Orange County, West L.A., and the Valley are the carjacking hot spots. That's where the nicer cars are, so that's where the carjackers go. A carjacking is a specialty of the real dumb car thief: generally it's done by someone who hasn't sat down to learn his profession. A professional car thief can get into your car faster than you can. Car alarms, safety systems, and clubs don't mean anything to a professional. To an amateur, however, they make it so difficult it's just easier to carjack you.

What makes L.A. perfect for carjacking is the same thing that makes it risky for the smash-and-grab type of robbery. New York's gridlock and narrow streets make it incredibly easy for someone to walk up and put a brick through your window and snatch a purse. A quick dart into a building or alley and the guy is home free. In L.A. (unless you're in Downtown), these ideal conditions don't exist. The roads are generally too wide, there's more than one lane of traffic, and, as we all know, stepping out into L.A. traffic is a dangerous proposition. In New York, the crim can bank on the person being trapped in his car; in L.A., he can get creamed by a motorcycle splitting lanes or a Hindi taxi cab driver.

Just because the criminal isn't likely to smash your window and grab a purse off the seat while you're sitting at a light doesn't mean that you're immune to car break-ins in L.A. Your average L.A. car raider isn't going to be as well prepared as his New York counterpart, which means he's not going to be as likely to pop your trunk and have a look-see, but I wouldn't bet anything expensive on it. A free tip: never be obvious about putting something expensive in your trunk and then walking away. If you're in a slimy neighborhood, drape a jacket over the item as you carry it to the trunk.

Once again, a hammer and screwdriver are all it takes to pop a trunk. Some people use crowbars, but that is even more obvious. The difference between L.A. and New York is that the former doesn't offer so many convenient hiding spots for the tools if the cops show up. That means you're less likely to get a popped trunk. Just as a drug dealer doesn't keep his drugs on him, only his gun, a guy carrying a screwdriver and hammer in a mall parking lot is sort of obvious what he's up to.

However, the airports are an exception to this trunk-popping rule, especially long-term parking. Although these lots are patrolled, the truth about patrols is that the criminal waits until the patrol is past and then gets to work, knowing the rent-a-cop isn't going to be back soon. It's never wise to leave anything of value in your car overnight, but it's especially true for over a longer period. It's better to have someone drive you or take a shuttle/cab to the airport. Failing that, take everything of value out of your car before you park it.

Incidentally, don't leave your house keys on your car key ring if you leave your car somewhere like long-term parking or a mechanic's. Many people who work at such places aren't of the highest character. This is especially true if you must fill out paperwork and have to give your address and acknowledge that you'll be out of town for a given period. I know it sounds obvious, but you'd be amazed.

Although you have less of a chance to have your trunk popped in L.A. than New York, if you leave something on the seat in a parked car you're just as likely to have it disappear here as anywhere else. Why not? You've left the proverbial "steal me!" sign hanging out where everyone can see it. This is especially true in South Central, East L.A., and, of course, every parking lot in the greater L.A. area. A window smasher doesn't give a shit that he set off your car alarm. The reason is simple: by the time anyone can respond, he's long gone. Once again, the myth of car alarms deterring a criminal is left sucking its thumb.

One thing to always watch for is the guy wandering around looking into car windows, especially in parking lots. That's not normal behavior; most people walking through parking lots don't even bother to look *at* the cars, much less inside. Most window smashers are cowards and will veer off if you spot them. Recently, I was coming out of the library and caught a guy looking in my car. Before I could get to him, he walked over to the next car, having decided the box of envelopes on my backseat wasn't worth busting the window for. When he saw me, he walked over to a pylon and waited for me to leave. I got in my car and did a loop around the pylon. He looked up and saw me sitting there watching him. I held out my finger and did a "Kapow!" gesture at him before driving off. I looped around the parking lot looking for a security guard or a cop to tell (naturally, I couldn't find one). When I came out on the street, the dude was legging it away.

I never got within 30 feet of the guy, but he knew he had been made. If you feel like doing someone a favor, from the safety of your running car you can let him see you spot him before you go get security. You don't talk to him or allow him to get near your car, just let him see that you know what he's up to. He's going to beat feet 99 times out of 100.

If you come upon someone looking in your car, there's a specific course of action to follow that will normally scare him away but not put you in danger. From about 30 feet away, whistle sharply while advancing, preferably with a look of death on your face. You're not running; you're just walking. He'll probably look up, see you, and shuffle off. It's that simple. Don't yell, "Hey, asshole!" while running forward, because many street scum become confrontational if you call them on what they are about to do. If he doesn't leave, stop and watch him for a second, then turn around and go get help. Don't approach him, however, because you never know if he is armed or willing to become confrontational.

If you see someone in your car, do yell, "Hey, asshole!" from as far away as possible while making it look like you are going to charge him. Usually he'll split, but if your thief is cornered, he will fight—which is why you want to warn him and have him run away rather than your catching him.

Now, I have to admit I have caught stereo thieves. One guy had broken into my car and was in the process of ripping out my stereo. I opened the door and put a knife to his throat and said, "What are you doing in my car?"

It was a hypothetical question. I knew what he was doing; I just didn't know how far he had gotten. The fact that the stereo didn't work and he hadn't damaged my car getting in (I'd left the windwing open—oops) made me hesitate to stab the guy. Also, human blood has a particular odor that is real obvious, unpleasant, and difficult to get out of upholstery. Besides having to endure my car reeking of blood, I didn't want to have to try explaining it to a cop. They don't mention these points in tough-guy movies.

This guy with the knife to his throat looked at me in wide-eyed innocence and said—and I quote—*"Your car?! I thought it was mah friend's car!"* Ever try to keep from laughing while holding a knife to a guy's throat? Let me tell you, it's hard. I dragged him out of the car and looked at the stereo; he hadn't gotten it out, and it looked fine. I told him to get the hell out of there and watched him run down the street. I got in and drove away.

The point to remember about that story is that the guy with a knife to his throat, caught red-handed in the act, tried to deny he was doing anything wrong.[1] I had the drop on him, so he wasn't about to become bellicose about it—but many do. That's why you should never get close enough to brace a car thief. Nothing fights harder than a cornered junkie, and unless you're going to hurt him immediately, always give him ample warning and leave him an out by which to escape.

NOTES

1. It wasn't his lying that offended me as much as the credence he gave my intelligence. Granted, he was under pressure, but he could have come up with something more credible.

L.A. New York

TRANSPORTATION

CHAPTER SEVEN

New York

There are two basic forms of transportation in New York: taxi cabs and the subway.

NEW YORK TAXIS

None of the travel guidebooks tell you this basic information, but here's how to operate New York City yellow cabs, which are also called medallion cabs.

The roof light illuminated means that the cab is empty and for hire—unless the "off duty" lights at the edge of the roof light are on, which naturally means the yellow box of tin is off duty. You wave and hail the cab, which stops. You pile in, and stow gear in the trunk if necessary. Give the driver your destination. Pay him, plus a tip, if he doesn't smell too bad or drive too loony, at the completion of your trip. Get a receipt, which comes from a digital machine mounted on the dash. The receipt contains the amount and the number of the cab, plus the time of the ride.

Anything else and you're in edgeville, as far as medallion cabs go. Medallion hacks are limited in number, and they carry a plastic badge, the medallion, bolted to the hood. They have numbers on the roof lights that correspond to the license plate numbers, and by law they are the only carriers that can take a hail—hail being a customer waving from the curbside.

Livery cabs—also known as car service—cannot pick up passengers hailing, under the law. This is rigidly enforced in Manhattan from about 110th Street down to the Battery. You're supposed to call a livery hack and have it come for you. (A little-known trick: if you're headed across the Hudson River to a New Jersey destination, call a Jersey cab. It's much cheaper. A medallion cab will take you, but you'll never forget the ride. It gets double fare, out and back, plus tolls in advance, and it's King Kong dollars.) Newark Airport is a little different, and we'll get to that in a minute.

Outside of Lower Manhattan, there are damn few yellow cabs running around. As for livery cabs, one car service says, "We're not yellow, we go anywhere," which is quite a boast, because livery drivers in the outer boroughs are robbed and murdered with alarming regularity. In fact, it's one of the most dangerous jobs in the United States—more lethal than working the bomb squad or clerking an all-night convenience store.

But, outside of Lower Manhattan, livery hacks are pretty much the only hacks you'll find. And they sure do take hails. If you find yourself in Brooklyn or somewhere and you flag a gypsy hack, negotiate a price first for the ride and try to sound like you know where you're going. But, as always, don't bluff to the point where you're playing too far outside your game limit. Car service and livery vehicles carry a plate beginning with T and reading "Taxi and Limousine." There's a third breed, the unlicensed and unregulated gypsy hack. Just say no. The regulated ones are bad enough.

Most cab scams involve the few moments between coming out of a place like Penn Station or the Port Authority and getting into the hack. A street scammer will try to piece off a couple of bucks for his "service" in hailing the cab, or, in the worst case, will get you all awkward, with part of your luggage in the cab trunk and part on the street, maybe your wife standing there nervously among all these icky winos, and when you haul out that wallet to give the man a tip, he grabs it and runs.

I've seen this happen by Penn Station. If you chase him—or them—you leave your luggage and your wife in a vulnerable position. Worse, no matter if you're man or woman and alone, you have to choose between running after your wallet or staying with your bags. And having been abruptly robbed like that will make you very fearful about leaving your bags. Even without the emotional side, you just lost your wallet; if the bags go too, you're stranded in this godawful Gomorra with el zippo squatto.

And, of course, what are you gonna do if you catch the guys?

Once you're in the cab, you usually only get scammed by a long route. Fast meters are so rare these days that you don't have to worry much. In the old days, when owners of the medallions actually drove their own cabs, they were prone to hot-rodding the meters. Nowadays, the owners rarely drive, and fleet operators cannot afford to get caught at a cheap scam like this. Besides, the way the business works today, a fast meter would benefit the driver, not the owner—and that makes it counterproductive from the owner's point of view. The new wrinkle (hey, it's New York) is pretty pathetic, but it happens nonetheless. The meter flips a little quicker in heavy traffic, figuring a balance between moving and sitting time. Some cabbies will engage in extra starting and stopping to jack up the meter. In extreme cases, this looks like Woody Allen (in his funnier days) at the wheel.

Your only defense against overlong routes is a thorough knowledge of the city from a driving point of view, which is tough to get without years of hard-won experience. There's just no quick fix here. Memorizing the map is fine, but it tells you nothing about one-way streets, dead-ends, and streets that abruptly become one-way the other way. I had a cabby do this in Amsterdam—10 minutes and about six guilders after I got in, we whizzed right by my friend's house again in a different direction, for a net gain of about 100 feet. We were going to the

airport, and when we got there I got my revenge. It came to 53
guilders, and I asked for a receipt for 65—a very generous tip by
any standards. The "yes sirs" flowed freely. We got out and I took
my handwritten receipt, then handed him 53. He gave me this
uncomprehending, openmouthed bovine expression. And I told
him I'd seen him bang me on the routing. He was not amused.

One thing cabbies occasionally do is pretend to misunder-
stand the obvious tourist and drive to a wrong address that sort
of sounds the same—an address which is, of course, really far
away from the correct one. I had this happen to me in Paris,
and I nipped it because I knew I had taken the Metro to within
three blocks of my destination—so when 10 blocks passed I
made the driver pull up. Language can easily be a barrier—at
present, only about 17 percent of the new cab drivers who take
the NYC city test are native English speakers. The rest speak
Farsi, Arabic, Haitian patois, all kinds of exotic tongues.
Manhattan is mostly numbered streets, but even for addresses
that aren't just write the address down and hand it to the driver.
Any wrong destinations then are on him, and if it happens
argue like hell. Usually, like my buddy in Paris, drivers pull
this kind of stuff on fares who have gear stowed in the trunk—
which makes you a virtual prisoner. Which is why I never put
bags back there unless there's no way out of it. Anything can
happen, and it's a good idea to be as portable as possible.

Here's the monetary situation for a medallion cab driver.
Unless they own the hack, they rent it by the shift, which is
usually 12 hours long. It costs anywhere from about $75 to
$120, depending on the desirability of the shift. Monday nights
are cheap. Saturday nights are expensive, but you don't get the
plums without the nettles, meaning you don't get Saturday
nights without working the dog shifts too. The owners have to
keep the cars in operation as close to 24 hours a day as possible
to maximize profits. I recently heard that most active cabs in
New York have 150,000 miles on the clock. They really get
driven and driven hard.

The cabbie has to cover his shift rent and his gas, and beyond that, he starts to make money. A good night is $100 take home. Some nights they yank down a sad $30 or $40 for their 12 hours. This is important to know. Your driver is an independent businessperson, the same as if he rented a store and sold apples. Instead, he just rents a car and sells rides under rigid legal guidelines. Taxi and Limousine Commission (TLC) cruisers patrol the streets and pull cabs over if they look like they're violating any one of the bazillion rules governing their behavior. The city realizes that cabbies are often the first line of contact for tourists and visitors, so they kind of care about keeping things square and looking good. Your ride receipt will include the number of the TLC to call if you have a complaint. And if you do, by all means call. Cabbies get away with all kinds of shit, like not stopping for black people (very common—partly out of prejudice and fear of crime, and partly because they're afraid that a black fare will want to get dropped deep in Harlem or Brooklyn where a return fare will be impossible to get) and not stopping for handicapped people, who require special handling.

So, your independent businessperson is cruising around trying to make a buck. By far the biggest arena for scamming an overcharge is when hacks take the long way coming in from the airports. Many are the tourists who've had the old wallet reamed by a cabby who took them 300 miles out of the way before hitting Manhattan. You don't have to be one of those tourists.

Arriving international passengers at Kennedy are always greeted by a mob of pushy free-lancers trying to take you for a ride. Don't do it. There are a lot of reasons, but the main one is that you have no control over the situation with a free-lancer—and that can get ugly in a whole lot of ways. The two safe methods of transport from Kennedy and La Guardia into Manhattan are by Carey bus and yellow cabs. But there's more to this than meets the red eye. A cab fare in from Kennedy will be anywhere from about $25 to maybe $40, depending on your destination in the city. The Carey bus is $11 as of 1994. Lone travelers who don't arrive in the wee small hours when Carey is off duty will obviously make out better financially by taking the bus. The buses are very clean, prompt, comfortable, and a good buy. Don't confuse this with the city-operated bus/subway link from Kennedy, which used to be the "Train to the Plane." Take it from an old, scarred hand, you don't want to ride that A train under Brooklyn with a pile of luggage, in either direction.

But if you arrive with a tribe of people, then the cab is usually a better deal. It's faster, and four people at the Carey rate of $11 quickly makes the cab fare look reasonable. But the wrong way to do this thing is on the meter. What we're discussing here is illegal, but routine. Here's what you're doing: you negotiate a price with the cabbie for you and your party into Manhattan. Say $40 or $50, tip included, and that should cover several destinations if the passengers are going to different places. The cash changes hands with the last party leaving the hack, not in advance. Then you take your ride. If you're in doubt or confused, lay $5 or $10 on a skycap luggage handler and ask him to please fix you up with a deal. They do this all the livelong day, and they're very good at it. But you must cross the skycap's palm with green—under no circumstances should you give this man less than a fiver. Maybe in Iowa they do things for free, but not in New York. The voice of the city, once again, is dead presidents. No matter what your financial situation or size of your party, either the Carey bus or the prearranged cab deal will get you safely into the big city. Remember, when cutting a deal with a cabby, that the meter fare—minimum—will be $25. And also remember that this independent businessperson, if he gets $50 for a half-hour trip and three destinations, just made half his shift rent. He's doing great. And you're safe at your destination.

Limos are always cruising the airports offering a ride to Manhattan for like $20—but they pack people in like sardines, and it's a terrible ride. I mean they'll jam you in mercilessly. It's the worst deal going. Just say no.

Following these guidelines, and watching yourself getting in and out of the cab, you will probably not have any problems. The old sage, philosophical New York cabby of legend is gone, replaced by a Sikh or a rastaman. But they are human, and it often pays to ask them about their night if you're in the mood to talk—ask if they're busy, that kind of stuff. For them, it's a break from having directions barked into their ear or listening to shit from drunks.

SUBWAYS

The New York City subways are electric trains running on 648 miles of track, both elevated and underground, served by 469 stations. There are currently 5,917 train cars in use. Subways are dangerous in a lot of ways. They are big, fast trains running right up against unguarded platforms, and there is an exposed high-voltage third rail on all tracks that carries plenty enough electricity to fry you as efficiently as Old Sparky if you touch it.

Compared to the subways in Paris, London, or Montreal, the New York City trains are pretty poor. They are also filthy a good part of the time—the stations more than the trains, but trains have their moments too. Inside the cars, you have about a 50-50 chance of getting heat or air conditioning—and sometimes you get heat in summer and AC in January. It is a genuine miracle to take even a short ride without hearing the universal panhandler's announcement to the passengers, "Ladies and gentlemen, I'm sorry to bother you, but . . ." Yeah, sorry, but I'm going to get in your face anyway. Recent court decisions hold that panhandlers have the right to work the transit system. Fare-paying passengers do not have the right to ride without having a change cup shoved under their noses. It's the New York state of mind, as dictated by people who never ride the trains. This is the heart of the subway curse, right here: the people who make the decisions don't use the system.

Many subway stations and the tunnels immediately adjacent are home to those famous MICAs—mentally ill, chemically addicted people—and other subterranean dwellers. Past the ends of the platforms in the dark tunnels, there is usually another platform, a vacant one that can be used as a dormitory or private boudoir. And MICA or not, everyone knows better than to shit where they live, so a lot of the regular platforms have become open bathrooms. Less than three months before this writing, in one of the stinkier stations in Manhattan—the 2nd Avenue stop on the F line—I saw a bum drop his crusty pants and squat in the middle of the platform as casually as if he were home in his private can, which he probably was. There happened to be a young cop upstairs by the token booth, and as I went by I said, "I know you don't want to hear this, but there's a guy taking a shit on the platform on the downtown side."

The cop immediately moved in that direction. "Where is he?" he asked.

"Don't worry," I said, "you'll see him. We all did." I don't know what police procedure is in a case like that. Rub his nose in it, maybe. Realize that although the bum pooping was an atypical event, no one went running and screaming away from the guy. It's unpleasant, but it just wasn't that shocking to the locals. They've seen it all before. And even though all the passengers filed out past the cop, I was the only one who stopped to tell him about it—which should teach you volumes about what people in New York will tolerate and what they think about their cops. Some years back, I wouldn't have bothered, either. Now I'm just sick of it. Why should anyone have to put up with that—literal—shit? And don't forget, there are kids on the trains who don't need to be exposed to that. And on top of it all, every one of us suckers paid for the privilege of being in the same public place as a bum pinching a log.

May 14, 1993, was a subway-oriented day in the New York

Daily News. There were several stories concerning the trains in the paper that day, and they covered a good cross-section of the system's problems.

The big front-page headline, in 2-inch-tall type, said, "THANKS, STRANGER: Mom Salutes Subway Hero Stabbed Saving Her and Tot." Right away, you're onto another mainline truth about New York City. Stabbed or not, when a stranger helps another person, it's a story. Be a woman of color and get raped, robbed, and murdered in the ghetto, and you might get an inch-tall story in the back pages. If it's an especially busy news day, your untimely demise might not make the papers at all. But be of any color and help a stranger in trouble and you'll be a front-page hero. In New York it's a man-bites-dog situation, because almost nobody ever lends a hurting stranger a hand. Unless they get paid. Remember, there is no tragedy so great that some New Yorker won't try to make a buck on it.

Page two of the May 14 *Daily News* featured a Mike McAlary column about a 16-year-old kid named Keron Thomas. Thomas really likes subway trains. On May 10, four days before, he had produced a fake motorman's ID and safely piloted a 10-car A train for almost a complete round trip, 45 miles, making all his correct stops. At the end, he ran into trouble by going a little too fast and triggering an automatic brake. Then, because he was afraid of rats, he wouldn't go onto the tracks and release the brake. McAlary said that Thomas was a natural-born hero and saluted him for his passion and for having the courage to pursue his dreams. Rush Limbaugh, McAlary wrote, also loved the kid for taking charge of his destiny and displaying the good old can-do spirit that made America great.

I don't love the kid. And I don't really think grand theft (train) is the kind of thing that strengthens America. Here again, it's subway philosophy from people who don't use the system. McAlary makes a big six-figure salary and has press plates on his car that allows him to park anywhere in the city and probably never rides the subways. Blimp Limbaugh definitely doesn't ride the subways. Consequently, neither of these assholes knows what he's talking about. I ride the trains every damn day, and the view from trackside is significantly different from the view from McAlary's car or Limburger's TV studio. Nobody in the trenches thought that Thomas was anything but a grand-slam menace to society.

Thomas' case was actually theft of our wheels. Picture the everlasting fireworks if Pork Limbaugh's car was stolen. It would be a dastardly, scurvy dog who stole Limbaugh's car—because that would directly affect him instead of a trainload of working joes and checkout janes dragging their weary butts home after trying to make a yankee dollar all day. Had Thomas heisted Limbaugh's car—or McAlary's car, for that matter—he would have become a two-bit television and tabloid symbol for everything wrong with coddling thieves and criminals in America. But instead he steals a train, endangering the estimated 2,000 passengers who got on and off throughout the route—and Limbaugh, the cardboard patriot, makes him out to be a hero. Limbaugh knows about as much about real life as he does about counting calories.

Thomas' case does help throw light on the tight security the Transit Authority (TA) keeps. A 16-year-old kid with fake ID walked right through their perimeter, fielded a couple questions, then boogied with a train. This isn't just an underage kid scoring a bottle of wine; it's fake ID carried past Pink-Panther-grade security—and there's nothing funny about it. In court, Thomas was given probation.

Back in 1992, a motorman sped his train off the tracks at Union Square, killing five and injuring hundreds. He was drunk when they found him a few hours later, but they weren't sure if he was bombed at the time of the wreck. Drunks can be kind of cute sometimes, like ambitious kids can be cute. But neither should be running trains. And no one made the drunk out to be a hero taking initiative into his hands.

Page five of the May 14 *Daily News* carried two stories about the front-page subway mugging victim and her shanked Samaritan savior. She had been mugged three times before on the trains. The station where she was assaulted, Lexington Avenue on the N line, is the ninth worst in the city, with 112 reported felonies in 1992—about one every three days. The Times Square/42nd Street station is the worst in the city, crimewise. It used to be two separate stations—now it's one huge, subterranean labyrinth that goes for blocks in all directions, with dozens of levels linked by staircases, blind corridors, mysterious platforms, ramps and escalators, and liberally laced with misleading signs. The Times Square/42nd Street complex is a stop for the A, C, E, 1, 2, 3, 7, 9, N, and R trains in both directions, and the shuttle to Grand Central. Really, it's like a spooky underground city. Those sly folks at the TA still consider the place as two stations when it comes to felony statistics. Riders reported 289 felonies in the Times Square part in 1992 and 254 in the 42nd Street part of the same station. Separately, they were the most-dangerous and second-most-dangerous stations in the city, and the two, which are actually one, weighed in with a staggering 543 felonies—and these were only the ones that were reported—in 1992, which is three every two days.

The second *Daily News* article on the good Samaritan was by columnist Amy Pagnozzi—a real rah-rah kind of story, about how the kid got stabbed, yes, but he did the right thing and really loves New York, and ain't this some exciting city, huh?

On page 7, columnist Juan Gonzales reported that TA emergency procedures caused delays that may have cost an 18-year-old Utah tourist his life. Instead of being able to call 911 directly, token booth clerks are required to phone their own Station Command, which is then supposed to relay the call. Gonzales said that in at least one instance, this third-party system translated the token clerk's report as a man being shot—a critical call—into shots fired, which is a far less important crime.

An old, experienced Brooklyn streetfighter and hood once told me, "I don't care if you're King Kong, you're taking your life in your hands in the subway." This from a seasoned bone-breaker, a guy who once made his living applying lengths of iron pipe to the heads of men who failed to pay their gambling debts, a guy who did two years in a state penitentiary, a guy who really, really likes hurting people. I believe him. So should you.

Here's a partial list of things I have seen on the trains: a coke sniffer pulling a knife on me; an insane, laughing, naked woman being led away by the cops; one man beating another with a big rock; a wig snatching; several fistfights; a forcible pickpocketing; and a wolf pack. This is over and above the usual overcrowding, reeking bums, panhandlers, weird vendors, menacing kids looking for a victim, drunks, insults, urinations, defecations, harsh words, rats on the tracks, loud and mysterious announcements, bad musicians, and delays. Of all the incidents, the pickpocketing and the wolf pack were the worst, and they were damn bad.

The pickpocket scene happened in Times Square (whattaya know?) on the E train during the morning rush hour, but it had been building up since the A line in Brooklyn about half an hour earlier. Five young guys got on, all dressed differently, talking. One had a dry cleaner's bag over his shoulder and was wearing a suit. Others were in jeans, casual stuff, or jogging clothes. At the next stop, they abruptly began to ignore each other. They all got off, then all got back on like strangers. They all got off and on again at every station into the city. To anyone who hadn't seen the first act, they would have looked like total strangers to each other, although getting off and on was a big red flag that something was seriously amiss.

If you see that happening, get off and wait for the next train or move to another car. The conductor is in the middle part of the train, opening and closing the doors. If you find yourself with a slow-building problem or someone following you, make it to the conductor and tell him or her.

These guys were so clearly out to make a score that I left the A train at West 4th Street and walked across to the local side and caught an E train. So did they, which scared the hell out of me. I only had a few more stops to Times Square, so I hung in and hoped for the best, ignoring the advice I just gave you. Today I wouldn't do that. I'd do what I said, get off, transfer again, do something to get my behind away from such an obvious oncoming felony. When you can see it coming, get the hell out of the way.

It turned out that they weren't interested in me at all. When we pulled into Times Square, I knew they were going to make their move because the jaw muscles on one of the thieves began to jump. This guy had been nervously clenching his teeth all along, making the muscles squirm visibly. Coming into Times Square, his jaw got so active that it looked like there was a nest of mice wrestling around under his skin.

The doors opened, and the crowd started to exit. Me too. The biggest of the thieves suddenly stopped in the doorway, blocking a man in a three-piece suit behind him. The rest of the gang jammed the suit from every angle and started grabbing at him. There was an old man in front of me who said, "What the hell?" but we were trying to get out the same door that the gang was using and I didn't want anything to do with them. I shoved the old man hard, just thrust him out the door and went with him. The sharks finished their feeding frenzy and became strangers in the crowd again. I didn't stick around for the aftermath. That was in 1990, and oddly enough, somebody else did stick around this gang starting in 1991. He saw them in action on the A line one day and began to watch them, approaching the victims afterward and offering to help identify these punks to the police. Almost nobody wanted to go to the cops, and the cops didn't really want to hear about this amateur sleuth work, either. Finally, in 1993, he got some willing victims, and the police made an arrest. The gang had been working the same train line, the same way, for three years, unmolested. Their trial is pending at this writing. And that just happens to be one I saw, purely by chance. There are a lot of other similar pattern crimes going on out there as regular as any other business.

A less violent variation of the subway gang is worked on buses in New York. A woman will walk down steps to exit the bus and drop something. She stoops to pick it up, immobilizing the victim behind her, also usually a woman. While the victim's distracted the man behind her slips the wallet out of her purse.

The key to avoiding situations like these is simple awareness. Watch your fellow passengers for unusual behavior. It doesn't matter if you're Jed Clampett; people are not all that different no matter where you go. New Yorkers are famous for ignoring their fellow human beings—if a stranger is showing special interest in you, it's probably either sexual or predatory (or both). Most people riding the subways are in neutral mode, more or less—running errands, commuting to or from work. And as bad as I've made it sound, most riders are not stressed up and quivering, and they don't do things like getting on and off the train at stops. Folks do drop things in doorways; it's completely natural. But your immediate concern in any kind of situation where you're hemmed in suddenly should be to inventory yourself and your possessions and protect them, if possible. You are the important person here. The woman bent over with her butt blocking you does not need your help. No one needs your help—the only thing you need to do is mind your purse or wallet.

When you see that something is going to happen, don't stick around to see what it'll be. This isn't TV, and crime is not a spectator sport. Helping people in trouble is a good thing to do but very unpredictable and dangerous. If you're the kind who likes to help out—and most of us are, really—pick your time and place. Most often, just leaving to call the cops is the best thing you can do. The victim you save may be yourself, and the surest way to avoid being involved in crime is by being outside its reach. Most pickpockets and sneak thieves are not violent types, but don't bet your life on it. Lives are hard to replace.

As a personal thing, I'll try and prevent a crime or help out if I think it's advisable. Other times I'll just do like other New Yorkers and ignore it. Leave the Superman action to Superman. There is a curiosity in all of us that wants to see action and adventure—you hear a gunshot and immediately want to stick your fool head out the window to see what happened, which makes your head a great target. When you encounter an imminent street scene that probably won't involve you, the desire to stick around and watch is strong. Fight it, in the trains or the streets. Just get the hell gone and forget it.

I'm writing this in August. It's hot. Yesterday, I turned a corner on the Lower East Side and saw four guys leaning up against a wall. They were about 20 feet apart, wearing light jackets and looking jumpy. Law-abiding citizens don't loiter looking like they know each other but want to stand far apart with jackets on in the middle of summer. Something was seriously potentially violent, probably involving the guns that were under their jackets. You just don't want to stick around and see what sort of nastiness develops, you really don't—if for no other reason than when you happen to be there sticking your unwanted snoopy proboscis into things and the feces hits the fan, somebody might decide to include you in the carnage just for the hell of it. In the street or in the subway, just get clear of situations and people that don't look right to you. Use your awareness and your common sense.

The wolf pack happened on the same local A train line, at 14th Street, in the evening. The train pulled in, the doors opened, and about a hundred teenage boys, yelling and waving beer bottles, streamed out of the train and ran down the platform and up the stairs. This was not youthful vigor; it was kids doing what they called "wilding." And if you wanna see something scary, that's it. They didn't touch any of the few people on the platform, but if they had, there wouldn't have been much I or anyone else could have done about it. I really wanted a pistol in my hand then. A nice big blue one with lots of bullets. Or a good short pump shotgun.

The only thing to do around a wolf pack is step back and let 'em run and hope they pass. The worst thing you can do is rabbit from them because if you weren't a target before, you will be when you flee. And be sure you report the incident to the cops right away. A wolf pack is a portable riot looking for victims to rape, rob, and beat, very ugly and very dangerous. Occasionally, wolf packs will pour into a store and strip the racks like piranha on cattle. Some years back, a wolf pack in Times Square chased some poor guy and yanked his clothes off and stole his money. He went to the cops, who got him some clothes, and then sailed back into that unkind night. The mob caught him again and chased him onto the tracks, where in despair he grabbed the third rail and fried himself while the mob jeered. Sad to say, the phrase "public spirit" in the Big Apple often means a mob shouting for some wretched, despondent individual to go ahead and jump from the roof just as he's threatening to do. It's not a kindly town.

There are some classic subway maneuvers to watch for and move away from. Often, you'll see a couple of teenage guys talking on the platform, but when the train arrives they split up, one going in one car, and another in the one just behind it. They meet again via the connecting door and sit across from each other and act like strangers. Even though this isn't overtly threatening, it usually means that they're ready to take a score if one presents itself. A lot of the crime in the trains and the streets is opportunistic. Thousands of people are walking around with the ways and means to do muggings, but they won't unless some situation arises that's too good to pass up. The phrase young hoods use is *getting paid*, which means stealing some money from somebody. If you hear somebody say it, it's code-red time. A mugging is imminent. Take steps to make sure it's not yours.

As with the streets, your best weapon in a train station or a train is awareness. If something or somebody looks strange to you—like really not right—don't make the mistake of thinking it's just some big-city piece of business you don't understand. Calmly and quietly move away. If it's a situation inside a train car, you can often either jump out at the last second before the doors close, leaving the person or persons stuck in the car, or you can walk out when the train pulls in and get back on at the last second, leaving your problem on the platform.

Don't get too cocky about either of these maneuvers. Every city kid knows how to get on a sealed train—you just peel back the spring gates between the cars and hop aboard, entering the cars through the connecting doors. It takes about a second. It can be very dangerous if the train lurches out of the station—but mostly it goes very smoothly, and there you are thinking you left your mugger on the platform, while he's actually still on the train. From inside the cars, it's difficult to see people between the cars, so someone could very well watch you from there and disembark down the line when you get off.

Not long ago a friend of mine got hit with a kind of trick subway lure. It was like 1:00 in the morning, and he was coming back from a party in Brooklyn with his girlfriend. They pulled into a station, the doors opened, and a teenage boy ran into the car and slapped his girl on top of her head, then ran back out of the car. My friend naturally jumped up to kick his rude little ass.

Waiting for him on the platform were 10 kids, the slapper and nine others. He caught himself a half a step from disaster, just inside the closing car doors. One of the kids did get on the train, in another car, but he didn't continue the confrontation. Had my friend taken that last half step, he would have been alone on a platform with a nasty gang, and the one kid on the train would have attacked his girl. He said the whole encounter was "like being lured into a trap by wild animals."

As a longtime subway consumer, just using the system and

coming into contact with its alleged employees feels like being trapped by wild animals.

TOKEN BOOTHS AND TOKEN CLERKS

Subway token booths are armored, bulletproofed vaults. They have their own air supply and air conditioning systems to prevent suffocating the clerks or smoking them out, and many are equipped with fire-suppression systems. Booths are targets because they have many thousands of dollars in cash and subway tokens at all times. Subway tokens spend just like yankee dollars in many businesses. The only successful violent assaults on token booths are by fire—they pour gas through the money slot and light it. It doesn't happen often, and when it does it's in the nastiest, loneliest stations in the wee small hours.

Clerks have strict guidelines on who they admit to their booths, which doesn't include transit cops unless they know the cops personally. Armor, of course, works two ways, and there was recently a case where people stood outside watching, unable to help, while a clerk died of a heart attack inside.

Being a token clerk is very much a 20-years-and-out job. No one grows up wanting to be a token clerk—it's the kind of civil service gig you get when you see that the future is not so bright (and the benefits aren't either) running a register at the local grocery store. Token clerks have power the way minimum-wage Barney Fife rent-a-cops have power. The attitude is absolutely the same—they are king of this little pathetic piece of real estate, and from this grain of power, they are going to get even for every injustice the world ever heaped on their suffering shoulders. A lot of times, it's hard to get the clerk to stop yapping on the phone long enough to bother selling you some tokens so you can go listen to the panhandlers on the train. Asking for directions is like inviting abuse—often it's like trying to have a discussion with a six-year-old child who is repeating everything you say back to you. Good thing they have bulletproof glass.

Clerks often cannot see the trains on the platform, and you can encounter mind-wrenching noncommunication with these people. After I was shot but still on crutches I lived off the F line in Manhattan. The F stops at West 4th Street, in the Village, on the bottom level below the A line. Every other day, the F would screw up and be rerouted along the A line to Brooklyn, which meant that it missed my stop. This would be announced over the loudspeakers. I would painfully climb the stairs up to the token booth and ask for a refund. The clerks would tell me—every other damn day—that the train was running fine and to go back down. They had not been notified. This, just after the goddamn loudspeaker system told us that the F to the Lower East Side was down. Usually I'd be so pissed off—and unrefunded—and in too much pain to crutch back downstairs and I'd go hail a cab. This resulted, later, in my not paying a subway fare for about a year. I figured that they had burned me enough, and it was time I did some burning back. I hate the New York City subways with a red passion.

Some clerks are very alert and knowledgeable. The great majority are uncaring, clock-watching morons. It would be in the direst emergency that I would seek help from a token clerk, and only then if I was so severely injured that I couldn't make it up the last steps to the street.

L.A.

When it comes to public transportation, Los Angeles sucks. Up to this point, it's been the RTD (retarded taxi drivers, as some would have it), although with the advent of the Metrolines the subway tactics of New York will soon be coming to L.A. It's a sad state of affairs that you can't get good service, safe service, and freedom from those on the Thorazine shuffle from public transport all in one package. The RTD is about as reliable as a politician's promise and the happy hunting grounds of a wide variety of scum and trouble-makers. Santa Monica buses are generally safer and more reliable, but the combination of the VA hospital and the Western Union for the crazies' mad money gives you a wonderful chance to ride with the screamers and droolers. Anything passing through Long Beach has a charming combination of all three: troublemakers, screamers, and droolers.

The back of the bus is home for the young, brave, and fool-ish (another threesome to avoid). If you have the bad luck to be forced to ride on the bus, stick to the front, unless you're looking for excitement. From the back door on is the land of the hunters. If you're female or male but not particularly interested in getting mad-dogged (receiving hard looks to prove whose penis is big-ger), stand in the front rather than going to a seat in the back.

It's to the back that the stoned, drunk, and belligerent head. A young buck will walk down and sprawl all over a seat and then proceed to mad-dog anyone he thinks he can get away with. This goes on until either he gets off or someone with more juice shows up and makes him move. If that newcomer doesn't have enough obvious *cojones,* you're about to see a fight. I have had more than one fight in the back of the bus myself, although the funniest one was back in the 1970s when my old running buddy and I were just coming back from the only sporting goods store where we had been able to find boxing wraps. Four young Crips came on and started woofing (whipping themselves up into a frenzy). My partner and I exchanged looks; we both knew where this plot was going. Without a word I tossed him one wrap, and I started tying one onto my right hand. He did the same, and when we were done, we just looked at each other and smiled that special feral smile that street fighters get. During the process, our little friends' volume dwindled—that smile just proved to be too much. They scrambled off the bus at the next stop.

You should know that not everyone who's throwing fists on the bus is going to be a young buck. The women on the street can hold their own, and, if given provocation, some give better than many guys. I was on a bus that was overcrowded but still admitting people. In the aisle was a fiftyish, short, fat Mexican woman who, when the bus driver asked for people to step to the back of the bus, replied in broken English, "I'm too fat." This despite the fact that she had stopped in the middle of the bus and that the entire aisle behind her to the back of the bus was empty. Finally someone got fed up with being polite while being jammed from behind. He pushed past her, knocking her into the lap of a seated passenger. The seated passenger shoved her back up into someone coming down the aisle, who immediately shoved her back into the guy's lap. This went on for about 10 people; I was number six. All the time, she's yelling at the top of her lungs, "I'm tooo faaat!" while bobbing up and down like a jack-in-the-box. Finally when the parade stopped, she regained her feet.

Let me tell you, this woman was madder than a wet hen and immediately burst out in tirade against everyone who had mistreated her, oddly enough in the wrong direction. We were behind her, and she started yelling at the people in front of her. She's hopping up and down screaming, "You think I'm afraid of you? I'm not afraid of you!" liberally laced with some choice Spanish profanities. She had totally terrorized a skinny gay guy in front of her, when she decided to take it to the rest of the bus. Sitting next to the gay guy was a tall black dude who had been doing his best to ignore the whole thing; in fact, he was looking out the window. With another announcement of "I'm not afraid of you," she hauled back and nailed the black dude with a solid right hook to the jaw. This dude jumped up and hollered, "What you hit me for, bitch?!"

At that point the entire back of the bus lost it. We were too closely packed together to be rolling in the aisles, but we were laughing that hard. She launched into a verbal assault against the guy. The black dude was about 6'3" and pissed off but not about to punch someone's grandmother, so he was in a quandary. In the ensuing hollering match, nobody noticed that the bus had stopped until the back doors opened and the bus driver reached in and grabbed her. As she was being dragged off, she latched onto the support bar. She and the bus driver engaged in a tug of war while she protested that nothing was going on. Finally a kid sitting in the seat near the door leaned over and gave her hand a rap across the knuckles. She lost her grip and went flying off the bus. For the rest of the ride, the black dude had to endure all sorts of ribbing about looking out for them grandmothers, they can be tough.

For the most part, the bus lines provide transportation for society's underbelly and cheap labor forces (although the downtown lines do carry many office workers). That means that you, as a bus rider, get to see the behavior of that segment of society in all its splendid glory. If you want to cure a bleeding heart liberal of his tendency to see society through rose-colored glasses, stick him on the RTD for a week and see how fast he loses respect for the downtrodden.

If you're female, that advice about staying up front applies in spades. Your purse is the prime target of that 15-year-old kid who can snatch it and be out the backdoor at a stop in a heartbeat. Always keep your purse away from the aisle. If it isn't too much of a discomfort, don't even take it off your arm. Jam it between yourself and the side of the bus if you're sitting by the window. If you're in the aisle seat and you think the person next to you is cool, move it between you and him. Not as a sign of territoriality, but to make it harder for someone to grab it and dash. If you're not sure about the person next to you, carry it on your lap with both hands on top of it. Never leave it on an empty seat because there is no way you could stop a fast teenager in time.

If you're planning to come to L.A. via the airport and you're not being picked up, understand that it's car rental time. They've simplified LAX so that now if you can find your way out of the parking lot, you will be routed out onto the Sepulveda, Century, or Imperial Freeways—that makes it easy. After you get the paperwork for the car, before you step outside the terminal, look at the map and figure out where you're going. You don't want to be sitting in your car reading the map. LAX is a relatively safe airport, but the wolves are there. If you take Century out don't go past I-405 (San Diego) Freeway because it lands you in Raymond Crip territory and then into the Crenshaw Mafia, a Bloods gang. Regardless of what you've heard, that peace accord isn't real or going to last.

If you need to travel east, take the the Imperial Freeway or I-405 to the Artesia (California 91) Freeway—which is to the south, somewhere in the vicinity of the I-405/110 and 91 interchange—or to the north the Santa Monica (I-10) Freeway. The trick to traveling Los Angeles safely is to stay on the freeways as much as possible. That way, the only thing you're really risking is an accident or, if you're an obnoxious enough driver, a freeway shooting.

LAX is pretty well patrolled, but nonetheless the dirt bags are out there prowling, especially in the long-term lots. They know you have everything with you that you need to make it wherever you're going, and that usually means stuff that's worth ripping off. I've seen more than one school of sharks cruising the lots, especially during off hours. While the short-term lot is relatively safe, I don't recommend venturing into long-term parking at these times. When flying into LAX, I always make it a habit to unpack my weapons before going into the parking lots or have people who are carrying meet me outside the security nets. I've seen way too much, and I don't feel comfortable in L.A. unarmed. The problem with LAX is that it is so close to Inglewood.

If you live in L.A. and can't get picked up or don't feel like risking the parking lots at LAX, the Super Shuttle is the van equivalent of a limo. It's cheaper than the limos or taxis, but it can end up taking more time—especially if you get involved with an independent company that charges more and goes all over. The good thing about Super Shuttle is that each area is served by one van. It advertises that you will have no more than four stops, and sometimes you can get lucky and be the first. You find the shuttle going where you want and tell the guy where you're going, and it's not likely that he'll get lost. This is a good, safe alternative to risking your car by leaving it in the parking lot at the airport.

Burbank Airport isn't too bad. If you're coming in on a business trip that takes you downtown or to the Valley, you should consider using it rather than LAX. Coming into Burbank, you won't get robbed or shot in the immediate area, just lost.

If you have business in the eastern section of the L.A. urban blight (in Riverside or San Bernardino), fly into Ontario. It's like landing in a small midwestern hick airport, but I've never had to drop-kick a Hare Krishna or deal with panhandlers there. It's convenient to both I-10 (yes, the very one that leads to Phoenix and El Paso) and the I-15 (direct service to Vegas and Salt Lake City—how can these two cities be served by the same highway?). It is also handy for dropping down into Orange County.

Arriving by train into Union Square is an adventure since most of the complex has been shut down and is now used as a movie set (it was the police station in *Blade Runner*). Union Station is kind of quaint and is located on the east side of Chinatown, just north of the governmental area of downtown, so it's not too slimy. Just avoid Olvera Street to the north because it's a tourist trap—then, again, maybe you want a stuffed pinata.

I don't recommend arriving in L.A. via the downtown Greyhound bus terminal at night. Come to think of it, during the day isn't too safe either. The terminal is next to L.A.'s skid row, and it's a lot like L.A.'s version of New York, just in case you want to experience that life-style. Whatever you do, don't arrive at the terminal without someone to pick you up, especially if you're female. Skip the downtown Long Beach bus terminal as well. If you're taking the bus into L.A., buy a ticket to Santa Monica, North Hollywood, or some other suburban station.

L.A.'s taxis run on a weird miles and/or minute scale and will eat your spare cash faster than a school of piranha. It's actually cheaper to rent a car than to get gouged by taxis in L.A. You're not going to get hustled by them, just driven to the poorhouse.

CHAPTER EIGHT

Times Square

I worked in Times Square for years, all hours of the day and night. The best line I ever heard came from a street hustler on 43rd Street, about nine o'clock at night. He said, "Hey, you wanna buy a switchblade? C'mere and I'll show it to you."

Right. Step into the shadows so a guy can show you his knife. I laughed for two blocks, but I'll bet he roped a lot of suckers that way—roped 'em and robbed 'em.

Everything you ever heard about Times Square is probably true, and then again, the magnitude of what you heard is probably wrong. Its glory days are gone. Times Square has always had a reputation as a center for prostitution. But the last real whorehouse in the area closed a few years ago, and believe me, as fleshpots go, it was pretty tawdry.

Then there's the fabled "Minnesota Strip." This storied area was a stretch of 8th Avenue where hapless runaway girls from America's heartland—wholesome, corn-fed girls who had strayed into the wicked city—had been conned by evil pimps and forcibly addicted to drugs, then turned out to walk the streets in degradation, their lives ruined. The Minnesota Strip never existed. Not that the story is untrue—pimps do watch incoming buses and prey on lost, runaway girls, for sure. But the Strip idea was the public relations brainchild of a priest who ran a runaway-help charity operation in the Times Square area. His clients were mainly inner-city kids of color, but he knew that didn't play too well to wealthy, white charitable contributors, so he invented the Minnesota Strip and painted a heart-rending picture, with strongly racist overtones, of the cream of young American white womanhood being pulled into unspeakable shame—and only his organization standing between a permanently ruined life and salvation. It worked, too. Money poured in. But the priest was later run out of the youth salvation business by allegations that he himself had engaged in sex with several of his male charges.

Which makes it a perfect Times Square story. Always a twist, always with the real facts concealed. Damon Runyon wrote the best Times Square tales, from the era of its real glory. Today, it's just a place for cheap hustles and porn. It's not even a real porn mecca. There are plenty of video stores and peep shows, and some strip joints—male and female—along 8th Avenue. But it's nowhere near as wild as Amsterdam's red-light district. The whole area, in fact, is undergoing a renovation of sorts, which has to do with big-deal real estate cloak-and-dagger machinations and the possibility of skazillions in profits if they can clean up the place. So the fight is on: porn versus big-money real estate interests.

For you on the sidewalk, the hazards are mostly the same as they are elsewhere in the city, only a little more concentrated. Most drug sales, switchblade sales, and so on are scams around Times Square. It's a prime area for muggings, especially chain snatchings. Gangs of young kids who specialize in this kind of business come into the Square at night and prey on the unwary. The hookers will try their best to get your money without coming across with any goods, and, depending on the season and the law enforcement climate, they do business openly in parking lots, rest rooms, and doorways in the neighborhood.

There are a lot of compelling reasons to be in Times Square. It's still the hub of legitimate theater in the United States, and the area is packed with flagship first-run movie theaters, along with cheap double-feature cinema grind houses that show New Yorkers the grade Z and Southern drive-in flicks they otherwise wouldn't be able to view. If your tastes run to low-budget flicks, watch yourself in the 42nd Street grind houses. The audience can get pretty rowdy pretty fast— since it usually consists of pimps killing time, welfare families killing time, muggers killing time, and a few cheap movie hounds. The audience talks. The audience yells. The floors and seats are sticky. And if you get into a confrontation with someone, don't expect Flashlight Sammy to come to the rescue. As a matter of good sense, I have always avoided the bathrooms in these places, and so should you.

Many tourists end up on 42nd Street—"The Deuce"— because the United Nations is at 42nd and the East River, Grand Central Station is located at 42nd and Park Avenue, on the east side of town, and the Port Authority Bus Terminal is at 42nd and 8th Avenue on the West Side. Foot traffic between Grand Central and the Port Authority is especially common for people passing through town. If you have a lot of luggage just grab a cab. It's worth it.

The Deuce is plagued with religious nuts using amplifiers and bullhorns, and black race-hate groups who also use amplifiers and bullhorns to out-shout the evangelists. Combine that with the general slimy, decayed tone of the place, and it makes for unpleasant strolling. On the other hand, between 5th and 6th Avenues is the famous New York Public Library and Bryant Park, now a drug-free remodeled showplace.

Grand Central Station is a beautiful building and something visitors really should see. It has a homeless problem, but no special crime concentration. The Port Authority (PA) is another matter altogether.

Covering two city blocks, from 42nd to 40th Streets, between 8th and 9th Avenues, the PA building is a magnet for all sorts of social and criminal problems. It teems with crackheads, prostitutes of both sexes, phone scam artists, and luggage thieves. Now here's a place with troubling bathrooms, at least the men's rooms. Pennsylvania (or Penn) Station, directly down 8th Avenue at 34th Street, has the same men's room problems. You go in and there's a crowd of guys who look like they're waiting for the urinals, but there are open urinals—and the guys aren't waiting, they're just spectating. Or something. Whatever they're doing, it involves some kind of sex kick that you either already know about or you don't want to know about. And there are usually homeless guys taking splash showers at the sinks—showers that they are way overdue for. The cops at both Penn Station and the PA have been patrolling the men's rooms with more vigor lately, which makes the experience a little less hair-raising for those who just want to pee.

Phone scammers have been so persistent at the PA that the pay phones do not accept incoming calls any more. These guys, as noted elsewhere, live to steal credit card and personal identification numbers (PIN) from unsuspecting callers, and, at the same time, they sell long-distance hookups via stolen card numbers to people who want to call places like Taiwan, Sudan, and Sri Lanka at a discount rate. If this sounds tempting as a customer, you do it at your own risk. It's a well-known scam at the PA, and the phone company is pretty aggressive about prosecution if it catches you.

Muggings inside the PA tend to be unobtrusive, and usually pistol or knife oriented. A guy slips quietly up behind you on an escalator, sticks something in your back, and demands money. You hand it over quietly, and he splits. Watch who's approaching you in the PA, Penn Station, and Grand Central even more alertly than you watch at other places in the city.

The Port Authority building has a number of signs in it that say, basically, "We have a heaps of uniformed personnel on duty—don't take assistance of any kind from nonuniformed free-lancers." This is great advice. Don't let them carry your bag, lest you see the kindly guy sprint off with it—use a red-cap. Don't let them give you directions or assist you in finding a bus. There is a taxi stand with official sanction on 8th Avenue—use it to get a taxi, even if you're headed downtown (8th Avenue goes uptown one way).

Penn Station is really the kingdom hall of taxi scams. At the 7th Avenue entrance to the Penn Station/Madison Square Garden complex is the same kind of official taxi stand you see at Grand Central on 42nd Street or the PA on 8th Avenue. But all the trains and Madison Square Garden are at the complete other end of Penn Station, on the 8th Avenue side—and there is a wide, inviting plaza there. Somehow, the rocket scientists that run Penn Station haven't figured out that the 8th Avenue side is a real convenient place to hail a cab—and they also don't seem to know that all those lowlifes in the plaza are there to try and beat tourists out of some money.

The scams there all revolve around some guy assisting you in some way with a cab. *Don't let anyone except the cab driver help you in any way.* Sometimes (and this happens all over town, especially around nightclubs) guys will run up to the cab and hold the door to help you out of the cab, like spontaneous doormen. They'll take a tip if that's all they can get, but the real purpose of being there is to reach in and snatch your cash when you pull it out to pay the driver. They always open the right-hand door, which is the side that the money slot is on in partitioned cabs (imagine that!). One fast grab and two fleet feet and your cash is history, gone into the night.

This also happens around the 8th Avenue end of Penn Station, where the bums will help you load your luggage into the cab trunk and then grab your wallet when you pull it out to tip them, and so on. Broad daylight is no deterrent.

Two crime prevention tips here. With the doorman scam, just refuse to pay the driver—like don't make a move for money at all—until the guy shuts the door and leaves. You're not in that big a rush; you're just not. Tell the cabbie to get rid of the doorman, if you're not forceful or threatening enough to do it yourself. Or insist that he drive up the block or whatever, if he's not able to chase the guy away. Some cabbies aren't willing to chase doormen away for one of several reasons: they're afraid of a confrontation, or—and this is increasingly obvious as time goes on and more surly immigrants take over the hack business—they hate their imperialistic, infidel, fat American customers who make money off the backs of the exploited millions/true believers of Islam and like to see the pig Americans become victims of crime.

I don't care who you are or how small you are, you're paying the freight here. Cabbies are vigorously regulated, and they're in financially desperate straits or they wouldn't be hacking. It's not a cushy job, and there's not much money in it. The cabby is not making money sitting and waiting for you to haul out the dough. Whatever happens here, make no move for money until the threat of the doorman is resolved in your favor. Holler for a cop, whatever. Knuckling under to a surly cabby and thrusting yourself into the hands of a doorman mugger is not what you want to do.

You just have to tough this one out. If you insist that the driver move the cab to get away from the doorman, the situation will come out OK. The cabby needs to skeedadle to make money. The doorman will get pissed off and go looking for another victim. You can go on with your life. Cash snatchers like this are cowards, and a later physical confrontation is very unlikely. Should you be female and threatened outside a nightclub, run to the huge bouncers that watch the door of every New York nightclub. They'll help.

The cabby should help you load or unload luggage, if you have so much that you need to put it in the trunk. Insist on it. Never use free-lancers. Correct handling of money is a help in all these situations. Keep a few bucks, like 40, in a money clip and use that for minute-to-minute purchases. Do not keep all your cash in your wallet. New York is a money town. It seems like you're buying something every other minute. With a money clip you don't have to pull out the whole poke all the time, which is dangerous. I clearly recall one fine St. Patrick's Day in the Grassroots Bar on St. Mark's Place, this green suburban kid stepped up to the mahogany and ordered a couple of drinks. When they came, he flipped open his tall wallet. Inside, neatly racked, was every precious metal credit card known to man, and their shining purchasing power, as he held his wallet aloft, beamed down the bar and caught every gin-soaked eye. He was a mark ready to take a pipe in the back of the head. The Grassroots is a safe, friendly bar (or I wouldn't be there, eh?), but not every watering hole is like that, and the kid was being stupid with a capital V for victim. Don't make his mistake. Just unobtrusively pull out a few bills and pay your way without showing the world your credit rating. This ain't Kansas.

Savvy money handling reduces a lot of opportunistic crimes. You are not nearly so much of a mark for muggers when you keep your business to yourself.

Another taxi scam I recently heard of happened to a fairly savvy out-of-towner I know, at Penn Station on 8th Avenue. From what I heard, a guy with a clipboard, who was actually inside the cab, made out like he was somehow in charge of managing the taxis. His pitch was that there were so many robberies recently that they had to start collecting a deposit from riders before the trip. They took seven bucks off this guy.

That's what I heard. The part that doesn't ring true is the participation of the actual cab. That bit, I think, might be a wee bit embellished, so that he could tell the story without losing too much face. It's always a good idea to note the roof number of the cab at least mentally, in case something goes wrong. From that, it's easy to tell who had the cab for the shift. And since taxis figure so heavily in scams around Penn Station and the Port Authority, reread the section on New York taxis in the previous chapter on transportation.

CHAPTER NINE

Beaches

Los Angeles doesn't have Times Square, but it does have beaches and boardwalks that New York—at least Manhattan—doesn't.

Ah, the joy of the beaches—the crowds, the traffic jams, the extortion of beach parking, the expensive yet terrible food, the bathrooms that look like they belong in New York subways, and of course the fun of toting everything across the hot, burning sand. Hmmmm! Beaches are so much fun.

Realistically, unless you still have a streak of macho in you, you're not going to get in a real hassle on the beach proper. Robbers avoid it, because the sand makes getting away quickly nearly impossible (even if you're a runner, running on sand will wipe you out fast). During the day there are too many people around anyway. If you're silly enough to wander around the beach at night, you'll run into the wandering homeless and drug-whacked babblers most often. You may run into a robber or rapist on the waterfront at night, but it's more often a crime of opportunity rather than one planned.

However, rip-offs on the beach are common and planned: when you go into the water, someone comes wandering up and snags whatever is worth stealing. These guys more often than not are roaming down the way rather than sitting there next to you, but the latter does happen as well. Usually, the guy walks up, grabs something, and walks away. Always cover your stuff at the beach with towels, and never leave wallets in pants pockets or purses because that's the first place the guy is going to look. When I used to hit the beach regularly, I'd wrap my wallet in a shirt and throw sand over it when I got there. However you can achieve the same effect by just burying your fanny pack. Naturally any time you go into the water ask the people sitting next to you to watch your stuff. Most beach rip-off artists are cowards, and if someone says, "Hey!" they're gone.

The kind of trouble you're most likely to get into on the beach is a run-in with assholes. The degree of hard-on you have will determine if there's going to be trouble between you and them. That and placement. There are certain areas that are staked out for the young bucks, and they defend these territories with vigor. Usually, they are at one end of the beach or near a breakwater or wall. By tacit consent of the local authorities, they go hang out there and leave the rest of the beach to everyone else. It is their area, and it is easier to steer clear of it.

However, now and then, you do get the traveling assholes, people who come to the beach and get obnoxious in a variety of predictable ways. Unless you're looking for a punchfest, it's easier to not set up near these groups, or if they set up near you, to simply move away. Drinking is verboten on the L.A. beaches, and (surprise, surprise) it carries a major ticket. Since most problems result from the "instant asshole: just add alcohol" sort of person, take a hike to the local lifeguard tower. He's got a phone, and the cops will show for this party. Regardless of what any tit-wagging TV lifeguard show might imply, those guys in the red shorts are not cops; if it gets real hairy, they're not going to play cavalry. That's what those dashing light blue shirts and guns are for.

Most of the trouble you'll see going down on the beach is between young bucks who have a hard-on for each other off the beach, but they just happened to run into each other and decided to dance there. This is especially true with Mexican homeboys who pack up in the Chevy and take it to the beach.

Another common reason for fisticuffs is that all that blonde hair and golden skin resulted in some surf rat parking his board in someone else's rack. Beach bunnies are closely guarded property by the local studs, and fur does fly over them. For the most part, though, serious beach boys restrict violence to their own kind, so unless you're a Mexican homeboy or a blond surfer out to play hide the sausage with a beach nymphet, you're not likely to end up scrapping on the beach.

That is not the case however on the boardwalks or areas near the beach. In fact, that is where it can and does get ugly with a capital UGH! Besides the bikepath, many areas have boardwalks that run along the beach—though why we call something made of asphalt and concrete a boardwalk is beyond me. The most popular boardwalks are Santa Monica, Venice, and Hermosa Beaches. The ones where you are most likely to get jacked are Venice and Santa Monica, although Hermosa can get furry now and then. Long Beach has a sporadic system of bikepaths and boardwalks that, depending on where you are, will either get you a pleasant stroll, a mugging, or toxic shock. The farther away from L.A. harbor, the smaller your chances of toxic shock or a mugging. In Long Beach, you're taking your life into your own hands trying to reach the beach anywhere except from the southern areas. Long Beach has areas of scuzzy with a capital, bold, and italicized *S*.

The boardwalks are a hotspot of tourism, free floor shows, hot juicy bodies, and all-around fun. They also are the home turf for a few gangs. The Shoreline Crips claim to hold the Venice boardwalk, but if you go too far inland you encounter other charming, like-minded groups like the V13s. If you're contemplating a quiet, moonlight stroll along the beach, you should know that certain difficult-to-reach places have been staked out by these charmers for their nighttime hangout spots. These places are chosen exactly like the park hangouts, far enough away from the main drag that a cop car cannot approach before anything illegal can be dropped into the shadows. When you pull into a beach parking area, especially at night, if you see a group hanging around cars, get the hell out of there. If you still want the walk, drive down the road a half mile or more and take your stroll in the same direction: away from the group.

Years before the color codes became synonymous with the Bloods and Crips, Mexican gangs had colors already staked out to tell people where they were from. Santa Monica was a yellow bandanna, Sawtelle was tan, Venice was dark blue, and Culver City was red. You were most likely to see dark blue, yellow, and tan bandannas along a northern boardwalk. This use of color coding pretty much disappears around Marina del Rey and doesn't pick up again until you reach Toes Beach and El Segundo, where the Culver City and Inglewood gangs hang out. Then it goes into remission again until you near San Pedro and Long Beach. When you see a group of Mexican guys moving along the boardwalk with bandannas around their necks or sticking out of their pockets, you know you're looking at a glee club and you should swing away from them. For the most part, though, these wolves aren't out to jam with anyone except each other and anyone foolish enough to cross them.

At the time of this writing, most of the black gangs had abandoned color coding, since the police were getting just a little too accurate in nailing them. Here's a guy dressed in blue from head to toe, swearing to the cop, "I ain't no gangster!" They now wear sports logos. Interpreting these can get kind of weird: "This means the Eight Trey Crips (83rd Avenue) because there're three dots and eight dashes in this logo." This switch did confuse the cops for about 30 seconds; now any young black man wearing a team logo is distrusted by the police, the public, and all the gangs.

What you really have to worry about is the beach rats. These are the lowlifes who live on or near the boardwalk. Many are on the skids or addicted to drugs. For some reason, homeless people seem to gravitate to the beach. While there is a solid racial mix of homeless addicts, a good number of beach rats are white. I haven't had time to make a run down there in the middle of winter in the last few years, but awhile ago a tent city was being allowed to set up during the week on the beach in Venice. Come Thursday, the cops would start rousting them out, and the tents would evaporate before the weekend crowds. Afterwards they'd pop back up.

Drunken brawls, screaming howlers, and roller-skating, guitar-playing Sihks all add color to the boardwalk. Fortunately, if you give the guitar player money, he goes away—but then again, so does a mugger. I have to admit that, if you have a strong stomach, some of the local crazies are sort of fun to listen to. I've met Jesus Christ, three CIA agents, and Richard Nixon on the Venice boardwalk. On the other hand the beach rats are looking to score off you. Any and all of the normal rip-offs that typify addicts accompany them to the boardwalk, so keep your stuff lashed to your body. Fanny packs should be worn to the front to prevent an attempted snatch, and purses should be left in the car's trunk.

Venice has a special problem when it comes to crime. The boardwalk has grown steadily in popularity over the years and is packed during the weekends. So not only are there the local sharks, but like any regularly crowded place, it draws outside predators. The closer you go toward Santa Monica, the slimier it becomes because the beach rats often head to the northern end. By the time you reach Rose Avenue, you'll be shooting a gauntlet of panhandlers, MICAs, street hustlers, and unidentified life forms. The southern end is pretty safe around the Plaza and Muscle Beach, but the sharks cruise there as well. If they see someone flashing cash, they will often follow that person away from the beach and into the alleys that abut the beach. Guess what is going to happen there? As always, you should keep an eye on anyone who is interested in you when you have your wallet out. And as a spot of common sense: stay on real streets and out of the alleys in Venice.

Santa Monica has its own special problem areas. Fortunately, the stretch from Venice to Santa Monica where P.O.P. used to be is not boardwalk territory, but it is full of serious beachgoers. The rats seem to float to the boardwalk areas. When the boardwalk picks up again around Pico, you start running into the charmers again. The boardwalk isn't terribly fun along this area because there are fewer tourists and more beach rats. The mentally tweaked tend to hang out more in the park along Ocean Boulevard north of the Santa Monica Pier, so what you meet along the boardwalk is a nastier breed. One thing you should know is that the base of the Santa Monica pier is not where you want to be. It gets real slimy under there, and the beach rats are always looking for an opportunity.

The floor show in both Venice and Santa Monica ends about 5 P.M. That's when the honest folks have mostly cleared out, and all that is left are the beach rats and hardasses. Even the run-of-the-mill hardasses avoid the Venice boardwalk at night. Popular it may be during the day, but at night Venice is the scene of some bad crazies.

Despite the circus setting up in the parking lot now and then, you also want to avoid the Santa Monica pier at night. It has not fared well since the big storm ripped off nearly a third of its length. While a nice newly constructed end perches on the water, the clientele has seriously deteriorated over the years. At night, young toughs and their teased-hair girlfriends cruise the arcades and cheap-food places busily looking for entertainment of some form. Although the guys are less likely to get violent with their girlfriends around, more than a few unattached toughs are cruising for trouble. Farther out toward the end, the fishermen generally ignore the whole goings-on, but late-night packs occasionally make it interesting, if not dangerous, for them. Because of this, most night fishermen clear out before midnight.

Going inland from the pier and park, this territory is difficult to describe. Downtown Santa Monica is a blend of chichi and winos throwing up in the alley. In certain cases, the drunk-in-alley ambiance extends to entire streets in a weird, unpredictable pattern. Unless you are a native and know this pattern, at night stay on the main east-west drag of Santa Monica as much as possible. In the north-south direction, the east side of Ocean Avenue is OK to walk down, but 4th and 2nd Streets get strange in pockets. I don't know about the promenade since they've renovated it.

The park that runs the length of the cliffs north of the pier is infested with homeless howlers and droolers both day and night because it is both home and hangout. This park is on the west side of Ocean Avenue, which makes it important to know your directions (hint: the big wet spot is to the west). A stroll along the park walkway to get to the pier is an olfactory experience. Remember that Santa Monica abuts the VA hospital, as well as hosting some sort of deal where the state sends the loonies their mad money. Both in the park and under the pier, you're likely to get panhandled, with the probability of it being more serious under the pier. In fact, if you're smart, you'll avoid the bathrooms down there; during the day that's wise, but at night it's imperative.

Speaking of bathrooms, the public restrooms along the northern beaches are a horror story. Never mind the eyeholes drilled in the stall wall that looks into the urinals. If some peeper wants to sit there and whack off that's his choice. It's the combination of the public service people not even going in there to clean up and the homeless using it as bathhouse and toilet (with no particular concern about which area is used as what) that makes the whole place the multisensory equivalent of a stockyard in July. A trip into these places causes flashbacks to biology class, with you trying desperately to remember if there's a cure for the creeping grunge that you're now convinced you're infected with (safety tip: *never* enter one of these bare-footed). Face it, male or female, if you're at the beach and you have to pee, go in the water.

Any other business you should take care of before you leave home or in a restaurant.

That's to say nothing about the pack of beach rats and toughs who often hang out and watch who goes into the bathroom alone. If for some godawful reason you can't find anywhere else to go, always look to make sure there isn't any pack of hardasses hanging around looking at you as you draw near the door. If you see a shark looking at you, don't go in there! Next to alleys, bathrooms are the prime spots for crime at the beach.

Running from Venice to Santa Monica is Main Street. In recent years, the area along this old thoroughfare has been renovated from old hippie housing and studios to designer stores and fern bars. Main Street is the cutoff point between beach and the rest of the city. What you need to realize is that beyond Main is someone else's territory, especially in Venice north of the circle. The farther past Main you get, the more likely you are to meet sharks. Brooks Street was the horror story of the 1970s and 1980s in Venice; now there is trouble aplenty all over, and the sharks are more than willing to share. By leaving the beach and striking off into these areas, you will discover people who will request your wallet or have already helped themselves to your car. If the parking is too crowded on the streets to keep you within three blocks east of Main, go pony up for the beach parking rather than risk the depths of Venice. Things mysteriously disappear from cars out in that place, and nobody is going to call the cops either. Remember the concept of the fringe area near crowded areas where the sharks prowl . . . guess what?

Also avoid the liquor stores on Main Street. Venice is a pit despite its pretensions of class. The liquor stores are magnets for the local sharks and beach rats and are therefore hot spots for trouble. You can get robbed or assaulted there faster than any place except the deep slimeholes of Venice.

Moving south of the marina, there is, of course, the ever-popular Toes beach on the Playa Del Rey side of the harbor.

Every few years, a gang moves into the jetty parking lot or park for its nightly hangout until the locals complain and they get rousted by the cops. For the most part, though, it's a locals-only beach, and nobody who doesn't live there can figure out how to find the place. The firepits near LAX offer a wide variety of entertainment at night if your idea of fun is drinking yourself silly, getting into a fight, throwing up, and, of course, being hassled by the cops for drinking on the beach. During the day, the families from Inglewood, Hawthorne, and Lawndale flock to that area and frolic under the charming oil tanks and sewage-treatment plants. Mariachi bands clash with rap music while children scream and holler; it's an enchanting place best enjoyed from afar. Here in the parking lots it can get real exciting, especially if you've had a previous run-in with a happy camper.

Hermosa and Redondo are nicer areas; they have relatively clean bathrooms that are even safe to go into. There you're more likely to encounter the beach bum than the beach rat. The beach bum is a relatively harmless breed of a golden-haired surfer boy who refused to grow up. Now in his thirties with skin that looks like a workboot and frizzy, sun-bleached hair, he roams the countless little bars that pepper the Southbay shoreline, supporting himself in ways best not examined too closely. The Redondo pier isn't as nice as it used to be, but it is relatively safe if you're into beach-bar nightlife. As with the Santa Monica pier, stay away from the underside (and even the lower levels) of the Redondo pier at night because that's where the rats gather. South of Redondo Beach pier is Torrance, which is well to do and whose beaches are safe.

The beach scene skips around Palos Verdes and doesn't pick up again until San Pedro. San Pedro is one of those places that unless you're a longshoreman, fisherman, shipyard iron worker, or biker, you really want to avoid. Although San Pedro has the only aquarium in Los Angeles County, it's easy to get lost down there and definitely a place most people wouldn't want to spend time in. I'm sure some local gang claims it as theirs, but as long as its members don't bother the rednecks they won't be exterminated.

Jumping the Los Angeles Harbor and River, you encounter Long Beach. Ever since they tore down the Long Beach pier and replaced it with the Queen Mary, a bunch of suicidal race-car drivers, and an occasional bash at the convention center, that section of town has been moldering. There is basically no reason to go down to the waterfront near downtown (unless you want to blow up the University of California offices; they're down there too). The beaches of Long Beach are long and scummy, with many of the local lovable residents coming to frolic in the surf and maul each other. I'm not sure if anyone claims the waterfront, since next to downtown is Long Beach's "Boy's Town," and you lose points if you claim that as your turf. The farther south you go, however, the better the beaches until you reach Belmont Shores, which, despite the fact that it abuts a drained swamp, is the ritziest part of the beach south of Torrance (Palos Verdes doesn't count because it sits on a cliff face). Everytime I go to Torrance, I personally get a nosebleed from the altitude, but that's just me.

Skipping over the bog, you encounter Seal Beach—if you can find it. You have to have a streak of Indiana Jones in you to really find your way down into that section. I did once, but I was drunk and don't remember exactly how I did it. It used to be a real cozy beach community because it was so hard to find.

From there south, you have Orange County and its ways. Orange County residents are different from most folks in California; they're an odd blend of Podunkee, Bel Air, Saigon, Mexico City, and the California Correctional Institute at Chino. Fun place; ask the locals for the rundown on the beaches there. I don't do Orange County.

L.A.

New York

CON GAMES

CHAPTER TEN

New York

There's a wide spectrum of New York con games in current use. Most of them are variations of old standbys, but they all work, and every day the operators find new suckers.

The basic advice is the same as always, and you've heard it since you were a kid: if it looks too good to be true, it probably is. Let's expand on that briefly. You're an adult, you've been to school, you have a job and a few life experiences stacked up behind you. Dollars do not grow on trees. You know this. You see it in action with every paycheck. Elvis is dead, so it's not very likely that a stranger is going to buy you a Cadillac because you have a nice face. And even when The King was alive he only bought a few Caddies for strangers. In other words, a sudden huge windfall is not a very likely occurrence. Oh sure, it happens—but probably, somewhere, hens grow teeth, too. Add to that the fact that if you're in New York, you're in a city where strangers literally don't even give each other directions, let alone hand them fountains of free money. To fall victim to a con game you have to suspend almost everything that you know to be real. In film and fiction, they call this "suspension of disbelief." You know that dragons don't burst out of your dishwasher and Freddie Kruger is imaginary. But you have to ignore that knowledge to enjoy the film or book. You disbelieve that the dinosaurs will walk the earth again. But if you're going to enjoy the films about modern dinosaur adventures, then you must suspend your disbelief for a while.

To get suckered into a con game, you have to suspend your disbelief and forget almost everything you know about life and money, and the paths that life and money flow along. Forget that money doesn't grow on trees. Forget that Elvis is dead. Ignore everything you ever knew about human nature. Now you're ready to get scammed by the found-money hustle.

PIGEON DROP

This is one of the silliest successful cons, but it is in use and still making money. Here's the deal: a person, probably a man, approaches you and shows you an envelope full of cash. He just found it, you see, and he's all excited and wondering what to do with it. After some deliberation, and being that you're the honest type, you and your new partner determine that the best thing to do is make an effort to find the owner. Actually he suggests it—insists on it, in fact. An effort must be made. Not a real gung ho effort, but a little something, like a balm for the conscience. And hey, if the owner doesn't show up—and it's pretty good odds that he won't—then you can whack up the money and keep it fair and square. It's a lot, and, boy, could you use it.

Now you can see your half of this huge windfall shining before you like a golden apple, waiting to be plucked. The money is right there in your hands . . . almost. There are just a few formalities to be taken care of before you get it. You are sweating and shivering with greed. Free money. Found money. What could be sweeter? At this point you have officially suspended disbelief.

Your new partner says that the best person to hold the money—in case the real owner shows up—is a lawyer. Lucky thing, he knows one. And he's nearby!

Right here, pause for a deep breath and reality check. You know lawyers. Lawyers steal the pennies off a dead person's eyes. They approach the court asking for $10 million in damages for mental distress because of collapsed elastic on a pair of underwear. And it was a lawyer who got your goddamn ex-wife/ex-husband all the property in the divorce. And, furthermore, the damn shyster will probably want 20 percent! Basically, lawyers suck. Everybody knows that. So how come this guy's all eager to throw his money to a shark?

Whatever reservations you might have, you'll find some way in your greed-driven head to rationalize them away.

Get back to the basic premise. If he found all this money in a bag with no witnesses, how the hell come he approached you and made you a partner? You've found money before. Did you run right up to the first stranger looking for guidance? My guess is, hell no. But this time it all kind of makes sense. And really, you don't want to think too hard about it because you might logic the money away—and we can't have that. Papa needs a new pair of Bentleys.

A call is made, and sure enough, the lawyer would be happy to hold the loot. Name a lawyer that wouldn't be happy to hold money.

Now comes the sting. Since your new partner is putting up so much cash—the cash he found—you should also put up something to demonstrate your trust and trustworthiness. The only thing that makes sense, of course, is a big pile of your own cash. Off to the bank, then, to make a sizable withdrawal: a few thousand, anyway.

You meet the lawyer in a coffee shop or somewhere, and you and your partner turn over everything, your cash and his. You get a legal-looking receipt, a business card, etc., and maybe go have a drink with them to celebrate the fact that after the honest 30-day waiting period, you and your new partner will be rolling in clover.

Naturally, you never see your pals or the cash again. This scam may sound silly on paper, but a good pair of actors can make it quite convincing.

A guy tried this on me once, and the best way to head it off is to tell the con man the same thing I told mine: "Screw the owner; let's whack it up and go party!" You never saw a guy beg off faster in your life. He was gone instantly. I wasn't playing the game, see. But I was acting like a normal person with a partly larcenous heart would. New wrinkles in this old scam include pooling the money (the mark's, the drop, and contributions from the hustlers) to buy a bond instead of leaving it with a lawyer—which eliminates the honesty element. In one recent case like this, the female mark was left standing on the sidewalk in front of a bank while the hustler "went inside to make withdrawals for their contributions"—and boogied out the back door, with her money.

GYPSY SWITCH

The famous Gypsy switch is still going strong around New York. This one doesn't rely so heavily on the victim forgetting everything he ever knew about life. The acting ability of the con artist and basic good will of the victim are all it takes to carry this off. Plus a little sex appeal from the main con artist.

Here's a common variation: you are a man and you encounter a beautiful foreign woman who is clearly lost. Foreign does not mean Canadian or British. Foreign means from Africa or from a small island in the Caribbean or the South Pacific. Someplace you're not familiar with. She will be beautiful, exotic, vulnerable, and lost. You will be her knight in shining armor.

She may or may not have some small luggage, but for sure she will have an address in her hand that is some distance from where you are, often in another borough. You will direct her or tell her how to signal a cab. She may be so fresh off the boat she can't even properly hail a taxi. A little conversation starts about why she is here alone, possibly because she had to flee political oppression in her homeland carrying only what she could. There might be a discussion about how unfriendly Americans have been to her so far. You don't want her to get a bad impression. And she is quite the looker, yes sirree. And all alone.

Here may come a dirty, disreputable kind of character who overhears your conversation and starts trying to give the vulnerable maid directions. He may even pick up her bag and insist on taking her to the address. You are Prince Charming. Her big liquid eyes implore you to save her from this vile lout. You speak up, and the lout throws out a few choice curses and moves away. Boy, was that ever easy. You are her hero! The look in her eyes says that her gratitude may have a physical side to it, big boy: she likes a brave cave man. You puff up with pride. When it comes to the ladies, no matter where they're from, you really got what it takes. And vanquishing bad guys is all in a day's work for an international stud like you.

There's another problem. She comes up close and shows you an envelope full of cash. Big money. She is scared and unsure about how best to protect it in this strange land. The banks are either closed or she has no address as yet. Would you watch it for her? You are strong; you are honest and honorable. You will surely keep it safe. You will not steal from her. She knows good character when she sees it. And there is this very distinct look in her eyes that promises some unbelievably exotic physical pleasures later on.

She will go on to her destination and call you later, to get her money and a little something else, too. But first, because you two are linked so closely now by mutual trust and honest caring, you must do something that is a custom in her country. It's such an intimate little ritual, almost like a blending of the spirits. You put all your cash into the envelope with hers. This means your futures are closely entwined. She seals the envelope and says something like, "I place the money close to my heart, so that my soul and yours are melded together the same way our money is mingled." She demonstrates by slipping the envelope inside her blouse, close to her heart. Possibly the movement exposes some cleavage. Then she brings it back out and tucks it into your pocket with a smile. Oh, the passion of faraway lands. You make sure she has cab fare. She goes on her way after a steamy good-bye, and you can't wait for her to call.

But wait you will, until Satan is ice skating. You have just been Gypsy switched. When the envelope disappeared inside her blouse, she left the cash there and pulled out an identical envelope containing cut paper. If you planned to rip her off and gave her a bogus phone number, she just beat you to the punch. If you were being a nice guy, she still got you for your dough. And that filthy unwashed scurvy brute you saved her from—that was her partner. Which explains why he was so easy to get rid of. A good actress can bend a lonely victim around her finger so thoroughly that he might even make a trip to the cash machine ("They're really very common in this country.") to have more good magic to put in the envelope, thus bringing your hearts closer yet.

SIDEWALK SALES

Here's another elementary but lucrative sidewalk scam: a guy comes up to your car at a traffic light with a VCR or a camcorder still in the box. He wants $50 for it. You hate to get rushed. You'd like to take a look at the goods.

"Hey, it's still sealed, man."

"I got the cash, but I want a look first."

Back and forth. Then he lets loose with one of several popular rope-a-dope lines:

"Shit, here come the cops." He moves away, but at the last second you stop him, throwing caution to the wind and hand over $50 for your VCR.

Or this one: "Shit, I'm not gonna dick around all night at this price. Take it or leave it, pal." He moves away, and you call him back and take it.

Or maybe the traffic light changes. You sit there deliberating, and the drivers behind you lean on their horns and cuss until you decide to go ahead and take a shot, because you're going to get a beating from these irate drivers if you don't move it soon.

And hey, $50 is a lot to pay for a box stuffed with newspaper.

There's an upscale version of this. A Styrofoam camcorder box is weighted down and the grifter cuts a life-size photo of a camcorder out of the Sunday newspaper color ads—or makes an appropriate one with a color photocopy machine—and sets it on the opening in the box. He also owns a shrink-wrap heater, with which he shrink-wraps the picture and the weight underneath it so it looks factory sealed. It won't pass muster in a good light, which is why the guy works cars stopped in traffic at night. Prices for this are slightly higher than the plain box scam because more work is involved in preparation.

If you're one of the many in search of a switchblade knife or some other illicit item, and you find a vendor willing to set you up, there are a few common, old, real obvious burns. And they still work. Rule one: when dealing with street merchants, make them read off the menu to you; don't you tell them what you want. Ever. As soon as you say you want a switchblade, then they are going to say they know where to get one, even if they don't. Street hustlers know good and well what they actually have in inventory or what they have access to.

Rule two: never front money. Front meaning the guy needs to get your cash from you first, then he's going to run upstairs and get the switchblade knives or whatever that you want. You'd be amazed at how often this works—a good actor can really make it sound reasonable. Then he takes your money and either boogies out the back door or, if he knows someone in the building, settles onto a couch and watches reruns of "F-Troop" while you stand in the rain waiting for your phantom merchandise.

THREE-CARD MONTE

Then there's three-card monte, a New York standby. Three-card monte involves cards, but it's really just the old shell game (actually, three shells and a pea) with a different face. You will see the shell-and-pea game on the streets, too, though played with three plastic bottle tops and a BB. It was good enough to grift our grandparents, and it's good enough to grift us. Three-card monte always involves at least two people—one to play and a shill to win. It's not a game at all, but a stone-cold hustle. Nobody wins except the shill. Without going into the gory mechanical details, the monte dealer—called a broad tosser in the business, broad referring to cards rather than women—makes his deceptive move right at the beginning of play, before the suckers expect it. He begins play by showing where the red card is, then turns them all face down and starts his moves. The object is to find the red card, just as with the shell game the object is to find the shell with the pea under it. Same game. Right at the start, he will pick up two cards, the red and a black, and make his secret move. From then on, the card you follow with your eyes that you think is red is really black. And if you pull out money, you're just another sucker.

Yet, people do all the time. A full-strength monte crew will include the dealer, a couple shills, and a couple watchers. There are lots of ways to get reluctant people to place bets, and, believe me, in capable hands, this game looks like a sure winner. But you will not be allowed to place a winning bet—through a variety of hustles—and the only people winning at this dodge are the shills.

Three-card monte is played all over the city, but it's especially prevalent along 14th Street and on Broadway below Houston Street. Tables are a few cardboard boxes, ready to be quickly knocked over if the cops come—or when somebody gets hustled for the milk and egg money and looks like he or she is going to cause a problem. Then imaginary cops are spotted, the table kicked apart, and the hustlers scatter.

There are other ways to cool upset marks, but that one works very well and is used often. Three-card monte is, naturally, illegal.

"STOLEN" MERCHANDISE

Another scam you probably won't encounter until you get out to the suburbs is the van full of "hot" merchandise. This is one of my personal favorites, because there's nothing at all illegal about it—it just plays on people's greed. A van pulls into a construction site, a car dealership, any kind of place where people are working. The guys inside say they have a bunch of stuff that "fell off a truck." This is New Yorkese for stolen. They might have cutlery sets, stereo items, even jewelry. And they have great prices. But what they're selling is just cheap stuff, not stolen swag. Phase Linear is (or was) a brand of very expensive stereo speakers. These guys will be selling Linear Phase. Because the customers think they're buying hot stuff, they grab almost anything. It's good merchandising.

Junkies and other street scum are forever wandering around with something or other for sale—bicycles, new cookware, whatever they've stolen. If you must buy something from one of these people, make sure it's something you can stick into a bag quickly—there's likely to be an angry victim somewhere nearby. I was once in the famous McSorley's Old Ale House having a libation when a guy walked in carrying a wooden extension ladder that he wanted to sell. He was quickly ushered back outside, still carrying the ladder, and we all sipped our ale and watched with glee as the pair of painters who owned the ladder caught the fellow and gave him a whupping he'll never forget, if he can ever remember it.

Aside from the legal problem of receiving stolen property, I don't suggest buying things from junkies on the off chance that karma really exists and that encouraging theft will later come back to haunt you.

All in all, the best advice on con games is the oldest: if it looks too good to be true . . .

L.A.

When it comes to cons, the L.A. street scene is pathetic in comparison with New York's. This has more to do with the layout of L.A. than the scumsuckers' desire to relieve you of the crushing weight of your money. Face it, L.A. is too spread out for effective street hustling. Unless you're talking about Hollywood Boulevard, the Venice and Hermosa Beach boardwalks, Redondo Beach Pier, or Westwood, there aren't enough people walking around on the streets to hustle effectively. Years ago, a band called Missing Persons summed it up well: "Nobody walks in L.A.!" If a monte con tried to set up in one of those corner minimalls, he'd be run off in a matter of minutes; anywhere else and he'd starve to death.

This doesn't mean that hustles don't exist. It's just that the con is directed at the government or businesses more than anyone else. California leads the nation in workman's comp frauds. Los Angeles is the insurance fraud capital of America.

STAGED AUTO ACCIDENTS

You must be wary of people with whom you have an automobile accident. The cars are usually big U.S.-made tanks (such as Monte Carlos, Impalas, or Cadillacs) that cruise around and ram into people. They specialize in zapping people who are pulling out of driveways, accelerating into people making left-hand turns (but in West L.A., drivers specialize in kamikaze left turns into oncoming traffic, so you never can tell), and, of course, the sudden slamming on of the brakes in front of you on the freeway or boulevard. In California each of these would be your fault. The American iron is big enough to withstand the five or so accidents in one day that it can rack up and keep its occupants safe and unhurt. Suddenly, however, everyone in the car (more than one witness against you) has some sort of medical problem stemming from the accident. In L.A., Mexicans are often used as the hitters, but an insurance fraud ring involves many people, and no small number of them are professionals. Doctors, lawyers, and Indian chiefs all have their hands in the scam.

Don't think that staging auto accidents is a small-time business. A professional ring involves buying and selling cars, filing lawsuits, issuing medical examinations, recruiting and organizing a group of drivers, doing the requisite clerical work, laundering money, and sometimes providing false IDs. This means crooked lawyers (any other kind?), dirty doctors, clerical support, automotive personnel, crew chiefs, etc. Those three people in the car are the low men on the totem pole. They take a small cut of the settlement, while the real movers and shakers score big time.

These guys aren't just nailing one person at a time; each hitter can be juggling several claims at once, all stemming from one, maybe two, trips out into accident land. I know of one ring that was taken down when the officer who took the report on one accident recognized the same driver involved in another incredibly similar accident the next day. Although the driver himself was Mexican, when the investigation was completed indictments went all the way to Bel Air and Palos Verdes. The lawyer who was involved in it was reported to have pulled in half a million clear profit. Another ring was busted because the same cop who had taken the above report got bounced over to another district to cover a manpower shortage. He showed up at an accident where the same guy had stepped out in front of another car. Something wrong with this picture? Cooould be!

The targets of staged accidents are usually nicer cars whose owners are more likely to have insurance. Drivers prowl more affluent areas looking for people who are alone, and women seem to be the preferred targets. They often ram the rear panels of cars pulling out of driveways. That way, the targeted driver is less likely to get hurt. A claim where both sides are pulling in money is more likely to be looked at than is a smaller single claim. Literally, the only way to avoid these setups is to be a good driver to start with and to be alert enough and able to whip out some moves that would make a stunt-car driver blush in shame. I worked with one girl who was driving the boss' car when someone tried the old slam-on-the-brakes-on-the-freeway trick. What they didn't know was that her boyfriend was a amateur race car driver and had taught her a few things. She came storming into work swearing at the guys she'd just missed. When I asked her how she knew it was deliberate she replied, "A young white female driving a nice car all by herself and a carload of Mexicans, what do you think it was?"

Another common routine involves two cars working in tandem. The two box in the target, and one suddenly slams on the brakes. The problem with this is if another party comes forth and says, "This is what I saw, and there was no reason for the guy to hit his brakes," the con is blown. Always innovative, the scammers have come up with a new version, called a "stoop and swoop." It is a refinement of the old cut-them-off-and-slam-on-the-brakes con because it involves a reason to slam on the brakes. Car A is in front of Car B, that is immediately in front of you. Car A does something stupid that makes Car B stop suddenly, and you rear-end Car B. Car A takes off. Suddenly, according to Car B's driver, you were tailgating and entirely at fault, or if the scam was done right, you both say the same thing: "Car A was at fault." Amazingly enough, nobody in the car you hit got the Car A's license plate number. If you ever get in an accident like this, take the officer aside and explain what happened in these terms (cops love it when you can explain things in precise terms). If not the beat cop, a bunco officer would probably like to see a copy of the accident report.

TRAVELING SALESMEN

Moving on to other kinds of hustlers you're more likely to run into in L.A., beware the wandering salesman. I'm not talking about the flower, cologne, or framed picture peddlers. I'm talking about the guys who walk in selling discount film developing or magazine subscriptions that you have to watch for. Sometimes they even have attractive wall clocks or vases that they give you if you sign up right now! With a $3.99 clock and $15 in business cards, they have a pretty lucrative con.[1] They come in and show people these great savings, and everyone goes pant, pant, pant! Of course, there's a small sign-up fee, anywhere from $20 to $75. The fee is not enough to make people uncomfortable, but if they sell 30 bogus contracts a day, these hucksters do pretty well for themselves. You write a check or hand them cash, and you've just bought a cheap clock for 50 bucks—and you never hear from them again.

These people can be real convincing. The acting, the business cards, and the "free gift" all add credibility. Calling the number on the paperwork won't do you any good because an accomplice usually answers with whatever business name is on his card. If the phone number is the accomplice's home number (sometimes they are that dumb), the next time you call you get an annoyed brush-off for bothering that person at home. Sometimes they post themselves at a pay phone where there isn't too much background noise. Other times, the crims use an innocent party's phone number, someone who will be at work or away from home all day. Before selecting the unwitting victim, they call to see if the guy has an answering machine in case you try to check on their credibility. If he does, they don't use him. So instead of an answer, you just get a ringing phone. That should set off warning bells, especially if it's during normal business hours. When you call at night, you get the "what the hell you talking about?" response.

One of the most important indicators that it's a scam comes during the discussion of payment. Naturally, a con man will accept a check—if he didn't it would be sort of obvious that something isn't legitimate about the deal. But since banking in California has gotten seriously anal (you can't open a business checking account without a complete DNA scan), the average hustler won't go this far for such a simple scam. Instead he'll tell you to make the check out to cash. Warning Will Robinson! Danger! Danger! A check made out to cash is a ghost; there's no way to find who cashed it or where that person is. A cash check can be signed over to anyone and more than once. By the time it gets back to your bank, it could have been signed over three different times! No way will you find the guy to whom you made it out in the first place.

CREDIT CARD RIP-OFFS

Another scam making the rounds in L.A. that you should know about is using the mail to get access to your credit cards. Although it's a bit of a hassle, don't mail your credit card payments from a local mailbox. Instead, mail them directly from the post office. One mailbox rip-off will give crims an armful of credit card numbers, signatures, balances, and credit limits—all without the card being reported stolen. If the box is full, all the guy has to do is reach in and start grabbing letters without having to break into the box.

There are all sorts of things the crook can order over the phone with your number and have them shipped to him instead of you. When it gets real interesting is when he splits to Vegas and starts getting cash advances off your card number.

Remember, if he got your payment he got your signature as well. It's a dog-and-pony show from hell to get the problem cleaned up. The credit card company is trying to palm the problem off on the vendor, who's trying to pass it back to you or raising hell with the credit card company because the card wasn't reported stolen and he acted in good faith. The credit card company will often not take the charge-off for months, and you'll find yourself locked in mortal combat to get them to do so. Whether this delayed fracas is to see if you'll get fed up enough to just pay the bill so the card company can pay the vendor, leaving everyone but you happy, or if it's because of bureaucratic apathy is anyone's guess.

Gone are the days where the enterprising hippie ran advertisements saying he wanted a million people to send him a dollar.[2] Now mail fraud more often involves straight rip-offs. A common ploy requires you to send cash (not large amounts though) to someone for a borderline service or opportunity, such as, "JOB OPENINGS—send $15 and a sample of your particular home skill [like drawing or sewing] to . . ." The question to ask yourself is why the firm needs money if it is reviewing your skill or offering you a job. That's the warning signal. If these guys are connected to a legitimate business, there's no reason for them to be charging you for what you can do for them! If the guys are smart, they'll at least send you a blow-off letter to cover their tracks. But other times, you and three thousand other people who answered the ad can kiss the money good-bye.

Contrary to what you might think, having a P.O. box for the address is reassuring, not a cause for suspicion. Because mail fraud is a federal offense, and one complaint brings the wrath of Uncle Sam down on the perpetrators, some con artists have caught on and now use mailbox services. You can spot these because they read, "Box number . . ." accompanied by an address. That's not a P.O. box; it's a box number—not the same thing. Most of these mailbox services are franchises, so you can call them up and ask if they have a branch at so-and-so address. You'd be amazed at how often the addresses are actually mailbox centers. That doesn't necessarily mean that you're getting ripped off, but it's generally wise to avoid paying for any type of service by mail.

SERVICE AGENCIES

One thing that has dug in like a tick in L.A. is the agency. These things range from writing critics (people who will critique your script or book for a fee) to model/talent agencies. These agencies will set you up with everything you need to make it in the glamorous world of show biz. Of course, there's a fee for that introduction, that makeover, that photo shoot, those classes . . . The guy commonly promises you a part in an upcoming feature that a producer he knows is putting together, but you have to be groomed for the part. That's where the hook comes in. You end up dropping a few thousand dollars to this guy and his "agency," only to be told that the show folded. Hey that's the biz, sweetheart.

My experience in the movie industry allows me to point something out: the real movers and shakers don't like amateurs. That goes for the crews, the directors, and the producers. This is a high-pressure, high-money industry where someone who isn't prepared can cost the company thousands of dollars. If you don't have your shit together, there are thousands of people out there who do. There's someone waiting tables who has all his head shots done, a long line of theater credits, stints as a movie extra, and walk-on parts. That person knows what to do when the lights are on and the cameras roll. That's the person the job will be given to, not some kid fresh from Podunk who's never been in front of the camera. When that fairy god-agent comes in and offers you the moon on your first job, something's wrong! Especially, when he starts talking about the money you're going to have to drop up front to get this juicy part (and he's taking a cut from all of those people he sends you to). The same thing goes for those writing, invention, and singing hustles. The second the guy starts talking about you paying him, something is wrong. An agent gets paid by making you money, not you paying him.

CREATIVE NAME EXCHANGES

Another fun-filled scam is for people who are listed in the phone book. There are several reasons not to be in the phone book, but the one that comes to mind is to keep conmen from using their same or similar name to leave you with the collectors. This is especially common with women who just use an initial, thinking that it will keep the bad guys from knowing that they're single females. I know a woman named Barbara Grant who listed herself as B. Grant in the phone book. Unfortunately a Brunelle Grant, using her address and phone number, left a string of collection agencies knocking on her door and ringing her phone. Nobody believed her that Brunelle wasn't her husband or brother and that she wasn't hiding him from them; after all, the phone was listed to B. Grant, and that meant Brunelle was around there somewhere, right? The similarity in names is enough of a red herring to keep the heat off the conman for months, if not years—and to keep it on you.

STREET VENDORS

You don't want to buy anything from someone on the street, especially something like a watch. The dude comes shuffling up to you and flashes you a chain or a watch, and you're looking at either hot property or a worthless piece of garbage. One thing you should know is that (if it is real) the more expensive the watch, the more likely it is to be registered. Yes, you may get yourself a cheap Rolex, but if anyone ever looks at the numbers, you're up on a possession of stolen property rap. This is the common way smasher burglars get rid of their hot property. That dude was inside someone's house not too long ago. Until you've been burglarized yourself, it's impossible to understand how infuriating that asshole standing there selling stolen property can be. I used to drop-kick people who tried to sell me hot stuff, but now I just snarl at them. I've gotten a whole lot calmer over the years (the electroshock therapy helped).

In addition to buying something hot, you could be setting yourself up for a snatch and grab when you pull out your money. He says 20 bucks and then books with both your wallet and the watch. That same watch or chain can score that dude all sorts of money. Snatch-and-dash crimes aren't as common in L.A. as they are in New York because people aren't crammed together as much, but the danger does exist if you let someone get close to you in a high-risk zone. Also, as Chris advised, don't ever step off the street with the dude! No! No! No! If he suggests you take care of business in the alley and you follow him, you deserve to get robbed!

In a more practical vein, do you realize that the dude can get $50 for a broken Rolex? You just bought junk, and he's laughing as he splits into the shadows.

The ghost vans full of goodies still infest the L.A. area, although to a lesser degree these days. The roaming days are gone. More often than not these hawkers pull onto a deserted lot and flip out stereo equipment and rugs. Often this merchandise is not hot; in fact, many of them have the owner's permission and sales licenses. They usually don't try to pass it off as hot when they do it this way. It's just a way to keep their overhead down: no rent or utilities. The stuff is cheap grade and won't last, but if you want to throw your money away, go ahead.

One thing that is legal and a great way to get good produce is the roaming produce vans in the Hollywood and Glendale areas. These guys get their produce from downtown and then have routes through the neighborhood. These vans go to the same farmers' market that the supermarkets go to for their produce, so their stuff is okay. If you don't mind conducting your business in a foreign language, you can get some great deals here.

There's a bit of a problem here, though. While some folks work for someone who goes to the farmers' market downtown, others sell produce that was shipped up here from Mexico. A couple of pickup trucks full of fruit over a back road, and nobody's the wiser. Mexico doesn't have anywhere near the pesticides restrictions that the United States has, and fruits soak up pesticides. God knows what else you're swallowing when you buy from these people.

"WILL WORK FOR FOOD"

One thing which you're going to encounter a lot in L.A. is "homeless" people standing by a freeway off ramp holding up a sign saying, "Will work for food." Evidently there is a thin but real line between looking for a job and panhandling. By saying they're looking for work they aren't hassled for bummin' money, which is actually more likely since people just drive by and hand them cash. First off, let's get something straight here: by standing on corners in more affluent sections (especially business areas), that person can make more money than by working a minimum-wage job. I know of one woman who turned down a prestigious Pasadena firm that offered her $40 to hold its place on Colorado Boulevard for the Rose Parade. She said she made more money on the off-ramp corner! Most of these people are basically honest because the cops only tolerate them as long as they don't get any complaints; however, you do get the bad apples.

Although I don't normally give people money, I'll pay someone to do a job.[3] All these jobs will be outside; never let a stranger into your house or place of business. If you have a tree that needs cutting, a garden that needs weeding, a garage to be cleaned up, trash to be hauled, or a car to be washed, you can use these people for extra help. For anywhere from 5 to 20 bucks, you can get these people to help you or do the job for you. You supply the tools and other equipment, and they supply the sweat. That's the extent of the deal; they aren't getting anything else besides that, and you should let them know this up front. Once the job is done, you pay the person (the amount already in your hand) and tell him not to come poking around looking for work: if you need him you'll come looking for him. If the guy shows up on your doorstep, remind him of that and send him away. It depends on the person and how convincing you can be about setting boundaries as to whether you've made a mistake in hiring this person. I can get downright surly when my gesture of kindness is trod upon, so I don't worry about them causing me trouble, but other people might. It's up to you.

I'm not a Muslim or a Buddhist, so I don't personally hold with giving money to someone who's just panhandling. On the other hand, I've seen certain business areas almost adopt these people as pets. All the local business people know the local bum and support him/her. If you are the sort who will give money to someone—which I admit I have done if A) their story amuses me, or B) it's a special case like runaway kids— here's the trick to doing it: long before you reach that person, have your money ready and your wallet secured away. If you're ultraorganized, do it before you start the drive to work. Take the money and fold it in half lengthwise, place it along your index finger, and hold it in place with your thumb. Curl your ring fingers into your palm and take off your watch, so nothing can be snatched. Hold the money at arm's length as you drive forward slowly. Your foot should be on the gas at all times, and if the guy gets frisky, you just punch it. If he tries to get closer than an arm's length, that same arm can be used to check him long enough for you to drive away. If that ever happens to you, immediately call the cops and register a complaint against the guy. He'll be run off immediately.

Another common trick, especially in Downtown, is for a bum to walk up behind you and mumble something. You turn around with a "What?" and that's the opening he needs to start panhandling. Another common dodge is for the guy to approach you and make a comment about something you are wearing, and once you acknowledge him, he starts bumming. A common ploy in nicer neighborhoods is the inquiry for directions to a local store. Once he's got you giving him directions, he hits you with the hard-luck story. Poor, poor pitiful me, do you got five bucks for my kiddy's shoes? Sure that kid's going to get new shoes—if you believe that, I've got a bridge I want to sell you.

The best response I ever heard to a panhandler was once when I was sitting on Biker Corner in Hollywood and a guy tried that approach with my friend. We were munching down on pizza, ignoring him. The dude had walked in, sat down, and began talking to himself about how he needed some money to get something to eat. When that didn't work, he mentioned my friend's shirt that had a rock-and-roll band's name on it. I was busy with a mouthful of food when the guy opened his mouth. My friend cut him off in mid-sentence by asking, "Do I know you?" The guy hemmed and hawed for a moment, and my friend asked again, "Do I know you?"

The guy answered no, and as I gulped my pizza my friend turned it right back on him: "Then what are you doing talking to me?" The guy started dancing around, and my friend said, "I don't know you, and you ain't got no business talking with me. Now leave!" By establishing that he didn't know the guy he reinforced the fact that the dude had no right to hit on him for money, much less talk to him. The guy thought about pushing it but realized that both my partner and I would happily smear him on the wall if he did, so he left.

Over the years I've used the same tactic because it elicits a scene less often than a more direct no. Many panhandlers rely on intimidation—not a threat, but the fact that you are uncomfortable around them—to get what they want. If you shoot off with a direct no, they will often try to extend the conversation to see if they can make you more uncomfortable. Only they know if this is to see if they can get you to change your mind about giving money or just to fuck with you for refusing them. Those who rely on guilt trips are harder for many people to get rid of.

A real common dodge in L.A. parking lots is the "car trouble" sob story. (It also plays well in small towns and in truckstops around the country.) Enter a guy whose car sits stranded in the lot. The car hood is convincingly raised, and his wife and sad-eyed child peer out the windows. (Hear those violins in the background?) He needs to get to some faraway place, and the alternator/transmission/starter (just pick one) has quit on him. He's almost got enough money, but he just needs . . .

There are ways to tell the difference between a con and someone honestly in need of help. The faraway destination might work on the freeway, but it doesn't ring true in the city. Be suspicious. See how the car is parked. Does it look like it just quit or was pushed out of the way, or has it been neatly parked? If it's in the middle of the night, just where does he think he's going to get the part? If he's "stranded" at a gas station, either check out his story with an attendant or offer to go in and pay the difference in how much he's got and what the part costs and stay there until the part is installed. If he's going from point A to B, is his car packed with all his worldly goods—well, why not? Lastly, if all he needs is (insert amount here), and you give it to him, why is he still asking people for the money?

NOTES

1.   These days, legitimate peddlers carry some form of company ID or pass. These things are often photo IDs, using four-color photos (an expensive process),

and the company often provides an 800 number for you to verify its representatives.

2. Hey, don't laugh. This guy raked in the money. It's amazing how many people sent him a buck just for grins.

3. My wife, on the other hand, won't give someone money, but she will give them food, especially women with kids. I sort of like that solution.

CHAPTER ELEVEN

Gangs

New York has a grand tradition of gang activity, stretching back to the New Amsterdam days. The early volunteer fire companies were nothing but territorial gangs with an excuse, who would happily beat each other senseless in the street while the structure burned to the ground. In the wicked heyday of the Five Points, the Dead Rabbits reigned supreme, even over the police department. The famous Hudson Dusters came, thumped, and faded away.

Today the city still has gangs, but it's not like the old days, and the straight citizen really has nothing to fear from today's team players. It's certainly nothing like L.A., and nowhere in the city is there a Crips/Bloods-type problem that creates trouble around a certain color of garment. A big sigh of relief, please.

There are street gangs in New York that wear biker-type colors, but with a few exceptions—notably the tough Savage Skulls—they are no-account chumps. The reason they stand around on their sidewalk all the livelong day is that they aren't smart or ambitious enough to afford motorcycles or even cars. Mind your own beeswax around them, and you're pretty much assured no trouble.

The same goes for motorcycle clubs. If you know how to act around bikers, then nothing we can say will add to your savoir faire. Tend to your own business, and all is coolness. Life is full enough of trouble that most bike clubs don't have to go looking for it. But jump salty or behave like a gold-plated dork, and you're in for trouble. And it'll probably look like an accident when the dust clears.

Chinatown is full of Chinese and Vietnamese gangs, but they stick to preying on their own community and almost never trouble outsiders. Tourists are safe as milk in Chinatown, unless a gunfight breaks out, which really could happen anywhere in the city—but as an insurance policy, I make it a point not to use the same few feet of sidewalk as knots of young tattooed Chinese guys, just in case their rivals choose that moment to do a little gunning.

Drug-dealing gangs and posses are united under the flag of profit and really don't give a good goddam about you if you're not in the drug chain somewhere.

Of course, any gang has the potential for violence, and if at all possible, physical distance should be kept. Wolf packs form sporadically and disperse the same way, a totally unpredictable occurrence. But they're not as common as they were a few years ago, and on this subject at least New Yorkers have wised up enough to call 911 and report these mobile riots as they occur.

Here and there in the city, one encounters bozos who claim to be "connected," meaning mobbed up or having some juice with organized crime. Organized crime is so powerful and entrenched in New York City that it's like a force of nature. As such, it moves in mysterious ways. But consider the forces of nature in their majesty. The breeze, even though it is capable of becoming a hurricane and leveling your house, does not brag about the fact. It is self-evident. And the sea, whose gentle, calming, rhythmic surf is so pleasant to watch, is able to rise up in fury and throw huge ships around like toys and pound bones into sand. But the sea keeps its wrath hidden most of the time.

So it is with organized crime. Some of the guys are flashy and easy to spot. Others not so. But none of them are so hungry to impress yo-yos in the street that they're going to brag about their business in some two-bit tavern, which is where never-gonna-bes usually hang out. Anyone bragging about being connected is a dangerous gasbag, someone to get away from quickly. The same with people who boast about membership in or association with major motorcycle clubs. Serious bike clubs are also like forces of nature, and genuine members and close associates do not lounge around bragging of their friends and exploits to strangers.

Not worrying about gangs in the city leaves you plenty of time to worry about other things.

CHAPTER TWELVE

Rape

Of all the topics we have have covered, rape is the most difficult. The women who are most likely to be raped are the ones least likely to listen to what we are saying *before* it happens, and then too emotionally damaged to listen *afterward*. It's a long, hard crash from "oh, it could never happen to me" to "it's all my fault for being raped," but that is what happens with most rapes. The trauma of having the assumption of personal safety ripped from her often throws a woman into a quagmire of self-doubt, guilt, and fear, in which she is convinced she is to blame for what happened. It is often years before the woman can confront the issue of what happened. The stronger the impression of safety, the harder the crash.

By refusing to accept rape as a real possibility, most women don't learn the predictable danger signs. Without this knowledge, they unwittingly find themselves vulnerable and then raped. It is terrible to realize, but most rapes could have been avoided. Like most predators, a rapist will not usually tangle with a prepared and aware person. Again, safety is found not in fighting off the attacker, but in avoiding situations where you can be attacked.

If you know, or are related to, a young woman between the ages of 15 and 25 who is A) a party girl, B) convinced it would never happen to her, C) contemptuous of men, or D) any combination of the above, hand her this book and have her read it.

Young women who have those traits are the ones most likely to be raped (though, of course, rape happens to all sorts of women; rapists are not respectors of age or persons). Rape is not a fun subject, so if the young female you're trying to impress with these rape facts resists, show her the video *Safe in the Street* (available from Paladin) and see if that opens her eyes and changes her attitude about reading this chapter.

Rape doesn't just affect the victim. It affects anyone who is involved with her. Since most rapes are committed by someone the woman knows, she will have difficulty trusting other people with whom she's intimate in the future. If you (a guy) become involved with a woman who has been raped, you will be dealing with fear, distrust, and emotional walls that have nothing to do with you personally, but everything to do with your gender. It's no fun when someone is bouncing off the walls because of post-traumatic stress disorder, though, and it's real hard not to take what they're saying personally.[1]

If the rape occurs while you're involved with the woman, we can almost guarantee that any normal male reaction you might have will be wrong. In fact, many women don't tell their husbands/boyfriends for fear of what he might do. So you're left dealing with your lady freaking out and not telling you what is wrong because she's afraid you'll go out and kill the guy. Incidentally, guys, the rest of this chapter is addressed directly to women. In many cases the advice won't apply to you. Read it anyway. You will find useful information for helping your female friends and relatives to stay safe.

As we all know, rape isn't a sexual act; it's one of rage, power, and aggression. It could be an expression of anger and rage at women in general, or it can be an act of rage against a specific female. There is some debate as to whether this also applies to drunken teenage date rape or just serial and forcible rapists. The theory most rape crisis centers now believe is that date rape starts out sexual, but turns into an act of power. What is clear, in any case, is that rape is an act of aggression, where one person physically forces his will on another. That particular remains consistent.

Rape is an emotional issue, and one that pushes people into extreme positions. Over the years, several excuses have been espoused to defend rapists. Many were offered by lawyers who were hired to defend them; others just reflect the rampant stupidity of a part of society on this subject. A common one, used by both of the above, is that the woman "invited" the rape by wearing provocative clothes or behaving in a come-hither manner. This opinion is popular among Neanderthals who haven't caught on that the Ice Age is over. Another frequently heard one is that although she says no, she really meant yes, and this is confusing to men. Exactly what part of no don't they understand? Or, how about this one: that the man was so drunk and horny that he didn't realize that she was fighting him rather than in the throes of passion. Yeah, right . . .

Unfortunately, the other camp has also brought forth some equally silly concepts. More than one extreme feminist has declared that all men are rapists at heart, and that they abstain only because of fear of the police. Another extreme opinion is that the woman could do nothing to prevent the rape, that she was a helpless victim. According to this theory, a rapist is an unstoppable force of nature that the woman cannot hope to prevail against (in his dreams . . .), and women are advised "not to fight back or he might hurt you." This one sends Animal into a frothing, howling rage when he hears it because 80 percent of all the women hurt by rapists are wounded or killed *after* the actual rape. Complying doesn't help.

The truth about rape lies somewhere in the middle, an uncomfortable middle where everyone has to accept responsibility for their actions, and where right or wrong doesn't matter half as much as not being raped in the first place! This may come as a shock to you, but apparently there are people out there who would rather be raped than give up being "right." They may deny this, but that's exactly what their actions indicate. They are so convinced that they are right that they walk right into the lion's jaws. Remember, the object of this exercise is avoid getting raped, not to have your opinion proven correct or to avoid an uncomfortable topic.

First, you need to drop the word *should* from your vocabulary. The most common resistance to many of the ideas presented here is voiced in that simple word. "They *should* . . ."; "We *shouldn't* have to . . ."; "Someone *should* . . ." Put bluntly, *should* expresses an ideal, not reality. It's what should happen, not what will (or can) happen. Granted, women *shouldn't* have to worry about being raped; women *should* be able to live their lives without constantly being careful; women *shouldn't* have to do these sort of things to prevent being raped.

However, reality intrudes. Reality isn't all fun and games, and that's what you have to base your decisions on. That means you have to be the one who's deciding what you're going to do, based on what could *realistically* happen when you find yourself in a precarious situation. When that happens, you do what you have to do to avoid being raped. The only thing *should* can do for you in this situation is allow you to feel justified after you've been raped. That is, if it didn't lull you into doing something that resulted in your getting raped in the first place!

That is an inflammatory statement, intended to open people's eyes about the fact that there could be as many as 821,000 rapes a year[2]—*most of which could have been avoided!* This is not a matter of blame, shame, guilt, psychological self-flagellation, or kung-fuing your way out of it. It's simply a matter of knowing the danger signals when a situation is about to go to hell in a handbasket. If you don't know them, the situation is going to continue unchecked, and you're going to get raped! If you choose to ignore them, you're going to get raped! And, practically speaking, it's easier to avoid being raped than it is to spend years healing from the trauma. It *can* happen to you. In fact, it happens to one out of every four women. That means between you and three of your friends, someone is going to be raped unless you do something about it!

By showing you how a rape situation builds up, we are offering you the tools to make sure it never happens to you—or never happens again.

The motivation for rape can generally broken down into three categories: anger, power, and sadism. What follows is our streamlined interpretation of this system.

An *anger* rape is exactly that: it happens when someone who is enraged at a person (or ideal) sudden strikes out. Basically, he explodes and attacks. You can see this in the number of domestic fights where the male attacks the female and rapes her not out of sexual intent, but sheer anger. It is a form of aggressive domination. It is not planned, and it's often a reaction to a fight with a specific person. However, it can just be an explosion of suppressed anger involving a stranger.

A *power* rape involves a slightly different motivation. It feeds the rapist's ego to have his way. A majority of rapes fall into this category. This kind of rape can result from temper tantrums or because of a crippling psychological image of women, the "need" to physically overpower a woman in order to make him feel empowered. These rapes can be either planned or opportunistic. Most experts place date rapes in this category. As with anger rapes, power rapes can be a matter of domination, which can make the difference between the two difficult for the layperson to discern.

The third category, *sadistic* rape, is mostly the province of serial rapists. It is a form of eroticized anger. In fact, in many cases, the rapist is not capable of functioning sexually without the rape. It is not the rape itself that excites these rapists; they get off on hurting people. These people are called "freaks" in the street and are usually beyond all hope of redemption. Fortunately these people are rare.

As you read this chapter, keep these three motivations in mind because they represent significant patterns—patterns into which most of the scenarios we describe fall.

As with every other crime in this book, rape involves a process. It doesn't just happen; things lead up to it. Very few rapes are the "jump out of the bushes" variety. Experts estimate that in 85 percent of all rapes the woman knows her attacker. And an alarming number of rapes occur in the woman's own home![3] Also, in nearly 85 percent of all "acquaintance" rapes, one or both parties were under the influence of alcohol. Looking at the numbers, one sees that nearly all rapes happen when social situations go amuck. The situation starts normally and then escalates out of control. The only good thing to be said about this type of rape is that it begins to head off into a recognizable direction long before it becomes dangerous.

Our objective with this book is to show you in what directions danger lies. Just think of this advise as: "You are here . . . that way's south . . . don't go south. If you find yourself in a situation heading south, turn around and head north."

Although the five stages of an attack (remember them?) do apply to rapes, they often do not occur in order. Instead of a nice tidy 1, 2, 3, they often can happen 3, 2, 1 (positioning, interview, and intent).[4] This is especially true with date rape. If someone has intent from the beginning, it's easier to see him trying to set up the other necessary steps. Unfortunately, with many rapes the situation "floats" to a point where the guy feels he can get away with it, and he says, "Why not?"

It is this "why not" attitude that members of the far feminist fanatics use to justify their theory that all men are suppressed rapists. What they don't take into consideration is that this is an extreme mind-set that takes time to reach—a mind-set that few men will adopt in their lives and that fewer still will remain in once sober.[5] Realistically, date rape usually results from a combination of youth, booze, aggression/frustration, and simple horniness—all combining to turn off the higher brain functions. Usually, it takes minutes, if not hours or days, for the situation to reach this point. Once you've read this book, the guy might as well hold up a sign that says "MOST LIKELY TO RAPE."

It is the flicker of intent that should set off your warning bells. In other words, when you see his intent brewing, look for signs of the guy interviewing you and positioning for the attack. If they are there, get out now!

Many situations are like boats that have slipped their moorings and floated away. If you're not aware that you're moving, you can float into dangerous waters without realizing it. Under those circumstances, when you do realize what is happening, turn your boat around and get out of there. The situation (and the guy) are the dangerous waters, you are the boat and you want to get back to port.

Safety lies in knowing where you *don't* want to be. Alone with someone with intent is a good example of where you don't want to be. If you see a situation begin to turn ugly, simply ask yourself this question: "If he were to attack me right now, would there be anyone around to help stop it?" Either leave directly or quickly manipulate him back to where other people are, but don't stay in a place where he would have the upper hand if he were to decide to attack. The words *quickly manipulate* are of critical importance. You don't have 20 minutes to argue about getting out of there because it may take him only 15 to decide to attack.

The most commonly perceived position for an attack is a young woman trapped in a car in some lonely place with a young, drunk, and aggressive male. Everyone recognizes that this is dangerous scenario. But it is less common than people think. Although women carefully avoid that particular trap, they walk right into another kind. Rapes in hotels, friends' houses, fraternity/dorm rooms, and parking lots all happen just as often, if not more so, as in a car. It is the basic situation, rather than details, that you need to watch for.

The interview in any of these situations can be subtle, but it is generally an escalating one. Often it is a blend of pushing your boundaries and seeing how you react to aggression.

Something happens–usually you turning down his advances—and he begins to push to see how you will react. Putting it bluntly, he was looking forward to getting laid, and he's vacillating between sulking and throwing a temper tantrum now that he's been rejected. This fits with the *power* theory of rape. He's upset and frustrated, and as far as he's concerned, he's determined to have his way. You need to recognize this pattern as it develops.

Your best chance to get out of this situation is to de-escalate it, usually by involving other people. Lie, if necessary, to avoid a confrontation. If you're alone with him, tell him that you need something that isn't available there. At a party, head back to the crowd. Don't think that just having someone else in the house is a sufficient deterrent. Many a woman has been raped in a separate room during a party or by a friend's boyfriend while her friend is passed out in the bedroom.

If he physically tries to stop you from leaving or follows you after you've left, the only way out may be through physical violence. It's not guaranteed, but you're looking at a nearly 50-50 chance of the situation turning physical. Try to talk your way out, but mentally prepare to defend yourself. It takes skills beyond those of the average person to prevent a situation like this from developing into violence, and even professionals have only a partial success rate with prevention.

If his attitude doesn't improve, it's time to leave. Drive yourself home or have a friend drive you home (tell your friend what is going on), find an excuse to be called away (baby-sitting a sick drunk friend works great), call a cab, or if necessary go sleep in your car. If you choose the last option and if you can (because alcohol is usually involved), drive a few blocks over, park, crawl into the back, and pass out (another reason why you should always have a warm blanket in your car). If the cops show up, tell them the truth: you'd rather sleep in your car than risk getting raped. They're understanding about that. Whatever you do, do not put yourself back into a place where you will be alone with a prospective rapist.

If you find yourself stuck in a place where both you and he will be spending the night, first see if the door locks. If not, put something in front of the door that will either stop it from opening or make a loud noise if it's knocked over. Also offering to share crash space with a friend (either of the same sex or a trusted male) can serve as a deterrent.

A major problem with a great many date rapes is that the woman is too drunk to realize she is in danger until the guy actually attacks her. If she's too drunk to spot trouble brewing, you can bet that she's too drunk to fight back effectively. On the other hand, it takes time for her to get that drunk, so again this situation didn't "just happen." It was during this time that the other two stages developed unnoticed, and then intent reared its ugly head. By the time the attack happened, it was too late to stop it except by physically overpowering the rapist.

Many date rapes involve the girl passing out and waking up with the guy on top of her. Go out and party and have fun, but set your limits. It will keep you out of trouble. Parents: if you have daughters in their teens or early 20s, get this information to them. Kids will party, you have to accept that, but help them establish the limits for their own safety.[6]

In the 1950s, before women regularly owned their own cars, a girl on a date was always told to carry "mad money" to get her home if the need arose. That way, she was never trapped, and she could always get home if her date misbehaved. It is unfortunate that more women today don't heed this advice. If you go out on a date in his car, slip a $20 bill into some recess of your purse and forget about it.

Many rapes brew for months, especially stalker rapes. Nonetheless, all of the stages will have been met before the attack occurs. For example, a female rejects a male's advances, yet he still fixates on her and tries to make contact with her on a sexual level. It doesn't have to be a date; it could be a coworker, neighbor, or fellow student. This near-harassment can go on for weeks or even months. One night, for what he tells himself are other reasons, he finds himself (usually intoxicated) in a place where she is likely to be alone, as in the laundry room or parking lot. He approaches her and, when he is spurned again, he attacks. If you have dealt with someone who continually makes sexual advances to you, be alarmed if you unexpectedly run into him in a deserted place—especially if he's been drinking.

It is impossible to be raped if you are not there. If someone starts escalating a situation, tell him to stop. If he doesn't, get up, get out, and don't go back. In the case of aggressive drunks, that not only means until he sobers up, it means you never put yourself in a position to drink with or be around mean drunks again. Many women make a mistake by allowing transgressions to go without repercussions or allowing the men to wiggle back into their lives once they've walked out. The idea is to end the problem, not just the particular event.

Oddly, the biggest problem women face when it comes to preventing a rape is committing violence to protect themselves. It is a well-known fact that the most dangerous creature on the face of the earth is a female protecting her young. We have both seen small women tear apart larger men who have either threatened or caused harm to her children. In those cases it was not a matter of size, strength, or gender. Sheer ferocity made up for everything else.

But few women apply this same energy to protecting themselves! A woman who can access this same energy in her own defense is a match for even a large martial-arts-trained man (which is, by the way, *not* the profile of most rapists). The myth that a woman can't defend herself against a man is complete bullshit. There is no physiological evidence to support this myth; it's just conventional wisdom. Remember, the world was also flat until 1492—so just because everybody believes it doesn't mean it's true.

We should warn you, however, that many women's self-defense courses will not help you prepare to defend yourself, because they don't deal with the issue of self-worth or combat training. The two most important aspects of an effective self-defense course are enhanced self-worth (to overcome hesitation about committing necessary violence) and simulated combat (to show you that you can do it). It is not the issue of how to carry your keys in your hand; it's a matter of having enough self-respect to allow yourself to access your instinctive abilities to stop a rapist. Your self-respect and boundaries must supersede your distaste for violence.

Women's self-defense has shifted its focus recently from the long years of required martial arts study previously offered to concentrated weekend courses. The latter deal with both self-worth and simulated combat, and although they won't train you to be a fighter, they will teach you how to defend yourself in a real situation. These cover "Awakening the Warrior Within," "IMPACT," and, of course, "Model Mugging." If you are worried about rape, we highly recommend you look into these classes. A weekend in exchange for your peace of mind is well worth it. With what you'll learn in this book, 80 percent of all the crime will pass you by. This weekend training is designed to handle the other 20 percent.

The patterns of the five stages remain true in the case of rape, with one minor addition: during the interview, the potential rapist will usually attempt to, or actually will, touch the person he is considering attacking (except when he uses surprise positioning and "jumps out of the bushes" and there is no time for it). This is a test. Just as a monkey will cautiously poke something it is not sure is a threat, the rapist tests to see if he can safely violate your boundaries. Like the monkey, if anything reads wrong, he will veer off. It is easy to visualize this happening during escalation- or regular-type interviews: the guy reaches out and touches your hair or arm while making some kind of comment, usually about clothing, hair, or personal beauty. Most women are so upset about the touching that they fail to realize the significance of the guy's action. He just proved that he can get away with touching you. Or they don't attach the correct significance to the frequency with which it happens (like considering the co-worker being a horny pest rather than a potential rapist). If you tell someone not to touch you and he's still got Roman hands and Russian fingers, you need to A) seriously enforce your boundaries before he can go spinning off into fantasy land, or B) immediately get out of there, depending on how far the situation has gone.

Touching can occur during a silent interview as well. There you are on a subway platform, and he comes close to you to see what you do. Often he will reach out and touch or brush against you. If you shy away (or even allow him to get close in the first place), he knows you're safe to attack. He drops out of sight and ZAP!

The hardest thing to do in a situation like this is *not* to retreat. Don't confuse this with the idea of "leaving" that we mentioned earlier. Retreating is backing up away from this encroachment and telling the guy to back off or stop, and it sends all the wrong messages. Leaving is getting out of the situation entirely, and it has to do with drawing boundaries. Many people would think that stepping back would be the best course. Unfortunately, it's just the opposite. By stepping back, even though it is followed by verbal aggression, you have shown him that he can get away with violating your space. When he violates your space, you retreat. That, in his mind, sets the precedent that you are safe to encroach upon. By meeting his physical moves with a verbal response only, you have made stopping his next invasion more difficult.

Instead of retreating, any attempt to violate your space should be met with an attitude that would freeze a bird out of the sky. The attitude isn't one that you'd normally use on a person; instead it's how you'd command a misbehaving dog. Often this can be accompanied with a snarled "back off" (whereupon he is the one that does the retreating). Or in extreme cases, slap the offending limb away with the same comment. (Don't go after the attacker's face because that can escalate rather than stop the attack.) By removing the offending limb from your space you are showing a willingness to defend yourself, but if you go after the face you are attacking. Even though that may sound extreme to you sitting at home right now, imagine the same situation when you are looking into the eyes of a predator. Whether it's a drunken acquaintance or a total stranger, it's still the same.

Rapes by strangers usually involve someone who is twisted about women rather than someone who is drunk, aggressive, and frustrated. Your goal is not to fight him, only to harm him enough for you to escape. The good news is that of all violent crimes, rape is the least likely to involve a weapon, even in attacks by strangers.[7]

That brings up a major point. You should be assertive when dealing with a potential rapist, but not aggressive. Assertive behavior does not challenge the attacker, yet it establishes boundaries—boundaries you are willing to back up with physical violence. It's the difference between being willing to do whatever you have to do to defend yourself and verbally attacking. The most common mistake that most women make, which crosses the line between assertion and aggression, is to tell the guy what they think (or feel) about him. Who cares what they think about the guy? What is important is that he violated your space and that he is not to do it again! Getting that message across is what's critical, not that you think he's an asshole. Once you bring your opinion into the situation, you cross over from being assertive to being aggressive. Being assertive will avoid problems; being aggressive will bring them on.

The danger of using verbal aggression is that, while it works under normal circumstances, it can lull you into assuming that it will work in all situations. What you consider the most extreme behavior isn't necessarily the most extreme someone else is willing to use. It only takes a slight twist in social dynamics for the situation to evolve to physical violence.

Many rapists have been verbally abused by a woman in a position of authority. In fact, many were raised by man-hating maternal figures. Many women can identify with growing up in an environment in which they were made to feel ashamed because of their gender. What many don't realize is many rapists grew up in this same environment. But the rapists have turned that hatred outward to all women or to women who remind them of that power figure. Rape proves to the rapist that by having a dick he is superior to the woman—even though deep down in his psyche he believes differently. Cussing or reaming out a person like this is about as smart as walking up and kicking a bear. Both will hurt you more than your target: the bear because you hurt it; the rapist because you've added to an existing pain or insecurity. You've just painted a target on your chest.

The next observation of Animal's is not going to be very popular, but it appears to have some validity. He interviewed several women who'd been raped more than once (in some cases, as many as four times). He found that many of these women—understandably enough—were extremely angry toward men, not just their rapists. What's particularly worth noting, however, is that in most cases this anger toward men was in place before the rapes occurred.[8]

Animal's findings coincided with his observation of young males who would go out looking for fights. Two aggressive males would find each other in huge rooms full of people. Like magnets, their aggression would draw them together. While we don't have enough data to make a definitive statement about rape victims, it would seem that a similar pattern exists in certain types of rape cases. Anger attracts anger. Whether the anger manifests as aggression or victimization doesn't matter; the basic pattern is there. This is not to imply these women "invite" rape. Rather, it is like two angry people crossing a room to slam into each other. Something about these people's energy or auras attract each, and one is willing to go further than the other in his anger. In neither case is this an "I'm pissed because I've had a bad hair day" reaction. It results from long-held, deep-seated resentment and behavioral expectations regarding the other sex by both parties. If this describes you, it is important to get professional counseling to help work out suppressed hostility toward the opposite sex. This applies to both men and women. There is a serious dysfunction in this society, and we all could use help about sexuality, boundaries, aggression. Men are not excused from the responsibility of working out their feelings of hostility toward women. However, the bottom line is that you, as a woman, are the one who is going to be raped. If you meet with a Neanderthal and you display this type of anger, you're going to have to realize that your words could be getting you involved in a fracas that you have a 50-50 chance of losing. Getting rid of this anger is the first step toward removing yourself from the rapist's criteria for a victim.

PROFILE OF A RAPIST

There are certain profiles to watch for to recognize some-one who might be a rapist. Many women who are raped notice this behavior in their attackers beforehand, but dismiss it as minor. *It is not minor!* These are extremely important signals. Make a mental note that if you see any of the following behaviors in someone, either cut off further socialization with this person or be careful to never be alone with him, especially if he's beendrinking.

ANGER

Is this person easily angered? Does he get mad over little things and overreact to them? Do annoyances provoke reactions way beyond what is warranted?

Excessive displays of anger are often an indication of suppressed anger deep inside a person. If anger were a pot on the stove, a normal person would have it filled up about one-quarter of the way. A good fire would be needed to get the contents to the point where they boil over. A person filled with suppressed anger, however, has his pot filled to the brim already, and any additional irritation causes him to boil over. This is why you need to watch how often someone gets angry over seemingly insignificant things.

Beware of physical manifestations of anger. This is the guy who lashes out at objects when he is mad, who kicks trash cans or punches cars and walls. It is a short step from hitting a wall to hitting you. If he gets angry enough, this type of man will often resort to rape as a form of dominance. Many spousal and/or couple fights result in rape from this type of anger.

We all get frustrated when we don't get our way. Watch how someone reacts over being denied something small, and you will see a critical facet of his personality. Someone who throws a tantrum over being denied something small is not someone you want to be in a vulnerable position with when you deny him sex.

HOSTILE OR VIOLENT LANGUAGE

Listen to what a person says. Speech reveals underlying beliefs. The words a person uses convey his opinion and beliefs on the subject. For example, it is extremely common among lower-class groups to refer to women as "bitches." It's not reserved for moments of anger or conflict, but used in everyday conversation. What does this reveal about a person's opinion of women? Often women will hear these warning signs and feel uncomfortable about them (as well they should), but then disregard them as trivial. *They are not trivial.* Listen for comments regarding violence, anger, aggression, and disparaging remarks about people—especially increasingly more frequent and hostile generalizations about "women." If you've just turned down his request for a date or sex, listen carefully for any hostility in his voice, especially if he's drunk.

BROODING

Watch for this like a hawk. When he gets angry does he

brood about it? Will he hang onto anger like a pit bull and not let it go? Someone like this will be pissed for hours or days over something a normal person would get over in 15 minutes.

Another serious danger sign is when someone goes deaf when mad. Does the guy get quietly mad and tune out anybody who's trying to talk to him? At a party the guy will stand in the corner glaring at someone who irritated him. Talking to this type is like talking to a shark that has zeroed in on a target. He becomes so wrapped up in his own anger and internal thought processes that he leaves the outside world and goes inside. The anger festers until it explodes, often not at the person who pissed him off but at an innocent victim who is nearby. This is especially true when alcohol is added to the equation.

Extreme Mood Swings

Avoid this like you would a poisonous snake! If the person can go from happy-go-lucky one second to extremely depressed and angry the next over something trivial, you are dealing with someone who has manic-depressive tendencies. If you see such a shift more than once or one that covers a giant leap on the emotional scale, backpedal. The movies *Sophie's Choice* and *Fatal Attraction* are about extreme cases of this mental illness, but they do an excellent job of showing how it manifests itself in behaviors. Someone in this sort of situation is capable of nearly anything in the downswing of this cycle. It is literally like dealing with a Jekyll-and-Hyde personality. While up, they can be witty, vivacious, and fun, but when down they are vicious and mean.

Insensitivity for Others/Emphasis on Self

How many times have you been shocked by a callous, ruthless comment by someone? Perhaps, more often, how many times have you seen that person embark on a course of behavior that benefits him at the expense of others? This could be either bullying behavior or a cold-blooded disregard for others in order for him to gain personal satisfaction. Does he believe in "might makes right" or in "his God-given right" to something? This near-sociopathic behavior is especially common among children of upper-class families. An alarming number of date rapes on campuses are committed by fraternity members and the off-spring of rich families. Why? Because they see no reason not to take what they want. We know of one example of the "most popular guy on campus" raping a woman "just to see what it was like!" The victim he chose was neither popular nor attractive, and, as such, he felt he could get away with it.[9]

A warning signal for this kind of selfish personality is someone who constantly invalidates or ignores whatever you say. The invalidation is much more subtle and harder to spot than the blatant ignoring. This type of person will say things like, "You don't really feel that way," or, "You don't mean that." How the hell does he know what you feel?

This behavior is dangerous because it often accompanies the "even though she said no, she really meant yes" belief. By invalidating your feelings and emotions, he strips you of your humanity. It's easier to rape a thing than a person.

The "ignore it" personality just totally disregards your feelings, thoughts, and boundaries. You say no, and he keeps on going. Watch for this behavior long before you ever end up alone with this kind of person. He may rationalize or try to trivialize it later, but it is important to watch for.

BULLYING

Does this person go out of his way to make other people uncomfortable or bow to his will? This can range from open confrontation to mental games he plays with people. This is based in our old friends, power and aggression. Watch for this behavior in a person because sooner or later he will turn this behavior toward you.

ALCOHOL OR DRUG ABUSE

What kind of drunk is this person? A happy drunk seldom rapes a person. However, a hostile or mean drunk is *not* safe to be around—especially when you are impaired yourself. We may be beating a dead horse by now, but all of these behaviors come out in spades when someone is chemically impaired.

• • •

By now you may have realized that the "jump out of the bushes" rape is relatively rare. Generally, it can be prevented by handling it like any other surprise situation. Be careful of people loitering and watching you. Anyone who watches you should be watched right back with the attitude of "I know you're there, but I'm not inviting you to talk to me, and I'm not afraid of you!" Always look around to see if someone is following you to your car or your apartment.

Be careful about following a routine too closely through high-risk fringe areas. The reason many rapes by strangers occur on college campuses is that the coed regularly parks in the same place and uses the same route to get to and from her car. After two or so days of observation, the guy has her schedule and route. He's done a silent interview (maybe even bumped into her), and now he moves into position. He chooses an attack spot, and all he has to do is check to see if her car is there and wait . . . she walks right into his trap.

A general habit you should cultivate is to stay in the middle of the walkway, away from any potential hiding spots. This makes the attacker take extra steps to reach you and gives you warning. Also, if one side of the street is well-lighted and the other not, walk on the illuminated side. It sounds obvious, but you'd be amazed at how often people space this out. Scout your route for potential ambush spots and avoid them if possible. If you can't and you do encounter someone in these places or following you, immediately head back to the lights and noise.

Although any woman is susceptible to rape, those most likely to be attacked are in their late teens or early 20s. With all we've talked about in this chapter, this makes sense. However, women in their 40s and early 50s are also frequent rape victims. Statistically, these are the women who are more likely to be attacked by ambush rapists or break-in burglars-turned-rapists. This makes no sense until one considers an important point: many burglars are in their late teens or early 20s, and their mothers are in the same age bracket as the women being attacked! The clinical term for this is "displaced hostility."

So, just because you've reached middle age does not exempt you from the likelihood of being raped. In fact, you are back in a higher risk. Many middle-aged people who find themselves in such a situation dismiss their younger attackers with a combination of condescension and lack of respect. Do not display this attitude of superiority or disdain to a potential rapist.

If the world were truly fair and just, the possibility of rape would not be a fact of life for women. Unfortunately, the world is neither fair nor just, which means your safety is up to you. Violence happens away from law enforcement officers and the courts. When you are out there on the streets, you have only yourself to rely on. If there was someone else bigger and stronger there, the guy wouldn't attack in the first place.

Your best defense against rape is to spot the early danger signals of potential rapists and avoid those people. With most would-be acquaintance rapists, this is simply a matter of cutting them out of your social circle and not socializing (or drinking) with them. There are lots of people to befriend in this world—you don't need a potential rapist as a friend.

With criminal or serial rapists, avoidance is harder. Fortunately, these types of rapists are few in number. The best advice for avoiding them is the same way you avoid all other types of criminals: learn to recognize their patterns and take appropriate action.

And remember, girls, as the comedian pointed out, when you hold a knife to a rapist's genitals and ask him if he wants you to cut it off, when he says no, he really means yes . . .

NOTES

1. Rape crisis centers regard rape the same way veterans' centers do war. Both vets and rape victims are subject to post-traumatic stress disorder for years afterward. Major trauma is major trauma.
2. Based on the 19 0 numbers of rapes reported to police, times eight. Estimated numbers of unreported rapes vary from between 1 in 7 to 1 in 10. There are two main sources for rape statistics available: the Justice Department and rape crisis centers. Each source has a different agenda and focus. The best we can do for accurate numbers is take numbers from the two sources and figure out a likely middle ground. The Justice Department deals with rapes reported to police nationwide; if it isn't reported it doesn't officially exist. The rape crisis centers, however, handle the traumatized people who come to them. Unfortunately, numbers from this source often vary, depending on the city, year, and who you're speaking to, and there's no real way to verify the numbers because confidentiality is a cornerstone of their services. Rape crisis centers say that only a minute fraction of the women who come to them want the incident reported to the police.
3. Some are from break-ins, but most result from the woman inviting her attacker in.
4. It might behoove you to go back and reread the Preface before you continue with this chapter. A clear understanding of the five stages of an attack is critical to understanding how rapes occur.
5. We don't consider alcohol an excuse—just a factor.
6. Not only against rape, but AIDS. Drunk sex is seldom safe sex.
7. 30 percent of all those reported to the police involve weapons. Remember though only one in seven

rapes are reported to the police and those more often than not are stranger or forcible rapes which accounts for the high weapons number from this source.

8.   This is true of approximately 70 percent of all multiple rape victims he interviewed and encountered. Another 25 percent were what could only be called professional victims; those in the remaining 5 percent were unique.

9.   He was convicted.

Bibliography

The following is a listing of books and videos by Marc "Animal" MacYoung and/or Chris Pfouts on the subjects of applied self-defense and street violence. All are available from Paladin Press.

Introduction to Street Violence:
Cheap Shots, Ambushes, and Other Lessons (MacYoung)
Lead Poisoning: 25 True Stories from the Wrong End of a Gun (Pfouts)
Safe in City (MacYoung and Pfouts)
Safe in the Street (video, MacYoung)
True Tales of American Violence (Pfouts)
Violence, Blunders, and Fractured Jaws (MacYoung)

For Women:
Safe in the Street (video, MacYoung)
Safe in the City (MacYoung and Pfouts)
Floor Fighting (MacYoung)
Street E&E (MacYoung)
Cheap Shots, Ambushes, and Other Lessons (MacYoung)

For Teens Having a Hard Time with Violence:
Cheap Shots, Ambushes, and Other Lessons (MacYoung)
Street E&E (MacYoung)

Floor Fighting (MacYoung)
Violence, Blunders, and Fractured Jaws (MacYoung)

Hand-to-Hand Fighting:
Cheap Shots, Ambushes, and Other Lessons (MacYoung)
Fists, Wits, and a Wicked Right (MacYoung)
Floor Fighting (MacYoung)
Surviving a Street Knife Fight (video, MacYoung)

Surviving in the Streets:
Cheap Shots, Ambushes, and Other Lessons (MacYoung)
Floor Fighting (MacYoung)
Safe in the City (MacYoung and Pfouts)
Safe in the Street (video, MacYoung)
Street E&E (MacYoung)
Violence, Blunders, and Fractured Jaws (MacYoung)

Weapons:
Knives, Knife Fighting, and Related Hassles (MacYoung)
Lead Poisoning: 25 True Stories from the Wrong End of a Gun (Pfouts)
Pool Cues, Beer Bottles, and Baseball Bats (MacYoung)
Surviving a Street Knife Fight (video, MacYoung)
Winning a Street Knife Fight (video, MacYoung)

ABOUT THE
Authors

MARC "ANIMAL" MACYOUNG knows the ins and outs of American violence. He is the author of eight books and has appeared in four videos on the subjects of street violence and crime. He writes, lectures, and teaches classes on a variety of topics ranging from crime avoidance to knife fighting for the police and military. Before settling down to a writing and teaching career, Animal worked as a bodyguard, bouncer, event security provider, and director of a correctional institute. He currently resides in the United States and runs Crime Avoidance/Applied Self-Defense, an alternative program for teaching people how to be safe from crime.

CHRIS PFOUTS is known to many as "The Fifth Bundy." He has written and collected a great deal of material on modern violence—much of it through direct involvement. His first book, *Lead Poisoning: 25 True Tales from the Wrong End of a Gun*, was published by Paladin Press in 1991. *True Tales of American Violence* followed it in 1993. Over a 10-year professional writing career, Pfouts has won several awards for his work. His reports on violence, social history, motorcycle history, travel, and tattooing have appeared in a number of American and European publications, and he enjoys a measure of notoriety as a music and literature critic. Pfouts resides on the edge of a high-crime zone in the United States and edits both *Tattoo World* and *International Tattoo Art* magazines.